"What evil lurks  Shadow Knows, and so do de-lighted readers of days of yesteryear ..."

Radio nuts throug. this data-filled memorial to the good old days of radio when heroes were invincible, villains dastardly, heroines endangered and kids of all ages thrilled to their adventures.

Did you know that Agnes Moorehead was once Margo Lane, companion to the Shadow? That Edgar Allan Poe wrote scripts for *Inner Sanctum*? And that *I Love a Mystery* was the greatest radio program of all time!?

Jim Harmon knows, and tells.

Along with an unbelievable collection of names, dates, and places, Harmon includes excerpts of radio scripts and most important re-creates the remembered boyhood enjoyment of radio days at their best and worst.

Read, enjoy and re-live the world of Raymond and the squeaking door, *Hi-Yo, Silver, Awa-a-ay!*, Tom Mix and Tony, Sam Spade, Captain Midnight, Sergeant Preston, and countless others.

—*Fort Worth Press*

ACKNOWLEDGMENTS

My foremost thanks to my fellow collectors and part-time historians of that lost art of radio: Bob Burns of CBS, John Cooper, Ed Corcoran, Richard Gulla, Professor Lawrence Sharp of the University of North Carolina, and William Thailing; and thanks to Robin Woods and Dave Dixon of the Canadian Broadcasting Corporation, and to Martin Halperin of the Hollywood Museum and Pacific Pioneer Broadcasters.

I am equally indebted to the memories and research of Redd Boggs of the University of California at Davis on the earliest days of Jack Armstrong, Jimmie Allen, and Orphan Annie; the Reverend Robert E. Neily on soap operas; and to William Blackbeard, Arthur Jean Cox, Don Glut, Richard Kyle, Richard Lupoff, Art Ronnie of the Los Angeles *Herald-Examiner* and other contributors to my publication *Radiohero Magazine*.

Those who actually created the programs of the era of dramatic radio also contributed directly to this book: Robert Bloch, Don Douglas, Mitch Evans, Tom Hicks, Forrest Lewis, and, foremost with every assistance, Carlton E. Morse.

Ron Haydock assisted me in editing the chapters on The Shadow, Captain Midnight, armchair detectives, and anthology drama.

Jeremy Tarcher was instrumental in the conception and execution of the entire project; my thanks to him are not only for that, but for his patient persuasion in making me see the value of biographical information on sound effects men in its true light.

—J. H.

THE GREAT
RADIO
HEROES

JIM HARMON

ACE BOOKS, INC.
1120 Avenue of the Americas
New York, N.Y. 10036

THE GREAT RADIO HEROES

Copyright ©, 1967, by Jim Harmon

An Ace Book, by arrangement with Doubleday & Co., Inc.

All Rights Reserved.

To

CARLTON E. MORSE

CONTENTS

CONTENTS

INTRODUCTION

"WHAT DID YOU LISTEN TO EVERY DAY AT FIVE O'CLOCK?"

You listened to the radio every day at five o'clock. Everybody in the United States of America over twenty-five years of age must have listened intently to the radio at that hour during some period of their lives.

I listened then and the sounds are with me to this day. Radio listening—primarily to dramatized stories—was very important to me. It was certainly more important than eating. How many times did I bolt down a meal to hear *Jack Armstrong?* Radio listening was infinitely more important than going to school. How many times did I make my cold last longer so I could stay home to follow kindly old Ma Perkins' courtroom trial for mass murder? Radio listening was as much a part of life as running water, runny noses, and recesses. How could you do without it?

If it sounds as though I had a love affair with radio, I did. I fell in love with radio at a very early age, and though the radio I loved is lost to me, my love has continued. I think you shared the same love.

When we were kids we sometimes talked about the radio world—the new premium offered by Tom Mix or the insidious trap Captain Midnight was about to fall into—but mostly we kept radio listening a private thing whether in the family circle about the living room, or in bed listening to table models. You had things your own way in Radioland. No one could tell 'you the monster on *Lights Out* was too gruesome, because you could make it as gruesome

7

as you liked. No one could suggest that Buck Rogers' girl friend, Wilma Deering, wore a spacesuit that fitted rather too snugly for a boy of your age to observe. You ran the show.

The heroes of radio were a faceless bunch, often lacking a first name, such as Casey, Crime Photographer, or any name at all, like the anonymous Mr. District Attorney. Was Lamont Cranston hawk-faced and black-haired, or a handsome, athletic blond? You filled in the details to suit yourself.

The results your imagination provided were good. There were no padded shoulders on the Lone Ranger, Superman flew with no jiggly trick photography, and the Martians whom Orson Welles helped attack the Earth were certainly more convincing than anything the movies have ever provided. It was all as true as a dream.

I wonder if I could have survived my childhood without the escape from it offered by radio. A fat kid, I could play on the same team as Jack Armstrong and still be reassured by the Fat Man that "heavy" guys could be heroes in their own right. A bookworm, I could be smugly satisfied that avid readers such as Ellery Queen, Sherlock Holmes, and I really won out in the end. And, in the midst of poverty, Jack, Doc, and Reggie assured me that the only good thing to do with money was to get rid of it fast so you could get on to something important.

"A child, simply to save his sanity," Jules Feiffer observed in *The Great Comic Book Heroes*, "must at times go underground. Have a place to hide where he cannot be got at by *grown-ups*. A place that implies, if only obliquely, that *they're* not so much; that *they* can't fly the way some people can, or let bullets bounce harmlessly off their chest, or beat up whoever picks on them, or—oh, joy of joys! even become invisible!"

Each of us found his own escape, his own reassurance in

radio. The world I found will not be identical to yours, but many compass points will be the same. There may have been musically inclined kids who liked little but *The Hit Parade* or *The Voice of Firestone*. Maybe a few other jovial tykes cared only for the comedy of stingy Jack Benny or the pompous Gildersleeve. As for myself, and most people I know, the vitally important part of radio was the afternoon serial heroes, the daytime serial heroines, and the nighttime killers, crooks, and detectives, and this book is primarily concerned with these.

Even in our "Child's Garden of Violence" we couldn't all pick the same flowers. There were rivals for the same time slot. Some shipped out with *Terry and the Pirates* as I leaped tall buildings with *Superman*. Others preferred being copilot to Sky King rather than Captain Midnight. Some liked the territory around Gene Autry's *Melody Ranch* better than Sherlock Holmes' London. Each has his own memories, only a small part of which I can share. Yet I think you will have listened to most of the same shows I did. My listening habits were devastatingly average.

Some were born for greatness. I was born for "trivia." Yes, somewhere, there is one grown-up kid who never threw away a radio premium, a secret manual, a comic book. Me. I even determined to regain the sounds of childhood that I had not been able to preserve. After some years of frustrating search and glad discovery, I have gathered, from actors and producers and folk with my same madness, scripts and recordings of most of the great shows of old-time radio. From these, I am able to offer actual samplings of the shows and in this book these are in script form, as:

> BILLY: Jumpin'-jiminy-gee-whiz, Jack . . .
> JACK: Quiet, Billy, there's no time for that . . .

Because of length, I have synopsized many sequences from

the old shows and paraphrased others from my memory or the memories of others.

Inevitably, some of these recollections may be off a cat's whisker, as conceivably may be the spelling of the character or actor names that I have only heard spoken and never seen in cold type. I look forward to hearing from all those who shared these adventures in body or spirit who will help me clear the static from these broadcasts of yesterday. No person I could locate had the actual scripts or sound recordings of some of the programs discussed. With the most negligent historical documentation of all popular art forms, radio was truly written on the wind.

Yet, as long as our generation lasts, radio will be one of the most imperishable art forms. As Tom Mix said to his sidekick, Sheriff Mike, on his closing broadcast, "How many times will the figure of big, burly Mike Shaw stride across the imagination of some grown-up child?"

So remember with me. Remember your own radio. Was it a small set in your room with a big yellow dial that also tuned in foreign and shortwave bands? Or was it the console in the living room, hulking four feet high, with a silky walnut finish and an intricately carved wooden frame over the cloth-covered speaker? In any case, it was yours. You could tune it in better than anyone else, for those "difficult" stations. You could even lovingly perform "the kick" or "the smash" with the fist that cleared the air of all crackle and hiss.

The air is cleared. You are on your stomach on the living room floor in front of the set. Or you are in bed listening with your head under the covers. With radio, with imagination, have it your own way.

Radio may not have been as good as we remember it, but it wasn't as bad as you might fear in your undeniably adult state. Return with me to those thrilling days of yesteryear. Have faith in what you once loved. You could never be that wrong.

Jim Harmon
Los Angeles, California,
and Mount Carmel, Illinois, 1966

I

"JACK, DOC, AND REGGIE"

You may know the sensation of waking up during a long winter's night and feeling a strange gnawing that can be satisfied only by reading a Sherlock Holmes story. Or riding along on a train, looking at the countryside wheel past and realizing you are ravenous for a game of Chinese Checkers! You may have caught yourself thinking as you read the news of the latest teen-age atrocity, "The Green Hornet would take care of that bunch in short order!" Or watching the latest spaceship take off on the television screen—"I went through all this long ago with Buck Rogers."

Such passing fancies are normal and natural. But years ago I discovered that I was a hopeless addict of *I Love a Mystery*. I read an Ernest Hemingway novel and caught myself thinking what a sentimental cream puff the hero was compared to Jack Packard. In the movies, during the shower scene of Hitchcock's *Psycho*, I murmured to my girl friend, "Now there was *real* gore on *I Love a Mystery* in 'My Beloved Is a Werewolf'!" Visiting the family of a friend, watching Gary Cooper in an old movie on TV, I say, "What's Coop trying to do? Give an imitation of Doc Long?"

As time went on, things got worse. I hummed *Valse Triste* as I shaved. I caught myself using Doc's favorite expression, "Honest to my grandma." And then it happened. I woke up one morning, feeling very groggy, with a strange dry taste in my mouth. I lay there for long minutes trying to get my bearings, to remember just what had happened the night before. Finally I looked at the clock. It was not morning. It was two o'clock in the afternoon. The events of the previous night came flooding in on me.

All evening, all night, until four in the morning, I had been recounting every story I could recall from *I Love a Mystery* to a group of party guests trapped in my bedroom! I had even—God help me!—I had even supplied all the dialects for the various principals involved, and no one knew better than I how terrible I was at doing dialects.

I staggered to the bathroom and let the cold water from the faucet run on my neck. Then I looked up into the mirror, into the reflection of my bloodshot eyes.

"You," I croaked, "are an *I Love a Mystery* addict."

Pacing the floor, trying to think, I decided I had to do something. The program had been off the air for a decade. I knew that. But maybe, just maybe, I thought, if I could hear some of the stories again, or at least read the scripts, I could get the program out of my system. Maybe I could find peace!

I wrote a letter to Carlton E. Morse, the writer-producer-director who had created *I Love a Mystery*, and waited for the reply as anxiously as I had waited for my *Little Orphan Annie* snooperscope. At last the letter from the creator of *I Love a Mystery* came! I was invited to his estate, Seven Stones, near San Francisco. Since this was only a trip of a few hundred miles from Los Angeles, I left immediately. After the long drive along the coast highway, I began climbing up into the mountains through stands of regal redwood trees. The mountain trail of graveled dirt hugged the slope with passionate ardor. Suddenly a small pylon marker loomed up, with the legend Seven Stones. The gate of a high wire fence was open, and the car climbed on, higher and higher. Past a small, comfortable-looking cottage, there was an abrupt break in the big trees, and I saw a huge baronial hall, dripping with moss. Within its stone niches stood religious statues. Surrounding the mansion like a moat was a dark green solitude that moved toward me like a living, lonely thing. There was a long driveway yet to travel, and along it I saw horses and cattle and sheep and pheasants.

Near a side door to the main house there was a place to stop. I climbed out and was greeted by a man in sun-tan work clothes. He was of sturdy build, with a high, domed cranium, a small moustache, and appeared to be of middle age. This was Carlton E. Morse.

As we entered the house the very first thing I saw was bookshelves in an alcove with over a hundred bound volumes of the collected works of Carlton E. Morse, including *I Love a Mystery* and *One Man's Family*. Properly awed, I was also saddened to think that this was the only set in existence of the works of the man I regarded as one of the greatest living writers of his kind. As we entered the living room, a clock struck the hour, just as the hour was always chimed at the beginning of one of Morse's episodes of *I Love a Mystery*. He took a leather chair against the backdrop of a picture window fully twelve by twenty feet that showed a panorama of part of the redwood forest on the estate.

"You've come a long way," he said. "Would you like to see some of my scripts of *I Love a Mystery?*"

Without small talk, Mr. Morse got a stack of the leather-bound volumes and moved to the couch. I sat beside him, and he turned the typewritten pages of the big books, reading a passage aloud here and there, explaining how he wrote the stories, telling an anecdote about the cast.

This was the first of a number of visits I made to Seven Stones in which I talked with Carlton Morse, and borrowed some of the original scripts. My addiction was not cured. It never will be. *I Love a Mystery?* Why, let me tell you . . .

A train whistle shrieks through the night . . . a voice calls

"I Love a Mystery, featuring the adventures of Jack, Doc, and Jerri Booker, specialists in crime and adventure, following the treasure map of P. Y. Ling to the pirate loot of 'The Island of Skulls' . . . A new Carlton Morse adventure thriller!" Then the music—haunting, somber, yet exciting—music of mint and chocolate. There's a name for it. It's called *Valse Triste* and it was written by Sibelius, but the name for it isn't enough. It's all the words the announcer is saying, and much more. It means . . . it will always mean to me . . . *I Love a Mystery.*

A clock strikes the hour, slowly, majestically. The announcer tells you it is nine o'clock at night in the Temple of the Jaguar on the Island of Skulls. Jack Packard and Doc Long are trying to rescue two girls kidnapped and imprisoned by the high priest of the temple and the high priestess, the beautiful but deadly Sunya. Jack has left Doc alone on the upper catwalks of the temple, and the Texan has just been confronted by Holy Joe, the outraged high priest.

> HOLY JOE: You have come to this island where you do not belong. You have ignored the religious taboos which are ours! You have invaded the Temple of the Jaguar and you have defiled the Temple of the Monkey Men—to let you live further is unthinkable! This is your appointed time to die, Señor Doc Long!

This sentence of death has been passed on Doc Long by one of a long line of temple officials beset with homicidal mania encountered by Doc and his partner, Jack. The high priest and Doc Long are facing each other as they stand on strands of rope that make up a huge, man-made spider web a hundred and fifty feet above the stone floor of a torch-lit cavern. Holy Joe is as big as two ordinary men, dwarfing even the tall, red-haired Texan. His eyes, as well as his deceptively soft, Spanish-accented voice, are filled with fanatical hate.

Even Doc Long was a bit nonplused facing a madman as he walked a rope that seemed halfway to the Moon. The Texan felt it necessary to mention his shooting pistol trained on Holy Joe's heart.

The high priest snorted in contempt. He was not interested in petty details. He was here to do murder.

> DOC: I warn you, Holy Joe—I ain't even going to take the gun out of my pocket. The first move you make in this direction, you're a dead pigeon. Lookee, if you're so anxious to fight me, wait until we're on solid ground. . . . That-a-way, I'll take you on bare knuckles and love it.

It certainly wouldn't have bothered Doc that Holy Joe was twice as big as he was—he hardly considered any fight interesting unless the odds were two to one against him. But Holy Joe was determined on having things exactly his own way. The fight was to be up here in these ropes he knew so well, the spider web that had been his home since he was no larger than a small monkey.

Doc Long assured the bloodthirsty priest that it wasn't his style to go around shooting down any man of the cloth regardless of the eccentricities of his worship, but that he had no mouth for being dropped down a hundred and fifty feet on his head.

The contempt of Holy Joe was unscathed. He didn't even believe the infidel had a gun in his pocket, and that he kept it there only so Joe wouldn't have a chance to whip it out of his hand. The high priest started forward. Doc Long warned him sharply.

The muffled crack of a pistol shot echoed through the

gigantic cavern. Holy Joe's eyes opened wide in chagrin at underestimating the infidel. He was only shot in the leg, but he had lost face. He let go of the ropes and dropped leisurely to the stone floor so far below. . . .

Meanwhile, Jack Packard had climbed to the very center of the spider web of ropes. In the center there was a bamboo cage containing the girls, P. Y. Ling and Edith, both traveling companions of an eccentric, invalid heiress who had brought this expedition to the Island of Skulls. Forcing the cage open, Jack Packard prepared to free the girls with his usual brisk, no-nonsense efficiency. He found the Chinese girl lying in a faint and Edith pacing the cage like a wild thing. She had been a prisoner of the Cult of the Jaguar longer, and had been prepared to be stretched on the Altars of the Monkey Men to make the "ultimate sacrifice."

In his usual authoritative growl, Jack demanded the attention of the distraught girl. But Edith seemed to prefer pacing the cage, gibbering to herself.

Calmly, though a bit impatiently, Jack Packard assured her that he had nothing but her best interests at heart, and that she need have no fear of him. Edith gibbered on, crouching in the rice straw that floored the strange cage. At last, Jack ran out of patience, and he took the arm of the crazed girl.

> JACK: You little hussy, you bit my arm! Stop it, Edith —stand still!
>
> EDITH: I'll bite you—I'll bite you!
>
> JACK: Look, we haven't got all day. When it gets around Holy Joe has been killed we'll have all the priests in the joint on our tail—now come here!
>
> EDITH: No! No!
>
> JACK: All right. Then I'll have to do it this way. (SOCK —BODY HITS THE FLOOR) Poor little kid. When

you wake up you'll be out of all this. Maybe knock a little sense back into your head too.

Jack leaned out of the cage and called up to Doc, who would help him lift the girls out of the cage and later lower them to the temple floor below. He informed Doc that reason had failed in the case of Edith.

DOC: Yeah, I saw it. You ought to make some woman a good husband, son.

By now it should be obvious to even the most jaded reader that *I Love a Mystery* was the greatest radio program of all time! Those who fondly remember the Norman Corwin dramas, or Fred Allen, or the Metropolitan Opera broadcasts may be surprised to hear which radio program holds this unique honor, but the information will come as no surprise to anyone who listened to it when he was between the ages of six and sixteen.

The program seems to have been especially designed to outrage the PTA, the Mothers of America, and to whiten the hair of child psychologists. The monsters and murderers were not cleaned and prettied up, as on television or in contemporary comic books. Even the heroes were hardly symbols of purity and justice. They were rebels against society and would probably be described as "kooks" or "beatniks" today. Few listeners could have grown up thinking that this was a safe, secure world where everything worth knowing was known, and with a firm knowledge that they knew just the "right way" of doing everything, and that was the way their elders had always done it. *I Love a Mystery* gave us the very wildest dream world possible, dwarfing the terrors of *The Hermit's Cave*, minimizing the exploits of *Captain Midnight*, making simplicity itself of the mysteries of *The Shadow*, and it was peopled with characters that had reality of a substance seldom found outside the printed pages of a novel.

On the surface of it, ILAM (as we initiates familiarly called the program) concerned the exploits of three young men, soldiers of fortune, sometime private detectives. They were Jack Packard, a relentlessly unsentimental tough guy who spoke a generalized Americanese; Doc Long, a woman-chasing, strongly accented Texan; and Reggie York, a highly traditional Englishman.

Their exploits took them with persistent regularity to more than one mysterious temple lost in the vast reaches of a forbidden jungle, and to rambling mansions owned by remarkably eccentric millionaires who were being plagued by ghastly relatives and even more gruesome murders. (In the case of some of the relatives, the homicides had to be *really* dreadful to top *them*.)

Jack Packard was the central figure of the story, and the central facet of his character was a dislike and distrust of women. Jack had a particular disgust for "women who got themselves in trouble," but he could not seem to escape from them. That might have been the irony of fate, because Jack had in pretty specific terms "got a girl in trouble" when he was in medical school. Even then, he had thought the girl should have had better sense, and he had refused to marry her. He was kicked out of college, and, like many dropouts, eventually found himself fighting a war, this one in China. Jack could have had any girl he wanted, and for that reason he held all of them in contempt for their accessibility. He represented that ideal of American strength, whether Gary Cooper's, Li'l Abner's, or Superman's, where, as Jules Feiffer has observed, one is "so virile and handsome . . . in such a position of strength, that he need never go near girls."

Jack was emotionally tough in many ways. Whereas the Lone Ranger would battle outlaws and killers without *kill-*

ing any of them with those facile silver bullets, Packard was man enough to take on an ax murderer barehanded, cut out the killer's heart with his own ax, and hand it to him.

What Jack lacked in ardor Doc Long more than made up for. An episode rarely went by without him making a pass at every girl in the cast, and, by implication, making several successfully.

Reggie York was less sharply defined and struck a middle course of cool but genuine chivalry toward the gentle sex. He was less important in the stories and absent completely from a number of them.

When Doc or Reggie, or both, were unavailable to the program because of other commitments or illnesses, Jack adventured with members of a group that could make up a roster of United Nations delegates:

Michael: a Frenchman. He had the movie manners and the rather sinister voice of Peter Lorre. He wasn't played by Lorre, but by Forrest Lewis, who assumed a voice so like Lorre's that Warner Brothers demanded Lewis be given name credit on every show to establish that it was *not* their star.

Terry Burke: as Irish as they come, but a bit brighter than Mr. Keen's partner, Mike Clancy, or the Green Hornet's bumbling nemesis, Mike Axford, and a bit more easy-going than Mr. District Attorney's hard-driving assistant, Harrington. When all of radio's second bananas got together for a St. Patrick's Day bash, Terry Burke had the most interesting stories to tell.

Swen: Swedish, of course. Somehow it was hard to take seriously a hero who said "Yumpin' Yiminy!" He lasted only for a couple of stories.

Then there was the distaff side:

Jerri Booker: Packard's secretary and traveling companion, played by Joan Blondell's sister, Gloria. *Her* voice was deeper than that of the heroes of some other programs.

Mary Kay Brown: she didn't have quite as much Dixie in her mouth as Doc Long had, but she was, according to Doc, "the cutest little ol' secretary ever to fill out a dress so nice."[1]

All of these characters worked out of or gathered together at the A-1 Detective Agency, which Jack, Doc, and Reggie had opened just before World War II started. (Its address, "Just off Hollywood Boulevard and one flight up," was until recently occupied by a real-life detective agency with another name.)

The shrill siren call of *I Love a Mystery* first sounded January 16, 1939, and the initial train ride ran to December 31, 1944. During this time, the format changed from fifteen minutes five days a week to one half hour Monday evening, then back again to the Monday through Friday serial when

---

[1] Jack Packard's friends owed a lot to radio's tradition of dialects, which was raised to its purest (and most non-libelous) form on *The Fred Allen Show*. Allen himself had a marked down-Easter accent, and the residents of his Allen's Alley were equally distinctive. For example, on one current topic, such as National Radio Week, Senator Claghorn (Kenny Delmar) might respond that the only radio programs he ever listened to were those on the "So'thern Broadcasting System"—*Mr. District Revenuer, One Man's Still, The K.K.K. in Peace and War.* "That's a *joke*, son!"

Mrs. Nusbaum (Minerva Pious) was almost as famous as Molly Goldberg. She told how her husband, Pierre, loved to listen to the radio, especially Toscanini conducting the NBC Symphony—so much so, he decided to become a conductor himself, and had at last succeeded. "A conductor on the NBC network?" Allen asked. "No—a conductor on the B.M.T. line." But it was left for that cantankerous New Englander, Titus Moody (Parker Fennelly) to make the classic observation about radio: "Nup—I don't hold with furniture that talks." Allen's Alley was to comedy what *I Love a Mystery* was to radio drama.

the series switched from NBC to CBS. Off the air for five years, in 1949 *I Love a Mystery* was moved from West Coast origination to the Mutual Network in New York as a daily program with a new and different cast. It went off the air in 1952.

In Morse's view, the original Hollywood cast was perfect. Indeed, he based the characters on the personalities of the actors who took the parts, close friends of his from drama society days at the University of California. So Michael Raffetto *was* Jack Packard. Barton Yarborough *was* Doc Long, and Walter Patterson *was* Reggie York. If not in all ways, at least in enough to make for thoroughly consistent performances over the years. Then, although the original Jack retired from the role, and Barton Yarborough and Walter Patterson met untimely deaths, the characters of Jack, Doc, and Reggie proved immortal.

A new cast was assembled in New York, and Russell Thorson and Jim Boles, familiar radio voices, became Jack and Doc. A youthful actor named Tony Randall auditioned for the part of Doc Long. After all, he told Morse, he had been raised in Oklahoma and he must have some of that western accent left in him. As he tried to re-create the drawl, it became obvious that Tony Randall had come a long way from Oklahoma. At last it became obvious even to Randall. "I just *cahn't* get it," he said in exasperation.

"By jove, I believe you have it!" cried Morse.

"Doc?" Randall asked quickly.

"No. Reggie," said Morse.

Tony Randall played Reggie for the run of the part, often appearing opposite various feminine characters portrayed by another performer who would also become celebrated in motion pictures, Mercedes McCambridge.

In New York, *I Love a Mystery* began repeating the scripts from the first episode on. In the original series, Jack, Doc, and Reggie met for the first time when the three of them had independently joined the Chinese in their war against the Japanese invaders. The trio came together during a pitched battle, surrounded by the enemy, outnumbered a few hundred to one. (It's too bad they didn't run into Pat Ryan and Terry Lee, who were always getting into similar Asian difficulties in *Terry and the Pirates* on the radio as well as the Sunday comics.)

Packard, Long, and York declared themselves to be "The Three Comrades" (those were the days before the grand term with the ring of Kipling's India took on a specific political connotation). They agreed that if they somehow managed to survive the war, they would meet at a certain San Francisco bar the next New Year's Eve. Grinning insidiously, the Japanese hundreds closed in on Jack, Doc, and Reggie, and then the haze of the battlefield obscured the scene.

After one of its rare scene-dividing "fades," *I Love a Mystery* took us to that San Francisco bar on New Year's Eve where Jack Packard and Reggie York sat discussing their wounds, their undesired decorations, and were preparing to drink a final toast to their missing partner. The toast was interrupted by Doc Long, who came crashing into the bar followed in steam-heated pursuit by the police. There was a moment of indecision. Reggie was all for slugging it out with the police, who outnumbered them only three to one, but Jack's cooler head prevailed. They would help Doc escape and manage to clear him later. They ran for it!

The three men hardly paused to catch their breath for the span of five glorious years, which were too wild to be called "woolly," constructed of fabric too tough, bristling, and durable to be anything but some new, man-made miracle fiber.

The titles of the thirty-eight serial stories in the series conjure up a lost time of adventure: "Blood on the Cat," "I Am the Destroyer of Women," "The Killer of the Circle-

M," "My Beloved Is a Vampire," "The Decapitation of Jefferson Monk" (which was made into a disappointing "B" movie), "The Deadly Sin of Sir Richard Coyle," "The Thing Wouldn't Die," "The Twenty Traders of Timbuktu" (the longest ILAM radio serial—twenty-two episodes), "The Graves of Wamperjaw, Texas," "The Corpse in Compartment C—Car 27" (the shortest serial—five chapters), "The Hermit of San Filipo Adavapo." The plots were as thick as their titles:

"The Million Dollar Mystery": Sunny Richards was a girl whose friendship brought about the death of any person she was emotionally near. If a man attempted to light her cigarette it seemed almost that he would burst into flame. Sunny was flirting with suicide when Jack and Doc found her. Here was a girl in truly desperate trouble, in need of a man, any man. What did woman-hater Jack Packard do? He became engaged to her. He might not love women who got into trouble, but he loved mystery and adventure. After run-ins with hoods and a half-crazed teen-age killer, Jack, Doc, and Reggie exposed the scheme of Sunny's jealous, demented, boy friend, crippled by chance in the first of the disasters. Jack then broke the engagement and began looking for another brand of trouble.

He found it in "The Secret Passage to Death": Jack and Doc were assigned to take care of that most helpless of heroines, the sleeping eighteen-year-old Chinese girl who has been placed in a hypnotic trance by an unnamed Someone. Their job was to take her entrancing and entranced body all the way from the Canadian border to the heart of San Francisco's Chinatown. Their enemy: every professional criminal in the country, out after the $50,000 reward on them offered by that criminal mastermind, the Enemy. Packard, complaining as usual, brought her through with the help of Doc and Reggie, and delivered the secret information implanted in her brain to the United States government.

The story of the sleeping Chinese girl was one of the rare serials on *I Love a Mystery* involving travel and a change of locale. While the stories might have dramatic lead-ins, a breakneck horseback ride to the first station on "The Secret Passage," or a plane crash, or a quick exit from a steaming freight train, when Jack, Doc, and Reggie got where they were going, they generally stayed until the trouble and all the troublemakers were cleaned up.

"The Thing That Cries in the Night" offered enough trouble to make a strong man weep. Grandma Martin asked Jack Packard and his two friends to stay in the Martin mansion until they found the fiend who was trying to murder her three granddaughters, Faith, Hope, and Charity. Packard (as usual) expressed the view that he didn't have much use for the kind of women who were always getting themselves into trouble. Besides, the sole interest he had at the moment was helping his partners "get rid of" $25,000 reward money that had been thrust their way. In fact, the only reason they had come to the Martin mansion at all was because they had been picked up by the beautiful Faith in a fancy car and had been offered an interesting time.

"You don't have much use for money, do you, Mr. Packard, or for people in authority?" the old woman asked.

"*No*," Jack Packard said concisely.

Grandma Martin spoke for the Establishment. "You are a very dangerous young man, Mr. Packard."[2]

[2]Obviously, the sentiments of some of the characters in *I Love a Mystery* might come as a modest shock to some listeners. It was not well to enter this world without some *preparation*.

Suppose the young listener was to be exposed to Jack Packard's sentiments after coming directly from those of good, old, storytelling, song-singing Uncle Don:

(*footnote continued on next page*)

Jack returned to his room to convey Mrs. Martin's request to Doc and Reggie. But before he could get very far, a knock at the door interrupted him. Opening the door, he found the gorgeous Hope Martin standing there without her dress, sky-high on something "decidedly *not* liquor." Her dress, she explained, was shredded and bloodstained in the hands of her lover, the chauffeur, who had just been murdered downstairs.

En route to the corpse they met Charity "Cherry" Martin, who had troubles of her own. Some mysterious figure was following her around lightly slashing her arms and thighs with a razor, and pushing her down stairs. Her sportive admirer did give her a bit of warning before his attentions by crying like a baby in some far-off corner of the old house.

Over the body of the chauffeur the three men discovered that Faith "Fay" Martin and her alcoholic brother were also being blackmailed by the Martins' driver for something they

(footnote continued)

"Suppose that some one of your little playmates has
    something that you would like to own,
"Now if you say, 'Dear Mother, may I have one just
    like that?'
"And Mother says 'No, dear,'
"Don't weep and moan.
"We can't have everything, dear,
"And there are many other pointers I could mention,
"You would not care for anything if you could have
    everything,
"I hope you are paying close attention. . . ."

Nila Mack's *Let's Pretend* may have offered the bridge from the spun-sugar world of Uncle Don to heartier stuff. True, the program began with a syrupy song about "Cream o' Wheat is so good to eat . . . Yes, we have it every day. . . ."

(footnote continued on next page)

were doing, separately or together. And about that time they discovered the much-slashed Cherry was missing. Doc discovered her in the basement, where she reported she had been dragged and was just about to be tossed, bound and gagged, into the roaring flames of the well-stoked furnace. And what of her abductor who cried like a baby from some unseen place?

"He was all in black," Cherry whispered. "And he didn't seem to have any legs, or any face!"

A missing part of the anatomy also had a place in "No Ring, No Ring Finger, No Husband": An unscheduled flight landed Jack and Doc in the sea off a small Pacific island. Soon they found themselves in the clutches of an old crone

(footnote continued)

The introduction from "Uncle Bill" Adams was pretty mild too. He would inquire of some Pretender like Sybil Trent how they were to travel to the Land of Let's Pretend this week.

Sybil would respond, "Well, Uncle Bill, we went in a PT boat last week, and in a camel caravan the week before— let's all travel on the back of a giant goose this week!"

"A giant goose you shall have," Uncle Bill would agree generously.

Whizz! Ga-Honk! Ga-Honk!

Not very hearty stuff? Once into the story, it was demonstrated that not even the world of fairy tales was all gooey cream puffs (or gooey Cream o' Wheat). After all, those giants were going around *killing* people. And being turned into a frog is no laughing matter.

I suspect some of the old castles and mysterious houses out to hell-and-gone may have prepared us for creeping through the corridors of temples and mansions in *I Love a Mystery*. As you faced the Giant along with young Jack, you got ready to stand up to Holy Joe with Doc Long. After you had a few witches under your belt you could even face Grandma Martin as she demurely demanded help in a matter of life and death.

who drank gin and laudanum, and inflicted various tortures on her guests and her stepdaughter, all because of her morose brooding over having "No Ring, No Ring Finger, No Husband." She had no ring finger because when a spot of leprosy appeared on the digit, she chopped it off with an ax. Memory fails me as to why she had no husband, but I have my suspicions.

In "Bury Your Dead, Arizona," a freight train took them to the town of that savory name (they were escaping police questions about a previous adventure), and there the Three Comrades stayed until they cleared up the matter of the incredibly fat magician known as the Maestro, who was terrorizing the village by turning his gorgeous assistant, Natasha, into a werewolf.

One story on *I Love a Mystery* proved so popular with the audience that it was retold several times, with slight variations in the international cast. Originally, it was Jack and Doc and Reggie who discovered the "Temple of Vampires." That was a well-constructed temple indeed. Its architecture may have resembled the Temple of the Jaguar on the Island of Skulls a bit, but it was actually built much closer to Earth than that, and on more solid foundations. The "Temple of Vampires" had such a solidity and reality that not only I but many people I know can still quote dialogue from this grandest of all blood-and-thunder adventures.

I still recall the scene where Jack, Doc, and Reggie, with the trouble-prone Sunny Richards and Hermie, the boy who stowed away on their plane, were coming out of the jungle where the plane was forced down and came upon their first view of the "Temple of Vampires."

> DOC: Jack, Jack, lookee here, we're at the temple.
> REGGIE: Jove—just stepped right out of the jungle into the courtyard.

DOC: Yeah, so busy not looking where we were going we doggone near run into it.

HERMIE: Hey! They's a *big* house, ain't it?

JACK: This is a courtyard, all right. We're walking on paving stones covered with heavy moss.

SUNNY: Trees and shrubs are growing right up through the stones.

DOC: And I was the one that thought maybe folks lived here.

REGGIE: Now there is a pile of stone that is a pile of stone . . .

JACK: Well, there's only one entrance. Shall we have a look inside?

DOC: Of course, we'll have a look. We come too far to stop now. Doggone, stone steps as grand as you please.

SUNNY: And what stone steps—fifteen or twenty steps up to the door, and they reach all across the front of the building.

JACK: Somebody put a lot of back-breaking work into this centuries ago . . .

Carlton Morse put a great deal of effort into the erection of his temple. Some of the strange old houses prowled by the maddest of murderers seemed a bit hazy on floor plans, with a new wing or an extra floor suddenly popping up as required, but the temple was built stone by stone. The trail to the temple, with every blood-drained corpse along the way, was followed step by step. You could almost feel that eroded stone flight under your feet as you climbed up with the Three Comrades, the girl, Sunny, and the boy, Hermie.

DOC: Big arch doorway, but not a door in the place.

JACK: Doors must have rotted away centuries ago.

(A GREAT BELL TOLLS SOLEMNLY)

SUNNY: Hey! Golly!

DOC: If I didn't hear church bells, you can call me a loony.

HERMIE: Yeah, I heard it.

JACK: Come on, let's go inside . . .

DOC: Well! Will you look what we found!

SUNNY: What a tremendous place!

REGGIE: The Nicaraguan government could hide its whole army in here.

DOC: Jack . . . Jack, did you see what I just saw?

JACK: What, Doc?

DOC: Something just flew from one side of the temple to the other, way up yonder.

JACK: Probably an owl . . .

DOC: Owl, my grandma! It was as big as a man and it didn't have no wings . . . and what's more, it was wearing a human skin, and that's all!

What, or rather who, Doc saw floating across the top of the temple was Manuel, the high priest. He did put on a black robe to greet his guests. It had been a long time since he had seen anyone with such nice white skin, particularly anyone as fair as Sunny. The high priestess, on the other hand, was more interested in the "leetle boy with seech nice red cheeks."

Later on, Jack and Doc discovered that the flying stunt was done Tarzan-style on long ropes hanging from the ceiling. They tried them out for themselves, but Doc, as usual, got carried away with all the fun he was having and nearly broke his neck.

Fun was certainly the main ingredient of *I Love a Mystery*. After all, what could be more fun (particularly when you were between six and sixteen) than saving a beautiful girl from a vampire, or riding a train out of town to get away from some gamblers who wanted to murder you, or getting into a fight for your life with the odds seven to two.

That's what happened in "The Battle of the Century," when Jack and Doc attempted to rescue the kidnapped Reggie from his hiding place in an abandoned silo on a California ranch. In this one scene, I would like to reproduce all of Carlton E. Morse's script. Part of the fun to Morse was getting everything exactly right. When another script called for a man to be heard swinging from a tree, Morse brought a real tree into the radio studio and had a real sound man swing from it on a rope. (Morse was at last persuaded to let the sound engineer *hold on* to the rope with his hands.) The same dedication to sound precision will be found in describing Jack and Doc's battle against seven rough and ready ranch hands.

> DOC: Here they come, Jack . . .
> JACK: Watch out, Doc . . .
> DOC: Whoooopeeee . .
> SOUND: (SOUND OF CONFUSION OF STRUGGLE . . .
>   EXCLAMATIONS . . . HEAVY BREATHING AND A RAIN
>   OF SOCKS AND PUNCHES UNTIL THE HAND OF EVERY
>   SOUND MAN IN MBS ACHES LIKE THE TOOTHACHE
>   AND IS SWOLLEN TWICE ITS SIZE ON CUE, STRUGGLE
>   FADES BACK A LITTLE)
> DOC: (BREATHLESS, CHUCKLES) How we a-doin', Jack?
> JACK: (GASPS) Save your breath for fighting . . .
> DOC: You bet you! (GRUNTS) Honest to . . . (GRUNTS)
>   grandma . . . (GRUNTS) I don't know . . . (GRUNTS)
>   when I've had so much fun!

My sentiments exactly, Doc, my sentiments about *I Love a Mystery* exactly.

II

CRIME LORD

Sirens howling in the night, the flaming clatter of sub-machine guns, and, finally, the marching tread of convicts headed for their cells! That was the beginning of *Gangbusters!*

Such a noisy billboard and such a program compounded of authentic police cases and violent melodrama was typical of the man who created this radio series and several other of the most successful crime shows on the air, Phillips H. Lord.

Lord was a writer, producer, director, salesman, and actor. His was the facile mind behind the creation of *Mr. District Attorney, David Harding, Counterspy,* and *G-Men,* the program which changed its plainclothes to police blue and its title to *Gangbusters.*

In 1935, Phillips H. Lord began what was to become *Gangbusters* by writing scripts based on the files of the Federal Bureau of Investigation. FBI Director J. Edgar Hoover was frequently displeased by Lord's heavy-handed use of gun play instead of patient police work to bring down public enemies, and he ended the association after twenty-six weeks. Unperturbed, Lord gave his investigators city police badges in place of FBI I.D.s and continued the program as *Gangbusters.* Mr. Hoover also continued his operation with even more lasting success.

The sirens, the rattle of the machine guns, and the cons' marching feet became the familiar trademark of *Gangbusters.* After this capsule view of crime and punishment, Commissioner Lewis J. Valentine, the host (who was succeeded in later years by his aide, Colonel H. Norman Schwartzkopf) interviewed a local official of the Rockport, Maine, or El Paso, Texas, police department, or some other privileged city. The interview faded down for a dramatization with a maximum of sound effects for the audio-conscious radio audience. Crooks would break into a store through a back window (*Smash! CRASH! Tinkle! Tinkle!*), walk slowly through the back room (*Thud-thud-Thud-thud-Thud*), open the door (*Snick-snack-screech*), only to discover the terrified old man who ran the place (*"Arrrgghhh"*), and proceed to beat the secret of the money's location from him (*Sock!* BIF! *Groan! Boffo! SMASH! Crack! Groan! Sock! "Arrrrggghhh!"*). After he told, obviously he was useless (RAT-A-TAT-TAT-TAT! *"ARRRRGGHH!" Slump! Thud!*). The dirty crooks would probably even blow up the store to hide the evidence (*KA-BROOOOOOM!*). Of course, they would be cornered by the tireless knights of the law leaving the scene of the crime (*Waaaaaaannnnn! Rat-a-tat-tat! Bang! Pow! BAM!* RAT-A-TAT-TAT-TAT-TAT!). And blind, and by then possibly deaf, justice would triumph again.

Producer Lord was asked in 1938 to name some of his favorite cases from the first three years of *Gangbusters*. His top favorite was the exposé of "Cardinella, the Devil."

"Cardinella, swarthy, with heavy eyebrows, which gave him a Mephistophelian appearance, took mere children and, by threats of torture, forced them to rob and murder for him," Phillips H. Lord explained. "But the angle of this story that shakes the imagination is Cardinella's attempt to come back to life after he was hanged and pronounced dead."

There was nothing supernatural in "The Devil's" attempt to come back from the dead. His gang tried only artificial respiration and various restoratives to his body, freshly cut from the gallows. No wonder Lord loved it. This was merely a simple story of murder, torture, robbery, and death—the perfect case for Phillips H. Lord.

Another Lord favorite was the case solved by a talking parrot turned stool pigeon. During a raid on a hangout of the Licavoli gang, the parrot was captured and turned over to Prosecuting Attorney Frazier Reams. He got the bird to talk, revealing many bits of information it had heard over the years, including names and phone numbers. Confronted with this information, gang leader Licavoli confessed. The heroic parrot was interviewed on *Gangbusters,* where it screamed right on cue, "Licavoli!"

Gangbusters told of how Dillinger, "Baby Face" Nelson, Willie Sutton, and the rest met their fate, but there was always a supply of dangerous criminals still on the loose, and *Gangbusters* offered nationally broadcast clues to aid in the capture of these bloodthirsty fiends who more than likely you would encounter sometime during the coming week.

I recall from my boyhood how at this point my mother always wanted me to switch off these police bulletins on the theory that, since one of the killers described was probably lurking outside our living-room window, he wouldn't like it if he knew we could identify him.

As for me, I only sneaked the tone dial down a notch, and listened in paralyzed fascination. These wanted criminals were animated portraits of Dorian Gray, their every sin seemingly reflected in an incredible array of physical deformities. One of the *Gangbusters* nationwide clues went something like this:

> WANTED: Oscar Leonard Butcher . . . fifty-three years old, six feet seven inches tall . . . weight, four hundred and eighty-nine pounds . . . *scar* from beneath left eye to right arm pit . . . *scar* from chin to left ear . . . no Adam's apple . . . no Adam's

> apple . . . six front teeth have gold caps . . six
> front teeth have gold caps . . walks in sideways,
> crablike motion . . . walks like crab . . . very
> high-pitched voice . . . high-pitched voice . .
> constantly uses phrase, "Goodness gracious sakes
> alive" . . . says "Goodness gracious sakes alive" . . .
> likes to play tennis . . . Oscar Leonard Butcher
> . . . wanted for questioning in mass murder . . .

At this point, *Gangbusters'* host, Colonel H. Norman Schwartzkopf, would break in and advise us, "If you have seen this man, notify the FBI, your local law enforcement agency, or *Gangbusters* . . . at once!"

Not me, Colonel! If I saw that man, I was going to run like hell!

I always wondered what would have happened if somebody called the radio station in New York and reported, "I just saw that killer you're after go into a grocery store. I'm outside in a phone booth. Can you send one of the announcers down to help me nail him?"

Even the alleged Colonel Schwartzkopf wouldn't have been much help in a genuine police operation. Like practically everyone on the show, he was there only "by proxy." Lord was worried about nonprofessionals hitting their cues and had the real Schwartzkopf impersonated by a radio actor. In most cases, the guest police official was also there "by proxy"—another actor. Real policemen obviously couldn't be expected to sound as stalwart as professional radio performers, Lord reasoned. The only actual principal of a police case ever to appear on *Gangbusters* and perform as he should was Licavoli's parrot who had been talking for his supper for a long time. As far as the public was concerned, *Gangbusters* was definitely not for the birds. They bought it, "proxy" policemen and all.

Lord, whose father was a minister, graduated from Bowdoin College and spent two restless years teaching school before he came to New York in 1927 to be a writer. The chief attribute of young Lord's personality was self-confidence. He believed he could write great books without ever having read more than a forced minimum of them. He considered himself an immediate master of anything into which he entered. His relentless drive could take him places that turned away other brains and talents. Handsome, well groomed, with dark hair and piercing eyes, a gleaming, dimpled smile, Lord could best be described by that word of 1930 usage, "nappy." He was right—the combination of his personality and appearance was irresistible.

During a visit to a friend's home, Lord heard one of the few radio broadcasts he ever took the time to hear (his nervous drive kept him moving too fast to do much listening to anything or anybody). The program was a sketch about life in a small rural town. Listening, Lord became exasperated at the exaggeration and hokum of the play. He dashed down to the radio station and pointed out all the mistakes in the backwoods program. Finally, he was so persuasive that the station gave him a chance to try out his own program suggestion, a program called *Seth Parker*.

By 1932, Seth Parker and his Jonesport neighbors were broadcast over the National Broadcasting Company network each Sunday night. Lord played Seth Parker, a character not unlike *Just Plain Bill,* a sort of masculine Ma Perkins with wisdom that sprang from the soil and disdained proper grammar. The Jonesport neighbors would tell kindly Seth Parker of their fears and hopes, defeats and dreams, and he would advise and inspire with fatherly devotion and with prayer to God Almighty. There were hymns. Lots of them. "Rock of Ages" and "The Old Rugged Cross" poured out of radios across the country, warming the cold of a New England winter, bringing refreshment to a tepid Ohio summer's night.

One devout disciple of Seth Parker penned a staggeringly long poem called "When Seth Parker's on the Air." Part of it went like this:

> A sort of wholesome atmosphere's lingering
>   'round this hour,
> As pure as morning dew that falls upon the fragrant
>   flower
> These gospel songs bring memories that haunt each
>   sweet refrain
> Refreshing as the summer breeze that cools the
>   coast of Maine,
> And when the neighbors "gither" and "Ma" Parker
>   strikes the chord,
> Somehow I feel I'm getting better acquainted
>   with the Lord . . .

Eventually the entire *Seth Parker* program was sold to NBC as a package and Lord became the first successful independent producer in radio. He parlayed the program into phonograph records, a Hollywood movie (*Way Back Home*), a nationwide tour of the Seth Parker Singers, original songs, magazine articles, books, and of course other radio programs.

In 1936, Phillips H. Lord had what appeared to be another stroke of genius. The back-country Maine minister, Seth Parker, would sail around the world, spreading his message!

Lord christened a three-masted schooner (renovated at a cost of $200,000), *The Seth Parker,* and set sail from New York harbor for the South Pacific. The ship anchored in at Baltimore, Charleston, and Savannah for broadcasts of homey philosophy and hymn singing. Afterward, the ship rocked with lavish parties full of bubbles, giggles, and hot jazz music. Disgruntled reporters (who perhaps had not been invited) suggested in the press that Seth Parker seemed to think he had already reached the Promised Land. Frantic messages began flying from the sponsor, Frigidaire. Evidently they were concerned over the large number of ice cubes being consumed by Lord and his party.

Lord's reputation was already seriously hurt, but the misfortunes of the ill-starred voyage were just beginning. While en route from Tahiti to Samoa, the renovated but still faulty ship was struck by a tropical storm. The captain, Constantine Flink, formerly of the Imperial Russian Navy, was consulted by owner Lord about whether to abandon ship. The Coast Guard was radioed for information about the location of ships nearest them. A request for aid was sent the nearby *HMS Australia*, which altered its course en route to Panama and made for *The Seth Parker*. The storm subsided and it appeared that the faltering yacht would be able to make the final three hundred miles to Samoa. Then a second hurricane washed over *The Seth Parker*. The *HMS Australia* was called back to take nine men off Lord's yacht, leaving on board the captain, two crewmen, and Lord himself. The ship limped the remaining miles to port, listing a bit, but arriving sound and whole.

The press and some government officials didn't trust Lord, however, and claimed it was all a publicity stunt, and that Lord would not have remained on board if he felt the ship were really in danger of sinking. "Although we failed in our original purpose, the journey—we got as far as Samoa—was by far the greatest adventure of my life," Lord later said blandly, "and if I had the chance, I'd repeat it."

Lord returned broke, with his image as a hymn-singing parson tarnished. *Seth Parker* went off the air, although it was later revived briefly and unsuccessfully before the last "Amen."

Heaven no longer offered Lord profitable employment. He turned back to the denizens of hell—the underworld. He attempted other programs with some temporary success. By the end of the thirties, Lord began telling real stories with real people via the interviews of Milo Bolton on *We, the People*. There was a soap opera called *Woman in Love* and true aviation stories on *Sky Blazers*. But by far his most lasting successes were two more crime dramas following roughly the pattern of his winner, *Gangbusters*.

The manner in which Lord came up with new program ideas was a thing to see in itself. He would breeze in from a vacation of sun and sea on his island off the Maine coast and announce he had a couple of new ideas for radio series. "One is terrific, it's wonderful . . . typical Phil Lord idea . . . what everyone expects from radio's number one idea man," Lord is quoted as saying. His second idea was not such an explosive one, however. It would only make a good, solid type of show to run a few years, according to one published account of the meeting. "It's about the idea an *average* man would have."

One of the newer writers on Lord's staff couldn't successfully stifle his snicker, and was fired on the spot. Yet Lord could deliver what he promised in the way of popular commercial successes. When *Amos 'n' Andy* left their daily fifteen-minute spot on NBC to go to CBS (for the first of two such switches), Lord and his staff began kicking the can around about a new daily serial concerning the career of a district attorney. No given name was immediately set for the lead character, and the staff began plotting the scripts by referring to the hero casually as "Mr. District Attorney." The name stuck.

The *Mr. District Attorney* series went on the air in 1939, with Dwight Weist in the title role, and with a young man named Jay Jostyn playing one of a gang of crooks who were terrorizing a helpless city for protection money, in open defiance of the newly elected, crusading D.A. Despite his youth, Jostyn's voice carried the dignity and authority of a much older man and he soon earned the starring role of the nameless prosecuter.

Jostyn was a dyed-in-the-wool footlights actor, not just a radio announcer moonlighting in a dramatic stint. He and his wife, Ruth Hill, had been starving actors on Broadway and in local theaters across the country in the thirties. When their second son was born, the Jostyns had had just enough money to buy some penny postcards for the announcements. Then they discovered they hadn't any ink to write the glad news. With not a dime to spare, the birth announcements might have had to be combined with graduation invitations if a salesman friend hadn't dropped by with a sample kit of office supplies, including ink.

With a background like this, Jostyn had a real appreciation of a steady job, and the skill to do it well. No one who heard him can forget his ringing tones as he orated the credo of Mr. District Attorney: "And it shall be my duty, not only to prosecute to the limit of the law all those charged with crimes perpetrated within this county, but to defend with equal vigor the rights and privileges of all its citizens!"

Jay Jostyn's sidekicks on the new half-hour series (justice could not be done in fifteen minutes) about the "champion of the people, defender of our fundamental rights to life, liberty, and the pursuit of happiness" were Harrington, his not-too-Irish cop, and the lovely and efficient Miss Miller. The staff was one up on the anonymous Chief. They at least had last names, if not given ones.

Miss Miller was played by Vicki Vola, who still does what little radio is left, commercials, religious dramas. Harrington was the late Len Doyle, a man who is remembered with respect and affection by almost everyone who ever met him. As Harrington, he could start (and finish) a fight with four to one odds against him. He was a tough and resourceful man in real life as well. According to one reasonably authenticated account, Len Doyle was attacked by a bobcat on a camping trip to the northeastern states and killed it with his bare hands. Harrington could have done no more.

While Mr. District Attorney usually let Harrington handle most of the rough stuff, the Chief himself sometimes stopped merely masterminding the war on crime from behind his desk and got in there with his own dukes. Sometimes he had no choice at all. Even the most staid attorney would defend himself when a murderer assaulted him in his sleep, or during an attack on his life by a blood-crazed midget, and especially if a mad Egyptologist tried to wall him into a sarcophagus!

At no time, however, was the D.A. more fighting mad than when a gangster kidnapped his secretary, Miss Miller. Mr. District Attorney tracked him down personally and, after rescuing the girl, almost beat the cringing hood to death. The depth of the relationship between the D.A. and Miss Miller seemed deeper than most between employer and employee. After office hours, perhaps there was a time when they did use their first names.

The average episode of *Mr. District Attorney* was not fraught with this intensity of emotion, just steady police work. Another kidnapping took place in "The Case of the Last Witness," a script by Jerry Devine, one of Phillips H. Lord's staff. In it a groom was abducted from his own wedding at gun point. The D.A. and Harrington followed up the reported sighting of the getaway car, and soon were following a trail of blood through the woods.

MR. D.A.: Harrington, do you see what I see?
HARRINGTON: Yeah, Chief, a bunch of chickens, and all dead. Their heads have all been cut off.
MR. D.A.: Not cut off, Harrington. They appear to have been shot off!

(HARRINGTON EXCLAIMS)

MR. D.A.: Yes, Harrington, shot off. And I know of only one person who indulges in a pastime like that . . . a gentleman named Boss Verona!

Of course, Boss Verona was eventually brought to justice. The D.A. had Miss Miller pose as the bride to deliver the kidnap ransom, and in the darkness of the meeting place she managed to snap some photographic evidence with that new marvel of 1942 science, infrared light.

Producer Lord was always ready to accept new inventions—even that invention that threatened to destroy his radio empire. In 1949, *Mr. District Attorney* became the first and only mystery radio series to move to live television with its original cast, Jostyn, Doyle, and Vicki Vola. On camera, however, Jay Jostyn looked younger and less stalwart than the image his voice created. *Mr. District Attorney* went to film with a Hollywood cast headed by David Brian in the title role. A youthful appearance is a difficulty that is outgrown, and eventually Jay Jostyn was promoted to the part of a judge on television's *Night Court,* a reasonable but too pragmatic progression for the man who was once, and for so long, the "guardian of our fundamental rights."

Phillips H. Lord added one more jewel to his Triumvirate of Tension 1942 with *David Harding, Counterspy.* A telegraph clicker clattered in the opening and a voice intoned, "Washington . . . calling David Harding, Counterspy . . . Washington, calling David Harding, Counterspy. . . ." Then after a moment of suspense came that calm, firm, reassuring voice, "Harding, Counterspy, calling Washington!"

The "United States Counterspies" were "officially appointed to combat the enemies of our country both at home and abroad"; this is, they were appointed by Phillips H. Lord. America had counterspies, but there was no agency of the government designated "United States Counterspies."

Nevertheless, many people believed that the *Counterspy* stories were official cases, just like the "true" stories on that other Lord production, *Gangbusters*. Of course, just as *Gangbusters* was a euphemism for G-Men in their peacetime work, so Counterspies was a substitute term for the FBI doing its counterespionage work in World War II.[1]

Phil Lord had had his troubles with FBI Director Hoover once, and that was enough. He wasn't going to have to worry about this program being "authorized." Lord was the real director of those heroic "United States Counterspies, especially appointed to combat the enemies of America both at home and abroad."

David Harding combated the enemies of America way into the mid-fifties, probably surprising even Phillips H. Lord, who must have conceived the program only as a wartime show. In later years, David Harding was joined by an assistant as valiant as Mr. District Attorney's Harrington, and one who also lacked a first name. Special Agent Peters carried much of the action on the program as David Harding took to directing the world of his agents on an executive level, just as efficiently as the famous and anonymous D.A.

In one of the very first programs in 1943, Harding took a VIP on a tour of Counterspy headquarters. "And these," David Harding announced, "are the cells where we keep

---

[1] The real G-Men were represented on the program *The FBI in Peace and War*. This program about the exploits of Special Agent Reynolds was only "based on Frederick L. Collins' great copyrighted book, *The FBI in Peace and War*," however, and was "*not* an official program of the FBI." Finally, the G-Men did retaliate with their own official crime program, *This Is Your FBI*. This lacked all the machine-gun work of *Gangbusters*, however, or even the theme of "L-A-V-A . . . L-A-V-A" to the tune of "Love for Three Oranges" that distinguished the unofficial *FBI in Peace and War*.

enemy spies before we take them out and shoot them!" Long before James Bond, Counterspies were evidently licensed to kill.

Espionage in World War II was tricky and dirty, but the American public was much more innocent in those days. It was particularly innocent in its eight-year-old members, like me. I was dazzled by the intrigue and counter-intrigue that enmeshed David Harding and his enemies. The denouement of one of the fabulous cases actually written by Phillips H. Lord reveals the true sophistication and complexity of these master plots.

Norma Braely, a European refugee, volunteers to help the Counterspies capture a Nazi agent who is posing as a British Commonwealth agent. Then she sees the man right in Counterspy headquarters.

NORMA: Sir Harold Palmer!

HARDING: That's right, Sir Harold Palmer to you, Miss Braely. But a Counterspy to me, George Davis.

NORMA: He's a Counterspy? But he's the Canadian you sent me to watch. He's the one I stole the papers from.

DAVIS: And a very good job of stealing them you did, too . . .

HARDING: Miss Braely, you are under arrest by the United States government!

NORMA: Oh no . . . no, no! I'll kill you! I'll kill myself!

(GUNSHOT, SOUNDS OF A STRUGGLE)

HARDING: Take that gun away from her, Davis . . . While you were stealing the papers, Davis here was putting blank cartridges in the gun you have in your handbag. Killing comes pretty easy to you, doesn't it?

NORMA: You rat! You swine!

HARDING: I wasn't absolutely positive that you were the woman, Miss Braely, until we heard that broadcast tonight . . . and your spies passed on word about the revised fortification papers being sent to the coast Saturday night. Then I knew that you were the one we wanted. Because that was just a made-up story! And you and I were the only two in the whole world who knew it . . .

NORMA: You rat! You swine, American swine!

DAVIS: She's about the most vicious spy we have taken in since the war began, Harding . . .

HARDING: I've a feeling she is responsible for a lot of information leaking out . . . but one thing's certain . . . she won't get out!

David Harding's voice rang with authority on the subject of doom to America's enemies. But the authority behind the voice was really actor Don McLaughlin. Simultaneously, McLaughlin was "by proxy" Colonel Schwartzkopf on *Gangbusters*. Somehow, he had managed to land the lead role on two of Phil Lord's greatest crime shows. The explanation for this two-out-of-three score was undoubtedly Don McLaughlin's fine talent as a radio actor; he was often said to have the "most American" voice on the air. McLaughlin was a Broadway actor, like Mr. D.A. Jay Jostyn. He had come from Iowa, and his clean-cut good looks (he is six feet tall and maintains his 175 pounds) had helped win him roles on the stage, and his voice was well suited to lead roles in radio. Not only the head *Counterspy* and host of *Gangbusters*, he played Dr. Jim Brent on *The Road of Life* and many other roles in soap opera and crime programs. Today he is still in a daytime serial, television's *As the World Turns*.

Occasionally appearing on the same television show with McLaughlin is his old sidekick, "Peters," Mandell Krammer.

Krammer, another active actor on the airwaves, certainly didn't go over to TV until the last gasp. In 1962, he had the title role of *Your's Truly, Johnny Dollar* in the last episode ever produced on a radio network of a drama with a continuing hero.

Phillips H. Lord had worked hard, but he didn't labor in radio as long as his actors. After Lord set the style and pace of his various series with the initial scripts he wrote and the production he keyed, he was content to sit back and let the civil service employees of *Mr. District Attorney, Gangbusters,* and *David Harding, Counterspy,* continue to earn money for him. Today, the first two programs are still doing just that, from reruns of the filmed TV episodes. Of course, *Gangbusters* has been retitled *Captured* (these days criminals are rehabilitated, not just "busted").

Lord lives on that island off the coast of Maine now, instead of commuting from it to New York with fresh ideas only "a genius like Phil Lord" could conceive.

I wonder if the waves pounding on the shore don't sometimes sound like the marching feet of convicts to him, and I wonder what he thinks when he fiddles with the dial of a television set and hears a commercial for toothpaste done in the ringing tones of a man who once pledged solemnly to "defend . . . the rights and privileges of all . . . citizens."

We know for certain that Lord was a man of his time. His talents and personality were exactly right for a medium and an era that offered hokum and demanded faith in it as gospel, for an art form that had to be believed in to be seen. For the short time that was uniquely his own, no one was ever believed in like Phillips H. Lord.

III

"WHO KNOWS WHAT EVIL LURKS"

"The Shadow, mysterious aide to the forces of law and order is, in reality, Lamont Cranston, wealthy young man about town who, years ago in the Orient, learned the hypnotic power to cloud men's minds so that they could not see him. Cranston's friend and companion, the lovely Margo Lane, alone knows to whom the voice of the invisible Shadow belongs. . . ."

There were electric thrills ahead when you heard that familiar opening, ominous and evocative as the theme of *Omphale's Spinning Wheel* that accompanied it. Mysterious friend to the law indeed was The Shadow. He was, and is, a classic figure of mystery itself. About him seems to hang the fog of Sherlock Holmes' London, and yet he is at home in the cheap dives frequented by the hard-boiled dicks of Dashiell Hammett and Raymond Chandler. And more than being a symbol of all this, The Shadow has become the chief fictional representative of all that was Radioland. After all, we knew even back then that here was the perfect hero for radio—the man you couldn't see.

This phantom avenger was never really created. Like Topsy, he just grew. Or more accurately, he was gathered out of those shadowy recesses of man's imagination. Long before the radio broadcasts and the magazine novels, The Shadow was a term used in many pieces of fiction to name a mysterious figure, sometimes hero, sometimes villain. In the nineteenth century, one writer speculated on "a certain shadow which may go into any place, by sunlight, moonlight, starlight, firelight, candlelight . . . and be supposed to be cognizant of everything." The Shadow would issue "warnings from time to time, that he is going to fall on such and such a subject, or to expose such and such a piece of humbug. . . . I want . . . to get up a general notion of 'What will the Shadow say about this, I wonder? What will the Shadow say about this? Is the Shadow here?' " The writer who speculated on using such a creature was Charles Dickens.

More recent predecessors of The Shadow in the early years of this century were the French villain Fantomos, who, like The Shadow, also lurked in dark recesses overhearing schemes and exchanging shots with adversaries garbed in black clothing and slouch hat, but with the distinction that, unlike The Shadow, he wore gloves; and Frank L. Packard's Jimmie Dale, alias The Gray Seal, who had a mask, signet ring, a civilian identity as a wealthy young man about town, a girl friend who sometimes used the pseudonym "Margot."

On radio The Shadow was the name given to a mysterious voice that introduced *Street and Smith's Detective Story Magazine Hour* by inquiring "Who knows what evil lurks in the hearts of men?" and then proceeded to answer the question by simply reading a story from the current issue of the crime magazine published by the sponsor.

The Shadow character became an instant hit and the whole show was devoted to his own exploits instead of merely introducing other stories. The program became a full-scale drama with actors, music, and sound effects. Street and Smith also issued a new magazine, *The Shadow Detective Magazine*.

In the first, Winter, 1931, the lead story was called "The Living Shadow." One of the early appearances of The Shadow on the radio was described in the text of this account from "the Secret Annals of The Shadow."

There were those, of course, who claimed that they had heard his voice coming through the spaceless ether over the radio. But at the broadcasting studio, The Shadow's identity had been carefully guarded. He was said to have been allotted a special room, hung with curtains of heavy, black velvet, along a twisting corridor. There he faced the unseeing microphone, masked and robed.

The underworld had gone so far as to make a determined effort to unravel The Shadow's identity, if it were truly The Shadow whose sinister voice the radio public knew, for there were doubters who maintained the voice was but that of an actor representing The Shadow. But all crookdom had reason to be interested —those without the law had to make sure.

So watchers were posted at the entrance to the broadcasting chain's building. Many walked in and out. None could be labeled as The Shadow. In desperation, a clever crook, whose specialty was wire-tapping, applied for and secured a position as a radiotrician. Yet questioning of his fellow workers brought nothing but guesses to light. Around the studio The Shadow was almost as much a myth as on the outside. Only his voice was known.

Every Thursday night the spy from crookdom would contrive to be in the twisting corridor watching the door of the room that was supposed to be The Shadow's. Yet no one ever entered that room!

Could it be, then, that The Shadow broadcast by remote control? That his voice was conveyed to the studio by private wire? No one knew. He and his fear-striking laugh had been heard. That was all.

The original scripter for the radio series, Harry E. Charlot, died under puzzling circumstances, a mystery the solution of which is known perhaps only to The Shadow. After him a long line of free lancers contributed to the broadcasts: Jerry McGill, Max Erlich, even Alfred Bester, one of the great names in contemporary science fiction. Walter Gibson, a professional magician as well as a prolific writer who penned most of the nearly two hundred (178) *Shadow* magazine novels under the name of Maxwell Grant, unfortunately played no significant part in scripting *The Shadow* radio plays.

The writers for the magazine and the radio script fashioners borrowed freely from each other. Fans of the novels still complain that faithful sidekicks of The Shadow never appeared on the air, though this isn't quite true. In 1937 and 1938, among others, Commissioner Weston appeared along with his fellow police department member, Inspector Cardona, The Shadow's ally and nemesis. Radio fans, on the other hand, insist they never cared for the novels because in them, they say incorrectly, Margo Lane was not Lamont Cranston's friendly companion. While Margo was first born on the radio series, she certainly did appear in many of the magazine stories.

Aside from Margo, and cab driver Moe "Shrevie" Shrevnitz, who was an in-and-out comedy relief on radio, only Commissioner Weston was a familiar character in both media.

And who was it who knew what bitter fruit the weed of crime bears? James La Curto for one, also Frank Readick, who were among the very first actors to assume the role of the airwave's awesome avenger. Following in their shadowy footsteps was Robert Hardy Andrews, prolific radio writer who first scripted *Jack Armstrong* and *Just Plain Bill*. Then, in 1937, there was an actor who was only twenty-two when he stepped before the carbon mike to pronounce The Shadow's warning to crookdom. His name was Orson Welles.

The very young Orson Welles gave a lot of vigor to the then youthful career of The Shadow. His ominous rumble imparted a Shakespearian depth and urgency to every line of outrageous melodrama. Welles was convincing. On his other program, *The Mercury Theatre,* he convinced a good portion of the nation that we were literally being invaded by monsters from Mars when he adapted H. G. Wells' interplanetary novel, *War of the Worlds,* to sound like an on-the-spot newscast. That one broadcast earned him too much fame and notoriety to allow him to remain the anonymous star of *The Shadow,* so in the spring of 1939 Welles spoke for the last time to radio listeners of the evils that lurk in the minds and hearts of men.

Bill Johnstone, who had appeared in character roles on the show, succeeded Welles as Lamont Cranston. Although Johnstone's voice was vaguely similar to Welles', it was lighter and much, much more mature, barely this side of elderly.

By 1944, Johnstone had retired from the title role and the part was taken over by Bret Morrison, who had returned from army service to radio. He had been Mr. First Nighter before Pearl Harbor. But obviously military life had strengthened him for hardier stuff than attending a new play each week in radio's Little Theatre off Times Square. Actually, Morrison probably sounded more like a "wealthy young man about town" than any who played The Shadow—the right combination of sophistication and forcefulness.

Morrison's Margo was Gertrude Werner; Johnstone had played opposite Marjorie Anderson; and Orson Welles shared the kilocycles with a Margo Lane played by Agnes Moorehead.

The Brooklynite cab driver, Shrevie, was Alan Reed, who hasn't learned any better grammar as the voice of the home screen's "Fred Flintstone." Santos Ortega as Commissioner Weston completed the cast of regulars.

In cast and story, *The Shadow* was designed to convince you that The Shadow was real, he was earnest, and that he might be very near, lurking somewhere in the shadows, aware of your every guilty secret. For some listeners he was so convincing that during the war they wrote to the network broadcasting the exploits of The Shadow demanding to know why Lamont Cranston was not using his secret powers to fight the Nazis and Japanese. What the network replied to these correspondents is not known.

Anyone who ever tuned in on Sunday knew that Lamont Cranston had "the power to cloud men's minds so that they could not see him." In the most brightly lit room, The Shadow was invisible. He chuckled merrily as he drove the murder suspects he visited out of their minds. He was here, he was there, he was everywhere. Once in a while he would lift a mad scientist's flask of elixir into the air, or pull a gun out of nowhere and leave it hanging in the air to prove he was corporeal. But most of the time, he counted on his eerie voice to cause his victims to jump at every shadow.

It is strange that none of the people The Shadow ever visited on the airwaves ever suspected mechanical trickery. The Shadow, when invisible, sounded exactly as if he were speaking over a telephone. For some reason, no one ever snarled, "You can't fool me, buster. Somewhere you got one of them tin cans rigged up with a tight string!"

Moreover, Cranston was always telephoning people—crooks, suspects, Police Commissioner Weston. No one ever bleated, "Cranston, huh? So that's who you really are, Shadow! I'd recognize that voice anywhere!"

Of course, all this was more than a stupid mistake. We all realized, I think, that The Shadow was more than a voice. It was the *power* of The Shadow to cloud men's minds that made him able to go unrecognized when he didn't wish to be recognized.

In the show's early years, the decade before World War II, there was a time of experimentation, a search for the limitations and scope of The Shadow himself. The Master of

Men's Minds was not limited to his power of hypnotic invisibility.

Those of the younger generation who think Shari Lewis invented ventriloquism would be surprised to learn that The Shadow was capable of projecting his voice up the entire slope of a volcanic mountain from its base. He did that in a 1937 radio episode called "White God" in order to cause a deranged scientist to blow himself and the mountain up in the mistaken belief that he would be taking his nemesis, The Shadow, along with him. The explosion didn't harm The Shadow, but it destroyed the volcano, which the scientist had turned into a gigantic magnet to pull planes and ships to their destruction. A madman in 1937, today he could probably get a good job with the government.

Many more purely psychic powers belonged to the youthful Shadow. The same year he caused the destruction of the "White God," he received a "Message from the Hills" delivered by sheer telepathy, the mind of an ancient native speaking directly to the mind of The Shadow to warn him of the forces of evil at work. The Shadow was able to answer the call for help both mentally and, at last, physically.

These were not all of the special powers of the Master of Darkness. When Margo was abducted by a lunatic who pined to be a vampire (another one of *those* weekends in the country!), The Shadow was able to silently "will" people he met to do his bidding and answer his questions. Finally, The Shadow located Margo just before the lunatic, a renegade medico, pumped the poor girl completely empty of blood. The "vampire" wasn't really thirsty, just greedy. He had gone a long way toward depopulating the countryside by siphoning the residents dry in order to sell their liquid contents to a blood bank.

After the thirties, the free-wheeling days of experimentation with The Shadow's powers were over. Someone decreed that Lamont Cranston was a detective and he would use his power as The Shadow exactly twice in each show. After the middle commercial, which urged you to rush right out and buy a ton of Blue Coal immediately, The Shadow would interview a reluctant witness to scare the bejabbers and the information out of him or her, and Cranston would become The Shadow for the second time in one show to capture the villain in the climax and, usually, rescue Margo Lane from his clutches.

Actually, it got so that The Shadow frightened people very little with his invisibility. It seemed everybody had been through that bit so many times that there were a few token lines about "Where's that voice coming from?" and "The Shadow has the power to cloud your mind . . ." and the interrogation would proceed in standard cops-and-robbers format.

Yet even into the forties and fifties an occasional broadcast of *The Shadow* had some element to help make it memorable—an interesting locale, a bit of business, a gimmick. The plays that were the most interesting were the ones concerned directly with The Shadow's power. While the furthest boundaries of his abilities were explored in the thirties, in the forties there was, on a rare occasion, a statement of his limitations.

The boundaries of hypnotic invisibility are known to science, since the feat can actually be performed by an expert. The subject, placed in a hypnotic trance and told "not to see" the hypnotist and his attire, will see a cigarette in the hand of the hypnotist eerily floating in the air. If the command is re-enforced by instructions not to detect any sign of the presence of the hypnotist, the subject will not even detect the smoking cigarette. Of course, any ordinary human hypnotist requires the right subject and careful preparation. Only the *superhuman* Shadow could cloud men's minds instantly. And even The Shadow was not infallible. Once he apparently neglected to instruct his subjects not to see any evidence of his presence, thus leaving himself open to being spotted in the home of a wealthy crook by the impressions of his feet in a deep-pile carpet. When guns came out, The Shadow's visible footsteps beat a hasty retreat, but, as I recall, he did catch up with the luxury-loving hood, no doubt in a place with hardwood floors.

Other much more complex methods were used to make The Shadow visible and expose his true identity. Aliens from space probed him with inspection rays and turned the data over to their calculators, which speedily beeped out a complete analysis when The Shadow hastily quit the scene. This happened back in 1939, when the audience must have really thought it was crazy Buck Rogers stuff.

Probably the highlight of all these "Shadow exposed" tales came in "The Shadow's Revenge," when Lamont Cranston stood mumbling furiously that he had the power to cloud men's minds while a pair of crooks were convulsed with laughter. "Hey, Cranston, you cracking up or something?" one amused gangster asked. It all seemed like a nightmare. And, unfortunately, (as far as a good story was concerned) it was exactly that.

As a listener, after those first few years of pre-teen innocence, the greatest mystery about The Shadow to me was exactly what was meant by Margo being Lamont Cranston's "friend and companion." The question can be answered a bit more realistically than the innuendos about Lois Lane and Superman, or even the Lone Ranger and Tonto. There does seem to be some real, not purely imagined, evidence that the relationship between Margo and Lamont was very companionable. After all, Cranston and Margo did travel around the world together several times, generally unchaperoned, and many of the radio plays began with the wealthy young man about town and his "friend and companion" having breakfast together at Cranston's town house or apartment. While there was never mention of the possibility of marriage, there were often suggestions of romance, and Lamont and Margo referred to each other as "darling." All in all, it is apparent that Margo had a deep appreciation of the skills Lamont Cranston learned in the Orient.

The question, if one ever existed, seems completely settled in one of the 1965 paperbound revivals of The Shadow novels. In *The Shadow's Revenge*, under the traditional by-line of Maxwell Grant, the Master of Darkness pays a call to Margo Lane's boudoir.

Margo Lane sat up in her bed. The slim body of the dark-haired woman was hidden by her light sheet. Awake, she smiled at the black-shrouded figure of her chief. The Shadow was not smiling, his great figure tall in the room, his glowing eyes piercing the dim bedroom light.

"I must go now, Margo," The Shadow said. "I must find The Demon before it is too late . . ."

So if Margo was The Shadow's "friend and companion," he was also her "chief" and she "smiled" at his entrance into her bedroom. Since The Shadow's prime motivation is power, he would exercise that power over the woman in his life. That part of the mystery of The Shadow seems solved.

Another "mystery" about Margo and Lamont that always interested me was why this companionable twosome never learned that no matter how bad the storm, no matter how perilous the road, they should never, never seek refuge in mysterious old mansions around which broke forks of lightning and winds of fury! They were sure to run into homicidal maniacs, gory corpses, and a legendary supernatural monster or two. It happened to them in "The Legend of Crown Shield Castle," "The House that Death Built," and "The Werewolf of Hamilton Mansion."

Hamilton Mansion wasn't the only place they ran into a lycanthrope menace. There was one in "Death Prowls at Night." There were zombies in "The Isle of the Living Dead," a relative of King Kong in "Night Marauders," and a crazy actor who thought he was the Frankenstein monster in "The Face."

Almost all of these creatures took after Margo Lane. It couldn't have been for her beauty alone. After all, so many of these fiends wanted to change her. One wanted to change her into a gorilla, and another madman tried to convince her to become a bitch—a she-wolf. She was menaced, tied up, tortured, threatened, and assaulted up to the point the censor would allow, and all because she traveled around the country with Lamont Cranston, who clearly wasn't going to make an honest woman of her. Such is the perversity of women!

The only other woman I can think of who has had to endure so much for a man is Lois Lane, perennial girl friend of Superman. With such a similarity in name and character, can there be any doubt that these two girls, so attracted to men who wear capes and mistreat them so, are sisters?

The perfect example of what Margo Lane had to go through appears in "The Ghost Walks Again," a script by Jerry Devine that was such a complete *Shadow* story that it was presented to writers as a sample of how to write the radio show.

When a ghost begins murdering the population of a small New England town, the town council gets together and comes to the only logical decision: call in Lamont Cranston. Needless to say, Cranston doesn't pay much heed to Margo (who is trailing him around again), and she is captured by the "ghost," who for kicks (there is no other reason) decides to put her to the torture.

EDWARD: In the days of the Puritans they had a very satisfactory method for dealing with meddlers . . . they branded them upon the forehead . . .

MARGO: No . . . no . . .

EDWARD: Soon, young lady, soon you shall feel the searing agony of that brand biting into your flesh!

MARGO: You're mad . . . you're mad!

EDWARD: (LAUGHING) You won't feel the pain too long . . . no . . . you see, after you are branded I have another treat for you . . . the press . . . the torture press!

MARGO: You let me out of here!

EDWARD: The branding iron is glowing now . . . it is ready to use!

MARGO: You can't do this . . . please!

EDWARD: (LAUGHING) Prepare yourself . . . prepare yourself, Miss Lane . . . I have the iron ready now . . .

MARGO: Keep it away from me . . . (SCREAMS) Keep it away!

SHADOW: Drop that iron, Mr. Darrow!

EDWARD: Who was that?

SHADOW: Release that girl . . .

EDWARD: No . . . no! Let go of my arm! Let me finish my work!

(IRON DROPS TO FLOOR)

SHADOW: There . . . your work is finished, Mr. Darrow!

EDWARD: Who are you?

SHADOW: (LAUGHS) I am The Shadow!

EDWARD: The Shadow! I've heard of you . . .

SHADOW: Then you know too that I am here to put an end to your career of torture and murder, Mr. Darrow!

And so, once again, The Shadow does prove that he knows "what bitter fruit the weed of crime bears" and that "crime does not pay!"

The Shadow's exploits took place originally in the thirties, forties, and even into the fifties. The radio program lasted until 1954, nearly five years longer than *The Shadow Magazine*. And perhaps that was where Lamont Cranston should have stayed—in the shadows of the past. But many people didn't think so. They wanted radio drama back and, in particular, favorite shows like *The Shadow*. Of course, for the most part, the old recordings had been destroyed long ago because the program originators never considered the possibility that one day there would be a public demand to hear the old shows once again. But a few people still had radio recordings—private collectors, members of the cast, production crews of radio programs, and especially Charles Michaelson.

Charles Michaelson had been involved in the production of the original *Shadow* broadcasts and he had picked up syndication rights on this program and others when big-time radio began going out in the fifties. He salvaged literally thousands of transcription discs that might otherwise have been destroyed for all time. For nearly a decade all he had been able to do with the old recordings was store them. "When we started to clean out our vaults around Christmas of 1962, I couldn't bear to destroy those old radio recordings," Michaelson recalled. "Maybe it was the sentiment of the holiday season. I phoned ten large radio stations around the country and asked if they'd be interested in airing some of the old shows again. . . . I got six affirmative answers."

Charles Michaelson, a man alternately nostalgic and practical, had his problems to solve, many of them with unions. A committee of actors was set up to agree on the identity of voices heard on various episodes for residual payments.

On some programs where the organist who played the theme and bridges couldn't be identified or located to sign an agreement, all the original music had to be edited out and stock transcription orchestrations inserted. In the end, Michaelson, the sentimental businessman, won over all obstacles. The Shadow returned!

WGN in Chicago was the first station to begin rebroadcasting *The Shadow*. Radio-TV columnists seized upon the programming idea and gustily informed Windy City citizens that "The Shadow is back on the air! Once again we'll hear of the evils that lurk in the hearts of men!"

Because of all the breezy banner waving that consequently drew audiences' attention back to radio drama, WGN's scheduling of the old *Shadow* shows received an overwhelming listener response as young and old alike, the neophytes and the nostalgics, all tuned in on Sunday afternoons in Chicago to brave the eerie adventures of the Master of Men's Minds. Students of the Pop Art culture at nearby Northwestern University even allegedly formed a Secret Shadow Society, complete with members garbed in black cloaks and slouch hats who huddled around an old Motorola floor-model radio, listening to *The Shadow*.

After this initial success, Michaelson added other stations to his list of customers and other titles to his catalogue of program offerings, including *Sherlock Holmes, Weird Circle*, and *The Green Hornet*.

The Shadow, though, became the most successful of the handful of old favorites the recordings of which had survived and were available for syndication, eventually reaching forty outlets. Though the market waxes and wanes, these old programs may be playing on some station somewhere as long as there is radio.

As one of the basic prototypes of what has come to be called Pop Art, The Shadow is unique and irreplaceable, a legend in his own time. A classic character who looms slouch hat and shoulders above all others of his kind, he is as inevitable as a guilty conscience, an unseen power that awakens within all of us our most deep-rooted fears of mortal retribution. There has never been a force quite like him.

None of the stories, or radio plays, or comic magazines, or motion pictures (and someday, no doubt, television programs), will ever be really good—not great art, not great literature. But The Shadow himself is great! For he is a creature of folklore, not created, but distilled.

Invisible as a radio beam, or cloaked in the blackness of night, The Shadow can achieve his full potential only in our imaginations. Whether by aid of a broadcast, or by the gift of memory, when The Shadow steals across the stage of our own consciousness, he *is* "the Master of Men's Minds."

A NOTE ON THE SHADOW MAGAZINE

Thundering automatics blasting red-tipped flame rumble in the night—answering blasts echo back—final volleys from automatics—silence. Then from the blackness behind automatics moves a deeper blackness—a shadow within a shadow—and disappears into the night. And on the chill night air is borne a peal of laughter.

The triumph laugh of The Shadow!

So runs the introduction to a 1935 Shadow novel, *The Python*. The scene is typical of the exploits of the night-prowling crime fighter in the pages of his magazine—his weapons were the night, his cloak of blackness, and his twin .45 automatics.[1]

[1] It should be noted that no other character in the novels ever carried a .45. They could only gape in awe at The Shadow's "big guns" while he snickered at the dinky little .32s and .38s with which gangdom constantly plinked away at him so ineffectually. If The Shadow had ever been struck in the heart by one of the effeminate little .32 slugs, he wouldn't even have deigned notice it.

In contrast to the radio program, where the Master of Men's Minds relied on his powers to cloud minds and to strike fear into stout hearts, in the magazine he was also a master of gunplay. On radio, without a lot of announcer's narration, The Shadow himself could explain how and why he was invisible to the eyes of men, but in print, The Shadow used his black cloak and the slouch hat and the shadows themselves to disguise his movements. He was *virtually* invisible, yet he was mortal, not godlike, and a penetrating gaze or a shaft of light could on rare occasion expose him.

The very first novel, *The Living Shadow*, explained, "It was as though the man's strength had been wrested from him," one character feels "when he faced a tall, black-cloaked figure that might have represented death itself. For he could not have sworn that he was looking at a human being. . . . The stranger's face was entirely obscured by a broad-brimmed felt hat bent downward over his features; and the long black cloak looked part of the thickening fog. . . ." And later, "The mysterious stranger had vanished—like a shadow!"

Only Moe "Shrevie" Shrevnitz, Commissioner Weston, and reporter Clyde Burke of The Shadow's faithful secret agents from the magazine were ever brought to radio life. In the magazine, there was handsome, dependable Harry Vincent, who, at some time in his long career must have asked, "Tennis, anyone?"; Burbank, who spent his life at a switchboard just to relay information when The Shadow called in, ordering "Report!"; and Kent Allard, who was never even mentioned on the radio program. Allard was The Shadow's true identity, according to the novels, Lamont Cranston being merely another false identity—an impersonation, just to make things complicated. The real Cranston left for Tibet or some other place long ago to let The Shadow use his name and fortune in combating crime. The only claim on fame Kent Allard himself had is that he was a World War I ace. It has been suggested, after hearing the cracked laughter that is his trademark, that The Shadow may be the result of a prolonged case of shell shock.

Street and Smith, the publisher of the Shadow novels, had a long career of creating fictional heroes the world thought real. In one of their dime novel weeklies in 1891, Nick Carter, the master detective, first saw the light of day. People believed in Nick Carter, wrote him letters to cheer or ask advice, and finally, even the creator, Frederick Dey, began to believe that he was the great sleuth. On a trip to Paris, Dey and a friend were attacked by a half-dozen hoodlums of the streets known as Apaches. His back to the wall, Dey shook a fist into their faces. *"Je suis Nick Carter!"* he yelled, identifying himself. The mob, it is said, fled in terror. Nick Carter was polished up in the 1940s to join his costumed colleague, The Shadow, in a series that followed that of the cloaked avenger on Sunday afternoons.

The Shadow Magazine began as a quarterly publication with the novel *The Living Shadow*, Winter, 1931, but within a few short years became so popular that Street and Smith started issuing the magazine twice a month. In the early forties the magazine once again became a monthly, then changed from its pulp-sized format to a digest-sized magazine, a bimonthly.

When The Shadow's reading audience began waning in 1948, Street and Smith decided to try and give the Phantom Avenger a shot in the arm for circulation's sake. Once again the magazine reverted to its original pulp size. But the hypo was short-lived and *The Shadow Magazine* lasted only four more issues, concluding seventeen years of publication with "The Whispering Eyes."

Recently, in 1964, The Shadow once again saw print, this time in the form of original paperbacks published by Belmont Books. The first title, *Return of The Shadow*, was written by Walter Gibson, who wrote almost all of the magazine novels, but the others in the new series, not written by Gibson, are under the time-honored Shadow author pseudonym, Maxwell Grant.

IV

"AND HERE IS YOUR HOST"

TURN OUT YOUR LIGHTS . . .

"Good evening, friends. This is Raymond, your host, welcoming you in through the squeaking door to the *Inner Sanctum*. We have another tale to thrill you, and to chill you. Won't you come in and have a seat? No chair, you say. Why don't you try that black box over there? It's nice to have someone here who really believes in black magic, the supernatural, zombies and goblins. What's that? You don't really believe in those things? Well, our story tonight is about a man who didn't believe in them either. But he found out that he was wrong—dead wrong. Ha-ha-ha-haaaa . . ."

Your host on *Inner Sanctum Mysteries* (brought to you by Bromoseltzerbromoseltzerbromoseltzer and its private, talking train) apparently had no last name. It wasn't necessary. One word, spoken in a sufficiently ominous tone, conjures up to anyone over twenty-five a whole lost world of shadow and stealth . . . "Raaaaaay-monnnnnnd . . ."[1]

As host of *Inner Sanctum,* he ushered us into an abode of mystery and a place of dread, but one where what you dreaded seldom turned out to be real. One week you might hear about a nice old man who seemed to be a vampire,

---

[1] Off mike Raymond not only had a last name, but a middle name, too—Raymond Edward Johnson.

but turned out to be just a nice old man or, at worst, a vampire turned out to be a deranged doctor with a hypodermic needle and a bicycle pump. Another week you might hear how a strange creature from the sea was killing off an entire shipful of men, one by one. But in the end it turned out to be the captain doing it all. ("Mad! He's stark, raving mad!")

On a very special week, you might hear Boris Karloff himself in an adaptation of Edgar Allan Poe's "The Telltale Heart."

> KARLOFF: His room was as black as pitch with the thick darkness (for the shutters were close fastened through fear of robbers) and so I knew that he could not see the opening of the door, and I kept pushing it on steadily . . . steadily. . . . Now I had my head in, and was about to open the lantern when my thumb slipped upon the tin fastening and the old man sprang up in the bed . . .
>
> OLD MAN: Who's there?
>
> KARLOFF: I kept quite still and said nothing. For a whole hour I did not move a muscle. . . . In the meantime, I did not hear him lie down. He was still sitting up in the bed listening . . . just as I have done, night after night, harkening to the death watches in the wall. . . .
>
> OLD MAN: (GROANS)
>
> KARLOFF: A groan! A groan of mortal terror. It was not a groan of pain or of grief—oh, no!—it was the low stifled sound that arises from the bottom of the soul when overcharged with awe. I knew the sound well. Many a night, just at midnight, when all the world slept, it has welled up from my own bosom, deepening, with its dreadful echo, the terrors that distracted me. . . .

Edgar Allan Poe wrote a beautiful radio script. The story-teller goes on in his painstaking work of putting out "his eye—his damned Evil Eye" and putting the dismembered body under the floorboards. But the old man's heart just doesn't know when to stop. The *sound* permeates all, driving the incomparable Karloff to higher octaves of terror.

Himan Brown was the man behind *Inner Sanctum*'s creaking door, whose ominous groan of massive hinges swinging open to reveal the terrible chamber of shadows was the perfect opening for every show. Brown, the producer, knew how to use the stuff of radio—the special sound effects in the opening and in the body of the show were equally well done. To get the proper sound of a head being bashed, for example, Brown devised a special bludgeon with which he would strike a small melon. The juicy, hollow, squishiness was much truer than the sound from the standard piece of foam rubber used on many shows. If nothing else, we all knew what a head being bashed *didn't* sound like.

Brown even used music as a sound effect. His organist was warned never to play a recognizable song, or, if he could help it, even an original snatch of melody. The man at the somber Hammond organ was to play sharp "stings"— a high musical note struck to emphasize an important piece of dialogue. He sounded "doom chords." He played "bridges" between scenes. There were two kinds of bridges; somber marches to disaster, extensions of "doom chords," and staccato frenzies of pell-mell movement, the chase.

Brown's biggest trouble was in his methods of killing people. The Federal Communications Commission objected if he got too specific. "The problem," Brown has said, "was not to reveal actual murder methods with such clarity and definition as to give the listener a good idea of how to erase someone he could do without, or even a half-complete knowledge of a known and effective method of killing with only a small chance of being caught." On the rare occasions when other radio programs did get too ingeniously specific, Brown implies, there was a significant influence on national crime statistics in following weeks.

Actually, anyone who followed the *modus operandi* on *Inner Sanctum* in real life would soon be heading, not for the "squeaking door," but the famous green door at the death house. The plots in which the true supernatural was generally explained away to make you "believe the story could really happen" were incredible combinations of strained coincidence, the possible but improbable, and the totally illogical. In scripts by such writers as John Roeburt and Max Wylie (who has himself pointed out how improbable his *Inner Sanctum* scripts were), a salesman might be driving along a highway and discover a dead body in the back seat. He drives on frantically for a time, then stops at a house where by chance he meets the wife of the dead man, who immediately falls for him. They are interrupted by a policeman who pulls a gun on the driver and puts him under arrest for the murder of the man in his car. The driver (a salesman by trade, remember), immediately disarms the policeman and knocks him cold. The widow and the salesman decide to run off together to Canada. Sometime later, the two are found in a northwoods cabin by the woman's supposedly "dead" husband, the man in the back seat. He has faked his "death" for insurance purposes, and now is going to kill the woman for running out on him. The salesman tackles the husband, and in the struggle a gun goes off and the husband staggers out of the house to the car and falls into the back seat, dead. The salesman is back where he started. For absurdity of plot, this could be matched only by Grand Opera, but the proper mood, the "logic of the instant," could carry this not atypical *Inner Sanctum* story on radio.

At the end of the half hour, Raymond would reappear, stepping over and around the litter of corpses, make his tongue-in-cheek apology for the puddle of blood on the floor, pass a few digging remarks about graves, and invite us to read the latest *Inner Sanctum Mystery* novel published by Simon & Schuster. Then it was time to close the "squeaking door" for another seven days. "Good night . . . and pleasant dreams . . ." Squeeeeeeeeeeeeel-KA-THUNK!

The Hermit's Cave was another radio chiller, but it differed from *Inner Sanctum* and the programs that imitated *Inner Sanctum*, shows like *The Haunting Hour, The Sealed Book, Weird Circle,* and, to some extent, *Suspense.* The difference was that *The Hermit's Cave* told stories of genuine supernatural horror without any contrived "explaining away" of the fantasy element.

The Hermit's Cave had for its occupant an elderly storyteller, the Hermit. In the days when radio was king, we did hear stories told by old people in real life as well as on the air. We listened to old people then, instead of driving them into senior citizen ghettos. Besides, you had damned well better listen to the Hermit or he would cut your heart out for your impertinence.

"Gho-o-ost stories! Weird stories! And murders too! The Hermit knows of them all! Turn out your lights. Turn them out, and listen while the Hermit tells you . . ."

The stories the Hermit told were perhaps less memorable than he was. They tended toward highly traditional ghost stories and occasional experiments in ghastly bad taste, stories of mad little men who hollowed out human heads, baked them, and used them for flower pots, that sort of thing.

A much superior fantasy series was another syndicated transcription feature, *Stay Tuned for Terror,* written entirely by Robert Bloch, who since the Alfred Hitchcock production of his novel *Psycho* has been fully recognized as a master of horror and fantasy. In spite of his talent for the grim and ghastly, Bloch is a humorous, almost whimsical fellow himself. He has the heart of a small boy. I've seen the box he keeps it in. Bloch has found, however, that it is difficult for people to keep him separated from the creatures he writes about: murderers, werewolves, transvestites, and other people in show business.

Bloch tells an amusing anecdote about his days in radio. During the time he was adapting such well-known stories of his as "Your's Truly, Jack the Ripper" for *Stay Tuned for Terror* in Chicago, he was approached about scripting another radio show that originated in that city. The attitude of broadcasting producers then as now seems that one writer is much the same as another writer. The producer in question felt that Robert Bloch must have some ability, since he had a series of his own. Bloch was therefore offered the opportunity of becoming the writer of *Jack Armstrong, the All-American Boy.*

During the time *Stay Tuned for Terror* was broadcast, other writers were doing horror series that achieved greater fame and currency. *Lights Out,* an NBC series from Chicago, offered an outlet in the thirties for the talents of both Willis Cooper and Arch Oboler. Cooper wrote many fine plays for this program and for another all his own called *Quiet Please,* but his work on *Lights Out* was overshadowed by that of the more grimly spectacular Oboler. The flashy showmanship of Oboler made *Lights Out* a byword in its time, something of a legend in ours. The fame the series generated has enabled Oboler as recently as 1963 to issue a record album of stories from the program under the title *Drop Dead.* The disc contains condensed versions of several *Lights Out* stories, including the one about the chicken heart that grows until it consumes the whole world, the most horrible fate envisioned for the globe in those dear, dead days before Hiroshima.

Following a good reaction on the record album, Oboler

revived a number of his *Lights Out* scripts in 1963 radio productions under the title *Arch Oboler's Plays*. The program met with as much success as possible in today's radio market, hostile to drama or other programming not involving phonograph records and many, many commercials.

One of Oboler's better *Lights Out* scripts concerned a young poet who was . . .

PAUL: The Ugliest Man in the World! All right, I'll think the thing for the last time, tear the words around in my head over and over the way they've torn for thirty years! Ugliest Man in the World. Ugliest Man in the World. Ugliest Man in the World! Press the trigger and stop it, press the trigger! No, no, I can't! Got to wait! Wait for what? Nothing if I wait! Press the trigger . . . No! . . . my chance . . . yes, my chance to think . . think it all out clearly for the first time in my life . . . how it started, why it's ending this way . . . think it all out clearly from the very start . . . then press the trigger . . .

MOTHER: (GHOSTLY—A MEMORY) School today, Paul.

PAUL: There's a start . . . first day of school . . . how old was I . . . nine or ten . . . she kept me home away from others . . . I didn't know why until that day . . . she took me to school . . . into a room full of more children than I'd ever seen . . . I was so happy I wondered why her face was white and set . . .

TEACHER: Your attention, children! I—I want you to meet a new classmate. His name is—uh—

YOUNG PAUL: Paul Martin!

PAUL: For a moment not a sound . . . row on row of children look up at me, staring at me, gaping at me . . . and then—one of them started laughing!

Another laughing . . . and another . . . and another! Laughing, laughing. I stood there, a little boy, looking down at their twisting mouths, my ears filled with the sound of them! Making fun of me, I knew that. But why? *Why?*

(THE LAUGHTER RUNNING UNDER THE PRECEDING SPEECH STOPS)

CHILD'S VOICE: (WHISPERING) Ugliest boy in the world!

With the simplicity and the strength of a fairy tale, Oboler went on to build the story of the ugliest man in the world who fell in love with a blind girl. Then, the blind girl lost her blindness. But, of course, she did not lose her love for Paul, who was no longer ugly once you knew him.

"You can turn them on now," the announcer said when *Lights Out* was over. Unfortunately, we can never turn the lights off again to achieve that purity of darkness, that blank state of imagination.

"STARS OF STAGE, SCREEN, AND RADIO"

"LUX . . . presents . . . HOLL-Y-WOOD!"

The Lux Radio Theatre had at its helm one of Raymond's rivals for radio's top M.C. of drama. "Ladies and Gentlemen, your host, Mr. Cecil B. DeMille!"

"Greetings . . . from Hollywood," Mr. DeMille would say warmly. He would then introduce a sixty-minute version of a then current motion picture, or of some well-remembered film from the past, generally with some or all of the original stars.

When a major motion picture was released into theaters in the thirties and forties, the producers were anxious to sell the story and the stars to *Lux Theatre*, letting the audience listen to a big new epic for free. Even though millions of people knew the story before they saw the picture, they still went to see it, perhaps feeling more secure, since they knew it was a good story and therefore wouldn't be disappointed.

The use of movie stars on radio had one great advantage: almost everyone knew what they looked like and mental images of them were easy to create. Most of them had good voices and performed well on the air. Clark Gable, Gary Cooper, and Lana Turner sounded just as they should sound, and their portraits could be drawn from their voices without ever seeing them. A few others, notably Herbert Marshall, gained depth and stature on radio over their visual appearance on the screen. On *Lux* as a guest star, and on other anthologies, as well as in his own spy series as Ken Thurston, *The Man Called X*, Marshall reached greater heights of popularity than he knew on the screen. In later years, after DeMille had departed, Marshall became host of *Radio Theatre*, the sustaining continuation of the *Lux* show.

Adaptations of movies hardly represented radio at its creative best. *Lux* presented modest, clean, and spare versions, however, of such classic books and films as *Les Miserables*, *Pride and Prejudice*, and *The War of the Worlds*, along with more standard fare such as *The Westerner*, *Murder My Sweet*, and *The African Queen*.

Lux did take advantage of the unique abilities of radio on a few occasions. Some twenty years after the release of the famous silent film *Seventh Heaven*, an audio version was presented on *Lux* with the original stars, Janet Gaynor and Charles Farrell. Although both had been retired for years and were past playing young lovers on the screen, their voices were firm and youthful and the play was a sentimental success.

A young Larry Parks was not needed on radio to play young Jolson. In *Lux*'s production of *The Jolson Story*, Al Jolson not only did the singing, but all of the acting of the story of his own life. The program received one of the highest ratings in radio history, and Jolson re-created many of his screen vehicles, from *The Jazz Singer* on, on the *Lux* stage.

In the mid-forties, a seemingly minor dispute with the American Federation of Radio Artists over a dues assessment caused C. B. DeMille to leave *The Lux Radio Theatre*. DeMille was one of the greatest names in Hollywood, one of that select group of producer-directors the general public knows and to whom it gives star billing (John Ford and Alfred Hitchcock may be the only others). He gave glamor and class to the program, which was, however, really produced by Lux's advertising agency. It continued without DeMille, first with guest hosts like Walter Huston, and then once again with a real movie producer, though not such a famous one, William Keighly, whose greatest recommendation may have been that he sounded a bit like DeMille. With Keighly and later replacements including Irving Cummings at the helm, *Lux* continued to bring motion picture adaptations to radio into the 1950s with adaptations of such films as *Gentlemen Prefer Blondes*, *Sitting Pretty*, and *Shane*.

The Lux Radio Theatre was a program for people who wanted movies right in their homes. By 1950, people could get real movies in their homes on television, and even the *Lux Video Theatre*, which had "live," cheaply done versions of old movies with small name casts could not compete with the real thing, and *Lux* went off both television and radio.

Lux, the most widely heard dramatic anthology, was never much of an achievement for radio, but it did inspire many imitations, some superior to the model: *Screen Guild Players*, *Screen Directors' Playhouse*, *M-G-M Radio Theatre*, *Ford Theatre*.

Indeed, the greatest accomplishment of *Lux Radio Theatre*

may have been in getting every star who appeared on the show, male or female, to come out and endorse Lux soap in an informal chat with the producer after the play. Hedy Lamarr, Lana Turner, Rita Hayworth, Ava Gardner, all owed their unique beauty to Lux. Even Humphrey Bogart said in his growling lisp: "We never use nothin' but Lux around our place, Thee Bee." It was Clifton Webb who declared in weary ad-lib enthusiasm: "Why, C. B., I wouldn't even go into a place to wash my hands if Lux wasn't there!"

As if in answer to Lux, DeMille, and Hollywood, the Broadway stage had its champion in Mr. First Nighter and *The First Nighter* program.

"Good evening, Mr. First Nighter!"
"Good evening, Vincent. I see there's a good crowd here tonight at the Little Theatre off Times Square. Well, we can always be sure of a good play with stars like Barbara Luddy and Les Tremayne. I'll see you after the first-act curtain, Vincent. Now friends of the radio audience, we have good seats, third row center, so let's go right in, shall we? Listen, from the lobby you can hear Frank Worth and his Orchestra playing the overture . . ."

Before the first curtain, Mr. First Nighter would leave Vincent Pelletier in the lobby to tell us all about Campana Balm cosmetics and go into the Little Theatre to take his seat. En route, the crowd would spot celebrities and ask those never-answered questions: "Isn't that Helen Hayes?" "Was that Walter Winchell?" while the usher urged: "Smoking in the outer lobby only."

Mr. First Nighter was played by a succession of actors, Vinton Hayworth, Bret Morrison, and Hugh Douglas, but on the Little Theatre stage one star, Barbara Luddy, appeared almost all of the time. Miss Luddy had a cheerful, bubbly quality and was, in a number of ways, the Doris Day of dramatic radio. Her co-star was originally Les Tremayne. After Tremayne left Chicago to play *The Thin Man* in New York, Olan Soulé became the leading man. The plays in the fictional "Little Theatre off Times Square" were almost always romantic comedies, with Miss Luddy and her co-star being forced into some kind of rivalry before their very pale "hate" could be turned to love.

Sometimes, however, the air would get a bit thicker on *The First Nighter*, with mystery and even that favorite soap-opera device, the girl with "amnesia." (Radio writers never heard of aphasia.)

> BILL: I want to take care of you, Ethel . . . forever.
> ETHEL: But there's something . . . strange about me, Bill. I don't know what it is myself. You must have realized it . . . and now you're trying to be kind.
> BILL: I'm only trying to be kind to myself, because I love you so.
> ETHEL: No. Wait. You must wonder how much I remember about . . . about the past. Things that happened before I knew you. And the answer is— nothing! I don't remember a thing, Bill. There must be months between the time I came to Grayfields, that I don't remember at all. That's the sort of woman you're asking to be your wife.
> BILL: I love the woman I'm asking to be my wife. . . . The only thing that matters to me . . . do you love me?
> ETHEL: I do! So very much. Only—
> BILL: Only nothing, darling. That's all I want to know.

Of course, Bill was being a bit hasty. Ethel had a bit of a secret in her past. On her *first* wedding night—to Oliver, not Bill—her groom had dropped dead as he danced with her. Oliver, we discovered, had developed an unnatural state for a lover on radio—*passion.* Radio morality being what it was in those days, nobody on radio ever expressed sexual desire. Oliver had paid the price for his passion—death! So Ethel had, in her unconscious, been afraid that the same thing would happen to any man who loved her. But no doubt Bill was a "nice boy" and would never be unseemly enough to get excited. In the end, everything worked out "nicely."

The curtain rang down. The audience applauded. Some cried. Miss Luddy and Mr. Tremayne took their curtain calls. And Mr. First Nighter announced that the play was another smash hit for the "Little Theatre off Times Square."

It was the "frame" that sold *The First Nighter* show. Mr. First Nighter arriving at the theater, the exciting trappings of an opening night on Broadway. For people in small towns, particularly, the adventure of going to an opening night in New York, on Broadway, was in itself an exciting experience. Interestingly enough, the program never did come from New York City, much less Broadway itself. *First Nighter* was originally broadcast from Chicago, and then later from Hollywood, and significantly, all those plays closed after the first-night performance.

Just as *Lux Radio Theatre* had its host of imitators, other programs copied *First Nighter's* theatrical format right down the aisle. There were *Curtain Time* and *Knickerbocker Playhouse*, among others.

The program that had perhaps the best "frame" on radio was one that dealt in stories similar to those on *First Nighter* —light romance, comedy, mystery—but with a rotating cast. The program was named after a culminating point of several railroads and had one of the great, classic radio openings.

"GRAND CENTRAL STATION! As a bullet seeks its target, shining rails in every part of our great country are aimed at Grand Central Station, heart of the nation's greatest city. Drawn by the magnetic force of the fantastic metropolis, day and night, great trains rush toward the Hudson River, sweep down its eastern bank for one hundred and forty miles, flash briefly past the long red row of tenement houses south of 125th Street, dive with a roar into the two and one-half mile tunnel that burrows beneath the glitter and swank of Park Avenue . . . and then . . . GRAND CENTRAL STATION . . . crossroads of a million private lives, gigantic stage on which are played a thousand dramas daily!"

The most famous play ever heard on this program was the annually repeated Christmas show. The story was of a spiritual entity who came to Earth and assumed the mortal guise of an intern who subsequently renewed a cynical and bitter ambulance driver's faith in humanity. Everybody in this world—and the next—eventually passed through *Grand Central Station.*

"As the old morning bugle call of the covered wagons dies away among the echoes, we bring you another story of *Death Valley Days*—presented by the Pacific Coast Borax Company, makers of 20-Mule Team brand of borax and Boraxo . . . and told to you by the Old Ranger. . . ."

The creaking of wagons and the braying of mules was a far cry from the commuter specials screaming through *Grand Central Station.* With its distinctly rural host, the Old Ranger, *Death Valley Days* was the only successful anthology series on radio without a big city setting, and the only lasting western anthology. It has repeated the same distinctions on television. Created by Ruth Cornwall Woodman for the makers of 20-Mule Team Borax, the TV series, claiming continuity with its radio incarnation, now proclaims itself to be in its thirty-fifth year on the air. Recently the program was opened by ten matched pairs of jackasses and Ronald Reagan, but for the first thirty years or so, the host was the Old Ranger, played by many radio actors, including John McBride, and portrayed on television by a former radio actor, Stanley Andrews.

The radio show had still another distinction. The stories the Old Ranger told were based on true incidents, their chief dramatic license being the introduction of the fictional senior-citizen narrator into the tale.

> OLD RANGER: I met Uncle Billy the first time in Los Angeles back in 1925. I was walkin' along the street one day, shortly after noon, an' I seen a big crowd gathered in front o' the I. W. Hellman Bank. . . . There by the curb, quite unconcerned about the commotion he was causin', stood a spare, leathery old feller in blue jeans an' a battered felt hat. He was a-tetherin' a string of burros to a fire hydrant. . . .

The Old Ranger went on to tell in this 1942 broadcast that this "leathery old feller" known as Uncle Billy wouldn't only hitch up his mules in front of a bank in the big city, he would camp anywhere he "derned well pleased," in city or country around Death Valley. Bank managers might object, but not most people in the hospitable plains and deserts. When one narrow-minded rancher did tell Billy to move on, the old man filed a legal mining claim valid even on private lands, and stayed as long as he liked. It was a lesson in human kindness and hospitality, the Old Ranger pointed out. These were values held high during the time of *Death Valley Days*.

The Mercury Theatre on the Air was the *compleat* radio anthology series, presenting fantasy often better than *Lights Out*, mystery a notch above *Inner Sanctum*, historical adventure more rugged than that of *Death Valley Days*, and certainly drama more likely to hit Broadway than those plays attended by Mr. First Nighter. An extremely creative and versatile program, it was produced and hosted by one of the most versatile and creative talents in the history of entertainment, Orson Welles.

Welles began the program in 1938 by putting his Broadway repertory group, the Mercury Theatre, "on the Air." The players were Agnes Moorehead, Joseph Cotton, Everett Sloan, and many other talented actors who went on to become stars. *The Mercury Theatre* show shifted from New York to Hollywood when Welles went to the West Coast to begin his illustrious but stilted film career with *Citizen Kane*. *The Mercury Theatre* began as a sustaining program, picked up Lady Esther cosmetics as its first sponsor, and metamorphosed into the *Campbell Playhouse* when Campbell Soup picked up the tab.

The series presented brilliant adaptations of Shakespeare, horror gems such as *Dracula* and *Frankenstein,* and originals that included "The Hitchhiker," a play about a phantom traveler who follows a lone driver clear across the nation. Lucille Fletcher's script for this became almost as famous as her "Sorry, Wrong Number" on *Suspense*. Of course, the most famous of all *Mercury Theatre* broadcasts came very early in the series and was the basis for much of the series' later fame. Indeed, *The Mercury Theatre* adaptation of H. G. Wells' *The War of the Worlds* became the most famous single radio broadcast of all time.

The broadcast began with a formal announcement that *The Mercury Theatre* was presenting an adaptation of H. G. Wells' *The War of the Worlds*. But then, the show seemed to turn into a dance-band remote as Latin music filled the air.

> ORCHESTRA ANNOUNCER: Good evening, ladies and gentlemen. From the Meridian Room of the Park Plaza in New York City, we bring you the music of Ramon Raquello and his Orchestra. With a touch of the Spanish, Ramon Raquello leads off with "La Cumparsita" . . .
>
> (MUSIC BEGINS)
>
> NEWS ANNOUNCER: Ladies and gentlemen, we interrupt our program of dance music to bring you a special bulletin from the Intercontinental Radio news. At twenty minutes before eight, central time, Professor Farrell of the Mount Jennings Observatory, Chicago, Illinois, reports observing several explosions of incandescent gas, occurring at regular intervals on the planet Mars. . . .

Slowly, the reports trickled in. It all amounts to the fact that strange cylinders from the planet Mars have struck the Earth. One lands near Grovers Mill, New Jersey. A radio reporter, Carl Phillips, and the man he was interviewing, Professor Pierson of Princeton (played by Welles) travel to the spot.

> PHILLIPS: Ladies and gentlemen, this is Carl Phillips again, at the Wilmuth farm, Grovers Mill, New Jersey. Professor Pierson and myself made the eleven miles from Princeton in ten minutes. Well, I—I hardly know where to begin, to paint for you a word picture of the strange scene before my eyes, like something out of a modern "Arabian Nights." Well, I just got here. I haven't had a chance to look around yet. I guess that's it. Yes,

I guess that's the . . . thing . . . directly in front of me, half buried in a vast pit. Must have struck with terrific force. The ground is covered with splinters of a tree it must have struck on its way down. What I can see of the—object itself doesn't look very much like a meteor, at least not the meteors I've seen. It looks more like a huge cylinder. It has a diameter of—what would you say, Professor Pierson?

PIERSON: (OFF MICROPHONE) About thirty yards.

PHILLIPS: About thirty yards—the metal on the sheath is, well, I've never seen anything like it. The color is sort of yellowish-white. Curious spectators now are pressing close to the object in spite of the efforts of the police . . . just a minute! Something's happening! Ladies and gentlemen, this is terrific! This end of the thing is beginning to flake off! The top is beginning to rotate like a screw! The thing must be hollow!

VOICES—She's a-movin'!

VOICE 1—Look, the darn thing's unscrewing!

VOICE 2—Keep back there! Keep back, I tell you!

VOICE 3—Maybe there's men in it trying to escape!

VOICE 4—It's red hot, they'll burn to a cinder!

VOICE 5—Keep back there! Keep those idiots back!

VOICE 6—She's off! The top's loose!

PHILLIPS: Ladies and gentlemen, this is the most terrifying thing I have ever witnessed—wait a minute! Someone's crawling out of the hollow top. Someone or—something. I can see peering out of that black hole two luminous disks—are they eyes? It might be a face. It might be—UGH! GASP! GAG!

The radio audience listened to what seemed to be actual news bulletins of an invasion from Mars, with on-the-spot remote broadcasts of battles between the Martians and the U. S. Army, with the Army taking a sound drubbing from death rays and poison gas. The audience listened—and believed it all to be real. In New Jersey people filled the streets, with wet towels wrapped around their heads to "protect" them from the heat rays of the Martians. In Michigan a housewife quietly prepared to commit suicide before the Martians could get their slimy tentacles on her. In New York State men reported to their National Guard headquarters to fight the war against the planet Mars.

How *many* really believed? Orson Welles has recently revealed in interviews that the initial reports of hysteria from the broadcast were actually minimized so as not to create further panic. For weeks after the broadcast teams were going about all over the country to lure people out of the refuge of the hills.

Why did people believe in the "Invasion from Mars"? Whole books have been written on the subject.[2] The public was less informed, more gullible in 1938, and there has to be a first time for everything, including Orson Welles' "Mars" hoax. International tensions had been building up in Europe. People were *expecting* invasion and warfare of some kind. Many thought the "invaders" were not really from Mars but from Nazi Germany. Finally, the program was an excellent job of documentary-styled radio drama. And the purpose of drama is to *convince*. This drama by Howard Koch did its job all too well.

Whatever the "Invasion from Mars" broadcast proved, it established the power and effectiveness of radio drama. For over thirty years, dramatic radio was effective, and then

---

[2] *The Invasion from Mars*, by Hadley Cantril and Associates, Princeton University Press, 1940.

with the September 30, 1963, broadcast of *Suspense* on CBS, it looked like it was all over. Since then, however, reruns of such old programs as *The Shadow* and *The Haunting Hour* have appeared. Arch Oboler did his short-lived syndicated series. And, most promisingly, the ABC Radio Network presented, in 1964 and 1965, an anthology series called *Theatre Five*, five nights a week.

A far cry from the skill and scope of such programs as *Mercury Theatre* and *Suspense* in their vintage period, *Theatre Five* nevertheless revealed some promise. The "live" series was canceled, however, in 1965 and the programs done to that date were made available for rerun on independent stations.

The anthology was a mainstay on radio, and radio had one for every taste—mystery, romance, historical, comedy, even genuine, drama.

One of the essentials of drama or of good fiction in general is that the characters develop during the story. They must grow and change. That is, in fact, the definition of what constitutes a story. Of course, the characters in a regular, continuing situation—Matt, Doc, and Kitty, in *Gunsmoke*, for instance—cannot change. They must be just the same for the next episode. They may appear to learn some new truth about themselves or others, but it has no real influence on the way they behave. There can also be little real suspense about continuing characters. You know they will live through the trouble, no matter how serious it looks. You know their situation isn't going to change radically or permanently. Matt Dillon will not be removed from his office as U. S. marshal and reduced to sweeping out stables —at least, not for more than one episode.

In the anthology drama, you never know for certain exactly how characters will behave or how they will eventually wind up. The audience can be and should be more fully involved with the fate of these unfamiliar characters, these unknown quantities. This involvement may require more work on the part of the audience, but it is worth it for those who tire of the same old motions and emotions of familiar faces.

There were stars in radio, of course, but not all of them were people like Barbara Luddy and Les Tremayne. Some of radio's stars were a gigantic, pulsating chicken heart and a battered old squeaking door. It was a world of faceless things and faceless people, but a master showman could bring it to life. The greatest impresario of radio was not Cecil B. DeMille or Orson Welles. The one who really ushered you into the world of strange and commonplace delight that was radio, the guide through the mind's inner rooms, was always yourself.

V

FULL-COLOR HEROES THAT WERE NEVER SEEN

"NOT A BIRD! NOT A PLANE!"

"It's the most serious thing that ever happened!" Robin, the Boy Wonder, said to Superman one spring day in 1945. "Batman has disappeared!"

"You'd better tell me about this," the Man of Steel rumbled.

This momentous and history-making conversation took place March 3, 1945, when Superman encountered Batman and Robin for the first time on the Mutual radio network. Looking back on it, the fact that the "Caped Crusader" had disappeared may not seem like the "most serious thing that ever happened," but it certainly did at the time.

On the day of that momentous meeting, things began in the usual way. Announcer Jackson Beck cried, "Faster than a speeding bullet! (*Kow-zing!*) More powerful than a locomotive! (*Chug-a-chug-a-chug!*) Able to leap tall buildings in a single bound! (*Whissssssssshh!*) Look! Up in the sky! It's a bird! It's a plane! It's . . . SUPERMAN!"

Quickly, we were advised by the announcer that Clark Kent had gone to a certain pier on North Bay, following instructions in a letter sent to his *Daily Planet* office. The letter asked Kent's help in locating the Man of Steel for an urgent mission. Near the specified pier, Kent spotted a drifting rowboat and a boy lying in the bottom, unconscious. Then, in the words of the narrator, "When the boy revived and identified himself as Dick Grayson . . . Clark Kent took Dick to his apartment, where he left for a moment, and then appeared as Superman. He told Dick that he had seen the cape beneath his coat, and the red leather vest with the letter 'R' on it, and recognized him as Robin, companion of the famous Batman! The boy admitted his identity and pleaded for help."

Dick Grayson, "Robin," explained to Superman that Batman was missing in action, and that he, Robin, had barely escaped a gang of crooks, one of whom mentioned the name of a man called Zoltan. Later, Superman, once again as Kent, took Dick to the place of business of Zoltan. Kent observed, strangely enough, "He's the only Zoltan in the telephone book." Zoltan's business was a wax museum, and through a window they saw what appeared to be a wax figure of Batman. Eventually, Superman discovered that this was the real Batman, sealed inside a super-hard wax alloy in a state of suspended animation. After being freed by Superman, the black-caped crusader vowed vengeance upon Zoltan to the Man of Steel and to Robin, the Boy Wonder.

"You'll forgive me for saying so," said Batman, "but no one is going to make a dummy out of me."

Zoltan was captured, his evil business of shipping great scientists to enemy countries in wax statues was destroyed, and Batman and Robin went on to help Superman in many other adventures, appearing in every second or third story between 1945 and 1952, sometimes having the stage much to themselves.

Any meeting of two separate heroes in comic books is known, in the language of comics collectors, as a "crossover," and is a rare, sought-after occurrence. The crossover where Superman and Batman met on the air was equally rare for fictional characters on radio, where almost nobody but comedians and singers ever visited each other's shows. Still, Batman and Superman getting together seemed "right" during the afternoon serial hour. The rest of that time on all the networks was saturated with successful adaptations of comic strips, including *Dick Tracy*, *Little Orphan Annie*, *Buck Rogers*, *Terry and the Pirates*, *Hop Harrigan*, and with programs original to radio but so like comics that they were destined to become comic-book material. Indeed, *The Green Hornet* and *Captain Midnight* both had second lives in the colored pages. Since all the available time in the afternoon was taken up by the serious, even stern, heroes from the funny papers, the doubling up of Batman and Superman was almost a necessity. There was simply no room for a *Batman* radio series separate from the *Superman* program, although no doubt the producers hoped that, given an opening, Batman and Robin would spin-off into a show of their own. But radio was plodding along at its own leisurely pace toward oblivion, and there was not to be time for Batman until television gave him his due.

Superman had been badly in need of a friend. He had stooges and foils, but no one he could treat as an equal, a colleague, a confidant. Batman filled this niche.

Batman won enough confidence from Superman to be the first person he ever let in on his secret identity as Clark Kent. Being a master of makeup, Batman thereafter sometimes doubled either as Kent or as Superman in order to help the real Man of Steel protect the secret of his identity.

But the prime reason, plot-wise, for the introduction of Batman and Robin was as an "antidote" for the deadly, radioactive element Kryptonite, to which even Superman was not invulnerable. The Man of Steel was immune to bullets, knives, poison gas, everything. To give the program some suspense, the writers brought in fragments of meteorites from Superman's home planet, which gave off radiation that robbed him of his superness and could kill him if he were exposed to it long enough. Ordinary radiation couldn't harm him, but super-radiation from his own super-planet could.

When Superman was un-supered by exposure to the rays of Kryptonite and lying helpless in a swoon, his reporter girl friend, Lois Lane, and her fellow *Daily Planet* employee, young Jimmy Olson, had to do a turnabout and rescue the once invulnerable Man of Steel. (Of course, Kryptonite didn't affect ordinary human beings). For the listener, this was certainly a startling development. You had heard these two inept reporters being trapped by the most transparent menaces conceivable for years and it was hard to believe they had enough initiative to blow their own noses, much less save Superman from the clutches of a mad scientist trying to destroy him with Kryptonite. Yet, somehow, they bumbled through a number of such adventures scattered over a year or so. In one sequence, the two of them managed to seal up the offending Kryptonite in a lead pipe pried from beneath a sink. Another time, Jimmy Olson returned a specimen of the strange element to its specially built container when he discovered Superman lying helpless beside the chunk of meteorite and its opened box, left there by a fiendish criminal. In still another adventure, the young boy and the girl reporter tossed the Kryptonite off a cliff into the sea so that it would be carried far from the Man of Steel and his superhuman powers could return. They had done it again. Miracles would, apparently, never cease.

More believable aides for Superman were clearly called for, and from the wings came the Dynamic Duo. While they were not from the *Superman* strip by Jerry Siegel and Joe Schuster, Bob Kane's *Batman and Robin* were both from the same publishing company. They were not immune to bullets, but at least they wore cloaks.

The most sterling rescue performed by the Caped Crusaders occurred when Superman was incapacitated in still another encounter with his elemental nemesis, Kryptonite, and kept a helpless prisoner in the attic of an old farmhouse. His captors sat around downstairs making bets on how soon their worst enemy, Superman, would die either from Kryptonite poisoning or starvation. Eventually, Superman became so weak he couldn't speak. For two whole weeks, he couldn't speak. Why, Superman might as well have stayed away from the radio station and gone on vacation to Miami!

Meanwhile, Batman and Robin were carrying the action, tracking down clues leading to Superman's whereabouts. When at last they located the old farmhouse, a terrific fight got under way in which the chunk of Kryptonite got knocked out of critical range of Superman. Weakened, dazed, he wandered off in a state of amnesia! Having forgotten everything, even his super-strength, the Man of Steel eventually found himself playing record-breaking baseball under the name of "Bud Guy."

Of course, the Dynamic Duo successfully captured the gang at the farmhouse and soon traced down their wandering super-buddy. The sight of the two familiar faces (or at least, the two familiar masks) brought Superman back to normal. Super-normal, that is.

Batman and Robin made such good sidekicks that it's hard to see how the Man of Steel had gotten along without them up to 1945. But he had, since *Superman* first began as a transcription series sold to individual stations in 1938.[1]

Before encountering Batman, Superman engaged in such varied adventures as searching for the lost explorer Alonzo Craig and the lost treasure of the Kuenaloki Indians (one of his first exploits in 1938), tracking down spies in World War II (such as the one spreading terror through the terrible Green Death), and voyaging to the planet Utopia, whose heavy gravity and nitrogen-free atmosphere first robbed the Man of Steel of his powers (this was before the introduction of Kryptonite).

The very first episode of *Superman* simplified the origin of the visitor from Krypton, "Who came to Earth with powers far beyond those of mortal men." In the comic books, the baby Superman landed in his experimental spacecraft

[1]The radio series began even before Superman became the star of a comic book devoted entirely to him—he only had the lead feature in *Action Comics*. The voice of both mild-mannered Clark Kent and his alter ego, the mighty Superman, was Clayton "Bud" Collyer, of television's *To Tell the Truth*, and then radio's *Renfrew of the Mounted* (*Renfrew* was to *Sergeant Preston* as *Tom Mix* was to *The Lone Ranger*; the first was a serial in modern times with airplanes and cars as well as horses, and the second, complete half-hour stories of the 1890s.) As Kent, Collyer always sounded as if the blue tights beneath his red shorts beneath his gray flannel trousers were too snug. When at last he found a convenient phone booth and he could cry, "Off with these clothes—this looks like a job for [*Sigh*] Superman!" the voice dropped an octave in relief.

His young friend, Jimmy Olson, also had a bit of trouble
(*footnote continued on next page*)

from the doomed planet and grew up with foster parents, the Kents, and slowly learned to use his super-powers. On radio, the baby apparently grew up during the flight and landed on Earth ready to combat evil. Although it was hardly a childhood to be envied, who could help but envy Superman's manhood.

Like Superman himself, most of the characters on the program were born full grown and developed no further. Lois Lane was always beautiful, pesky, aggressive, and, best of all, unobtainable. (That's exactly the way you wanted it when you were ten.) Perry White was always the gruff but lovable editor, a bit more whimsical some times than others. Only teen-age Jimmy Olson was given a chance to mature.

When Jimmy started to work on the *Daily Planet* as a

(footnote continued)

with his voice cracking at times. (It was more noticeable when Jackie Kelk was playing his other role of Homer on the *Henry Aldrich Show*.) The fact that Superman, super as he was, was the only adult still going through a change of voice may have helped some of the slightly older of his young audience identify with him. As usual in such shows, the sidekick was not needed for identification. We wanted to be the hero, not some star-struck kid trailing him around.

Others in the cast whose voices remained pretty much the same were Joan Alexander as Lois Lane, and Julian Noa as *Daily Planet* editor Perry White. The voice of Batman did change from time to time. Completely. Because the role was not sustained, being offstage for weeks or months, a variety of actors assumed the cape and cowl. These included Don McLaughlin (also *David Harding, Counterspy*), Bret Morrison (*The Shadow*), and Richard Kolmar (*Boston Blackie*, and now a Broadway producer). Robin was played by a variety of youths including Ron Liss and one who also did Jimmy at times, Mitch Evans, whose father is Vinton Hayworth, the first Mr. First Nighter. The radio family tree was a complex one, indeed.

cub reporter, he was cynical, tough-talking, and rude. He was particularly contemptuous of the "old fool," Perry White. Along with seemingly everybody in the thirties (Pat O'Brien, Babe Ruth, Jack Armstrong), White considered sports the way to rehabilitate all lost souls. In White's case, outdoor sports seemed particularly effective. He took Jimmy up to his hunting lodge to teach him healthy outdoor living. Things weren't going too well until Jimmy and White were attacked by a giant grizzly bear. The gray-haired editor immediately sprang to the boy's defense with a hunting knife, and though considerably past the age of Steve Wilson or Brit Reid, White upheld the honor of newspaper editors, the heartiest professional men in dramatic radio.

Superman arrived at last to finish the great beast, rescue White, and hear Jimmy's tearful vow that he would never fail to respect his elders again. That must have been a difficult resolution to keep, since White thereafter seemed to be treated as something of a comedy relief. And Mr. Kent's bumbling was only exceeded by Miss Lane's total imbecility. He must have thought it took a Superman to just be a man.

Even Superman himself seemed only a foil for the villains who kept him jumping tall buildings and racing faster than a locomotive to stall their plans. "The Yellow Mask" was one of the first of the master criminals he encountered in 1941, and a prototype of the breed. The Yellow Mask was running ragged the city of Dyerville by creating "earthquakes, fires, and floods." His mysterious voice came over the radios of the townspeople with warnings, but no demands. Reporters Clark Kent and Lois Lane went to investigate. Crossing the bridge over the Jefferson River, Clark and Lois heard a voice on their car radio: "Go back, Mr. Kent . . . go back . . . go back. This is the last warning of the Yellow Mask!"

Halfway across, the bridge began to collapse beneath the car carrying the two reporters. Lois screamed and fainted (just like a girl!) and Clark Kent took advantage of the situation by taking off his clothes. Leaping into the air, his voice sinking to a solemn bass, Superman (who like many of radio's great heroes, had the habit of talking to himself) said, "Got to save the bridge—and save Lois—not much time—good thing it's dark—no one saw Clark Kent change into Superman—Great Scott! The bridge is rocking like a pendulum—if I can get down underneath it—down on the piers—quick—it's going—matter of seconds—down—down!"

Then the narrator informed us, "Red cloak streaming in the wind, Superman plummeted down through the darkness like an arrow. . . ." While the bridge swayed above him, the Man of Steel dipped beneath the water and discovered with his X-ray eyes that the foundation had been blown apart. If he could twist the girders that were hanging loose back into place, Lois and the bridge could be saved. But could any man, even Superman, do that? "I don't know . . . it's pretty far gone . . . but maybe I can make it. If I don't, the whole thing will fall, crash into the river, and take Lois along with it. Now then . . . one more pull . . . *did it!*"

You never really doubted that Superman could save the bridge, or that, later on, he could save Dyerville from onrushing flood waters and ultimately expose and capture the Yellow Mask. If there was any suspense, it was in how Superman would do it. The program was one long stall until the predestined conclusion.

When finally *Superman* was adapted to the complete-in-one-half-hour format, the new policy worked better for the show than most others that tried it. There was little need for stalling tactics on a half-hour show. Kryptonite rarely appeared. Batman and Robin were seldom required to lend aid. You could easily believe that Superman, like the Lone Ranger, could wrap up any kind of trouble in half an hour.

The *Superman* radio series ultimately vanished faster than

a speeding bullet. Now there is even a Broadway play about the Man of Steel, as well as filmed live-action and a cartoon series on television. The not-deliberately-funny cartoon series has offered a unique revival for the original radio cast. In 1966, Bud Collyer returned as Kent-Superman along with Joan Alexander as Lois and the familiar narrator, Jackson Beck. If you close your eyes, it seems almost the same. If Collyer's "Up, up and *awa-a-ay*" doesn't take us quite as far away, perhaps the fault lies not in the star but in ourselves.

"THAT CRAZY BUCK ROGERS STUFF"

Buck Rogers must have been wildly jealous of Superman, who could rocket between planets stripped to his colorful underwear, while he required a full-fledged spaceship, spacesuit, and a beautiful copilot to do the same interplanetary voyaging. Still, the twenty-fifth-century adventurer must have taken some pride in the fact that he did his first flying in a 1929 newspaper strip, nine years before Superman appeared in comics and on radio. The program began three years after his first comic-strip flight and started with a strange thundering rumble that represented a time machine taking us into the future, forward in time to share the adventures of "Buck Rogers . . . in the . . . twenty-fifth cen-tu-reeeee."

After the commercial, which assured you that that syrupy chocolate stuff, Cocomalt, you stirred up in milk was really good for you, Buck Rogers and his lovely sidekick were constantly getting ready for a blast-off.

"Wilma, does all your equipment check out?" Buck Rogers inquired.

"Yes, Buck, I have my Thermic Radiation Projector, the Electro-cosmic Spectrometer, and the Super Radiating Protonoformer all set to go."

"Let me check the tubes of your jets," Buck suggested. "On a trip like this, we can't afford to have anything go wrong."

"I'll say not!" Wilma agreed. "The future of the whole universe depends on you, Buck, and Dr. Huer."

"And you, Wilma. Don't forget you are an important part of this mission for the peace and security of the planets."

Those were the immortal words spoken by Buck Rogers around 1932 and they were written by the same man who years later was having Superman save merely the inhabitants of the planet Earth from disaster. The author of both *The Adventures of Superman* and *Buck Rogers in the Twenty-Fifth Century A.D.* on radio was Jack Johnstone, who also produced and directed the programs.

Radio, like movies and television, tended to type-cast people, and for years the broadcasting world seemed to think Johnstone was ideal to write and produce science fiction thrillers for the juvenile audience. Nevertheless, he managed to escape that limitation and survive in dramatic radio as long as it lasted. He was the regular scripter on the very last radio drama with continuing characters, *Yours Truly, Johnny Dollar*. Today, he is more interested in washing machines than time machines—he owns a string of Laundromat-type establishments.

Johnstone liked inventing "all those gadgets. The Molecular Contractor Beam Projector was one of my favorites," he recalled. "One shot from that and you found yourself knee-high to a Lilliputian. A Molecular Expansion Beam Projector took the shrunk out of your shrink and you were returned to normal." *Buck Rogers* also employed death rays (forerunners of laser beams), guided missiles, and atomic bombs, all in the early 1930s.

The radio programs borrowed liberally from the original comic strip by Phil Nowland and Dick Calkins, but developed some of the ideas in interesting fashion. The relationship between Buck and Wilma Deering, his blonde assistant, so antiseptic in the comic strips, became more human through the added dimension of live voices. When they were marooned on an Arctic ice mountain, they were far from cool. Contemplating the moon and stars, their voices got lower and lower, ever more intimate. Outraged mothers, overhearing their children's radio program, wrote in letters of protest about the scene as they imagined it.

The stories were set in an interplanetary future and had whole planets at war with each other just to sell first Kellogg's Rice Krispies, and then Cocomalt. Although the warfare was symbolic and bloodless, there were a lot of protesting letters about Buck's adventures, even the non-amorous ones. It's surprising that anyone bothered, since even the "menace" on *Buck Rogers* couldn't really upset anyone. His archenemy, Killer Kane, was a pathetic, henpecked boob, who was always being pushed around by a villainess named Ardala. She not only had all the looks in the outfit, but all of the brains. Without her, Kane was helpless, and on those rare occasions when he succeeded, it was only by blind luck. Like the time he was trying to burn up an entire planetoid two or three miles in diameter. He tried matches on the coal-like rocks, a cigarette lighter, a blowtorch, and finally a flamethrower. No luck. In disgust and fury, Kane drew his ray gun and blasted the offending rock. It burst into flame. A typical Kane victory.

With such "opposition" from Killer Kane and Ardala, Buck, Wilma, and kindly old Dr. Huer ("Heh! Heh!") roamed the planets by spaceship and flying belts, venturing into a fourth-dimensional oblivion during World War II when the program was off the air.

I heard the show for the first time when it was revived in the mid-1940s. The new opening ran:

"Beyond the atomic bomb!"
Booooooo-oo-om . . .
"Beyond rocket power!"
Ka-zoo-oo-om . . .
"Beyond the future!"
Ooo-eeeee-oooooooo . . . [VERY WEIRD!]
"Buck Rogers in the Twenty-fifth Century A.D."

The first episode had Buck returning to Earth top speed to join Dr. Huer at a session of the World Council at Niagara Falls, New York. (Phil Nowland's comic strip set up a world organization at Niagara Falls long before the United Nations met at Flushing Meadow.) There was a bit of a problem. The Sun was going out. Just to make matters worse, as the episode drew to a close, Buck's rocketship went out of control and seemed about to crash into the cascading falls!

Buck pulled out in time (next episode) and went on to discover the Sun wasn't really going out. A mad scientist in league with his old enemy, Killer Kane, was creating a gigantic cloud in space to stop the Sun's rays from reaching Earth. Buck found the cloud-making machine and destroyed it, thus solving the interplanetary smog problem. But there were other problems still to be solved.

Buck, Wilma, and Huer crash-landed on a mysterious planet in a later sequence, a world inhabited solely by robots. The robots were programmed to look after and guard all human beings. Unfortunately, to guard them, the robots had to see to it that they never left that world. Not wishing to remain in such delightful company forever, Buck managed to break into the factory where new robots were programmed with information tapes and to change those tapes so that the robots would obey him. The reprogrammed chief robot, called One, became a new sidekick for Buck and followed him through later exploits.

Then came the day when Buck had just bested Kane in a terrific fist fight and turned him over to the "Rehabilitation Center," which always seemed to fail miserably where Kane was concerned. Buck was cruising along in his rocketship with Doc Huer, Wilma, and One. Wilma was saying how happy she was. Doc was happy too. Buck, battered and bruised though he was, was feeling particularly manic. And One? "As you know, robots are incapable of emotion. However, I can report that my lubrication system is functioning unusually well today." With everyone feeling well lubricated, the rocketship blasted off into the sunset. Then the announcer intoned, "This concludes the present series of adventures with Buck Rogers. Watch your newspaper for the announcement of Buck Rogers' return to the air."

I'm still looking.

CALLING DICK TRACY

During his first trip into oblivion in the early forties, Matt Crowley,[2] who played the twenty-fifth-century adventurer, made as amazing a change as any time machine ever effected. Trading his rocketship for a police car, and his ray gun for a police .38, Buck Rogers became *Dick Tracy*.

Dick Tracy was one of the three Chicago *Tribune* comic strips to appear on radio. The others were *Little Orphan Annie* and *Terry and the Pirates*.

[2]Curtis Arnall and John Larkin also played the role of Buck Rogers during other periods. Matt Crowley not only played Buck and Dick Tracy, but virtually every other comic-strip hero to make it to radio: Jungle Jim; Mark Trail; and Batman on *The Adventures of Superman*.

Many of the adventures of Terry Lee in the Orient would seem remarkably similar to those of Jack Armstrong if related here at length. Pat Ryan, his sidekick, an older Soldier of Fortune, played much the same wise, heroic mentor as Uncle Jim Fairfield, although he was much handsomer, a rugged dark-haired Irisher contrasting with Terry's own blond, boyish appearance. The women in the serials adapted from the Milton Caniff strip were equally good-looking, the beautiful but "regular fellow" Burma, and the delightfully dangerous, Eurasian she-pirate, the Dragon Lady.

Occasionally Pat Ryan turned his charge, Terry, over to another old China hand, aviator Flip Corkin. Once Flip and Terry aided a female spy for the Allied cause who was registered in an intrigue-ridden Calcutta hotel. The narrator cautioned us, "A girl can get into a lot of trouble in the Hoobli Hotel." Yet the two Americans were able to save the girl from the Nazi killer who cut down the opposition with a non-regulation issue poison dart gun. (I wonder how Quaker Puffed Wheat could resist offering the dart gun as a box-top premium.)

At the end of the war, Terry Lee had grown to young manhood but he continued to associate with his old friends like Pat, Connie, and Hotshot Charlie, although he no longer needed their spiritual guidance, not even where the apparently ageless Dragon Lady was concerned. In the postwar era, she attempted to steal the fabulous Pirate Gold Detector Ring (this *was* a premium, of course) in order to locate and seize a secret gold mine belonging to a young American boy. Terry and his friends made short work of the D.L. and her crew of Chinese pirates who seemed almost laughably out of place in the Atomic Age.

Unquestionably, among these celebrated comic strips it was the indestructible detective and the round-eyed waif who made the greatest impression on radio audiences. Although they appeared on the very same funny-paper page most places, they were in marked contrast.

Little Orphan Annie was the most juvenile serial star, the only sub-teen-age protagonist ever to be successful as an adventure character on radio. On the other hand, the hero of Chester Gould's great strip was the most relentlessly adult of all heroes. Although not then married, Tracy had an adopted son, Dick Tracy, Jr., and, as a full-fledged policeman, Tracy was the sternest father figure of all. There was no hedging. Tracy was no uncle, no guardian. He was a genuine father. He was no secret agent, no leader of a secret flying army. He was a cop. You didn't fool around with Dick Tracy. Even the news service seemed to tread lightly with Tracy. When one of the major events of World War II occurred, there was no strange voice interrupting the Tracy program with a bulletin. First came the standard opening: machine guns, sirens, and a filtered voice "Calling Dick Tracy! Calling Dick Tracy!" and then, "This is Dick Tracy on The Case of the Stolen Safe! Let's go, men!" After this vital introduction was completed, Tracy's own announcer read the war news.

A British news service has announced that Adolph Hitler just committed suicide in his bunker in Berlin. This, predicted one spokesman, will mean the virtual end of the Second World War in Europe. And now, back to the adventures of Dick Tracy!

In the important program that followed, Tracy and Pat Patton, another member of radio's League of Dumb Irish Sidekicks, were weaving a dragnet around a safe-cracker, Spike Connelly, and his moll, Gert. As Tracy closed in from the front, Pat guarded the rear exit with his usual efficiency. Tracy came through the house and discovered the Irish cop on the ground.

TRACY: How are you feeling, Pat?

PAT: This head of mine feels like it had stopped a Nazi shell. That dame certainly put everything she had into it when she hit me in the head with her shoe. Look at the bump on the top of me head. I can't even get my hat on, Dick. Wait till I lay my hands on that pair again.

TRACY: Let's get back to the car. I want to contact headquarters.

PAT: They certainly made a sucker out of me. Imagine the dame getting into the scrap—that's what fooled me . . .

TRACY: Here's the car, Pat.

PAT: Isn't that our signal, Dick?

TRACY: That's us, all right. I'll turn up the amplifier. Inspector Tracy, go ahead.

ROSS: (ON RADIO) Sergeant Ross speaking, Inspector. Flash just came in from the highway patrol. Alan Preston of 575 South Street reports he stopped to help two motorists who seemed to have trouble with their car.

TRACY: A man and a woman?

ROSS: That's right. The minute he got the chance the man slugged Preston, dragged him into the bushes, and took his car.

TRACY: Sounds suspicious!

ROSS: I questioned Preston. Description of the man and woman tallies with your bulletin.

TRACY: Any more details?

ROSS: The license number of Preston's car is four-one-five-nine-dash-M, as in morning. It was a black sedan, four-door, 1938 model.

TRACY: Good work!

ROSS: Here's something else that may help, Inspector. Just as Preston was coming to, he saw the car turn around and start back in a northeasterly direction . . .

TRACY: Thanks, Sergeant. Pat and I will take over. Keep all men on twenty-four-hour duty. Have them stand by for instructions. And pass the word to the rest of the cars to have them converge on Area B. That should take in enough territory to cross their trail. Let's go, Pat!

The dragnet seemed extensive enough to trap a safecracker. To consider what measures Dick Tracy would take against, say, a bank robber staggers the imagination.

Tracy never failed to get his man, but someone higher up on the force decided he was working too hard five days a week. The daily fifteen-minute serial was dropped and was replaced by a half-hour nighttime program once a week, which used even more characters from the comic strip. Besides Pat, Tess Trueheart, and Chief Brandon, Vitamin Flintheart, B. O. Plenty, and Flattop entered from the wings. It was too ridiculous for radio (although perhaps we'll find it won't be so for television). Tracy went off the air, back into the funny papers, just above *Little Orphan Annie*.

LITTLE LEAPIN' LIZARDS

"Who's that little chatterbox,
The one with the pretty auburn locks?
Who can it be?
It's Little Orphan Annie!
Always wears a sunny smile,
Now wouldn't it be worth the while
If you could be
Like Little Orphan Annie?"

The singing of that "pop" masterpiece by an unidentified group began the radio broadcasts of *Little Orphan Annie*. Just as she usually appeared below *Dick Tracy* on the comics page, Annie directly followed the hawk-nosed hawk-shaw in the radio schedule for years.

The popularity of *Little Orphan Annie* can be attributed to the fact that the program was the only one to deal with really young children, Annie and her pal, Joe Corntassel. If you wanted to listen to a show about your age group, told on a level you could understand with no difficulty whatsoever when you were a child in the thirties, you listened to *Little Orphan Annie*. Even *Jack Armstrong* was about teen-agers.

With radio's typical fidelity to the comic-strip original, one of the earliest sequences was lifted directly from the newspaper story line. Annie met Joe Corntassel on the farm of Mr. and Mrs. Silo. Annie and the boy seemed to hit it off well—even Sandy gave him a friendly "Arf!" He carried through in most of the later stories, joining Annie and that fascinating figure Daddy Warbucks on trips around the world.

Even though he had risen from their ranks himself (according to the comic strip he was a "self-made man") Daddy Warbucks always seemed to have trouble with the rabble. He had made his fortune in World War I (he represented munitions wealth—war bucks—you know). During the 1930s Depression, he was down and out, in a state of mental depression himself. But Annie never would accept his defeat. "We may be down, but we ain't out, Daddy!" she assured him. Inspired, Warbucks fought his way to the top of the business world, considerably aided by two oriental experts in homicide, the gigantic servant Punjab and the slinky little Asp. It was not merely implied, but clearly demonstrated, that Warbucks would kill anybody who got in his way en route to money or power. Intended as a symbol of "rugged capitalism," Warbucks seemed far more a ruthless gangster. His place in society was completely outside. He made his own rules, ran his own private army equipped with planes, tanks, and submarines, and consistently ordered the executions of those who opposed him.

While this portrait is based on the comic strip, his image on radio was directly derived from the comic page. He would get along fine with the crew of his yacht as long as they did their jobs and took their pay with a smile. But for indolent complainers against the status quo, Warbucks had little truck. After all, they were a shifty lot with bushy hair who said "Yi!" especially when Punjab sliced off their heads with a scimitar. Not surprisingly, on one occasion the crew mutinied and declared themselves to be "pirates." They made Warbucks, the girl who called him Daddy, and the rest of the passengers walk the plank! Fortunately for Annie and her friends, there was an island nearby that the mutineers had presumably not noticed. (You could be sure that Warbucks would never make such a mistake where *his* enemies were concerned.)

On the island, Annie, Joe, Punjab, and Sandy took refuge in an abandoned stockade. Warmed by a fire, things were looking up for the little orphan and her company—until they were attacked by cannibals!

"Leapin' lizards, they want to eat me, Sandy!" Annie cried out. Frightened, but tough in only the way born Republicans can be tough, Annie worked frantically to fashion masks of her own face. Big circle, two little circles, squiggles for hair; big circle, two little circles . . . over and over. These masks Annie stuck in the loopholes of the stockade to make it look as if every firing position was manned by an Annie. Terrified at this army of little red-haired girls, the ignorant natives fled in a rout.

(Back in those early days, it came as a surprise when a copy of one of those Little Orphan Annie masks was made available to listeners for a dime and the inner seal from a jar of Ovaltine, another in the long line of Ovaltine premiums climaxed by the immortal Shake-Up Mug.)

While Annie and Joe roamed cannibal islands and other exotic ports with Warbucks, many of her adventures were of a tamer sort, nearer to home. Once, Annie and Joe were falsely accused of lifting a few dollars for candy (maybe even "chocolatey-flavored" Ovaltine!). They skipped town under this black cloud, hopping a freight to the big city, where they uncovered the real thief and proved their innocence.

These *Little Orphan Annie* serials ran a neat thirteen weeks and were written and produced by the staff of Ovaltine's advertising agency in Chicago, following the characters and story line developed by Harold Grey in his great comic strip. The radio program began in such pioneering days that there were no coast-to-coast networks, so two separate casts did each day's script, one in Chicago (for the east), where the cast was headed by little Shirley Bell, and one in San Francisco (for the west), with Floy Margaret Hughes, who reports she still drinks Ovaltine.

With the establishment of coast-to-coast broadcasting in 1933, the Chicago cast became the permanent one. Shirley Bell was still Annie, and, surprisingly enough, she was also the dog, Sandy. She got an assist on some of the "Arfs" from announcer Pierre André. Her Daddy Warbucks was originally played by Stanley Andrews (later to be the Old Ranger, the original host of television's *Death Valley Days*). As for the "gosh-wow-gee!" boy, Joe Corntassel, that role was played through his noted velvet fog by youthful Mel Torme.

The mellow tones of Pierre André introduced each day's broadcast, following the equally mellow strains of "Who's that little chatterbox?" His voice was magnificent; wise, kindly, strong, commanding, enthusiastic, good-humored, interested.

> ANDRÉ: *And now* . . . LITTLE ORPHAN ANNIE . . . a **bomb** has *destroyed* part of the town hall of Sunfield! And that *mysterious* gang of boys known as **The Blackjackets!** is suspected of having set off the bomb! *However*, Annie and Joe set off to trail a woman she was sure would lead them to the persons who were really GUILTY! And *now*, we find **Annie** and Joe still cautiously following the woman along one of the *back streets* of the town. **Listen** . . .

ANNIE: Look out, Joe, she's turning around to look back again. Let's stop and pretend we're interested in this store window.

JOE: All right, but this is about the fifth time we've had to stop and look into windows. Do you think she suspects we're following her?

ANNIE: Welllll . . . no. I just think she's being careful. We wouldn't have to be so particular about keeping out of her sight if we were complete strangers to her. But if she caught sight of us, she'd know we were the two kids she saw back there in the mayor's office.

JOE: She'd recognize us, all right.

ANNIE: You bet she would. We'd better be moving along again. She's getting pretty far ahead of us . . .

JOE: Hey . . . she's getting into that black sedan with a man . . .

ANNIE: We've let a swell lead on that bombing get away from us. I bet you anything we would have that crime practically solved if . . . *suffering sunfish!* We even forgot to notice the license number of the sedan!

JOE: Hey, look what's coming here—a taxi!

ANNIE: Golly, so it is. And empty, too.

JOE: But this is luck! There aren't more than a half a dozen taxis in the whole town!

ANNIE: I'll say it's luck! Hey there!

(TAXI PULLS UP TO A STOP)

CABBIE: You want a cab?

ANNIE: You bet we do! Come on, Joe, pile in. It's lucky the mayor gave us some expense money.

JOE: I'll say! Turn right here, driver. North on Pepper Street. There's a black sedan somewhere up ahead there and we want you to follow it!

(CAR DOOR SLAMS, THE TAXI PULLS AWAY)

ANNIE: The sedan has a big head start on us so you'll have to go like the wind to catch him. And we got to catch him, it's terribly important!

CABBIE: Okay, I'll do my best!

The cab driver certainly did do his best, never once questioning two small children who ordered him to follow a black sedan in the middle of the night. Annie and Joe kept hot on the trail of the mysterious woman, tracing her first to "the worst cafe in Sunfield" run by a man with a sinister foreign name (Italian), and, finally, to the very headquarters of the gang of boys known as the Blackjackets.

Pierre André urged us to tune in tomorrow. As if we needed to be told!

In 1940, Quaker Puffed Wheat Sparkies (a brand name since dropped) took over the guardianship of *Little Orphan Annie* from Ovaltine and introduced a new character, Captain Sparks, as a companion to Annie on her adventures.

Sparks, a heroic aviator, soon took over the entire show with Annie as his stooge in fighting enemy spies and the like. Even Annie's club, the Safety Guard, soon became the Secret Guard under Captain Sparks' direction. Just as Vic Hardy's Scientific Bureau of Investigation would take over

Jack Armstrong some years later, Captain Sparks absorbed Little Orphan Annie into a militaristic-government agency in the early forties.

There was a strange kind of irony involved here. Ovaltine had dropped Annie in favor of sponsoring *Captain Midnight,* whose chief lieutenants, Joyce Ryan and Chuck Ramsey, and his Secret Squadron fought enemy spies and master criminals. The producers of *Little Orphan Annie* combined with the new sponsor to borrow *in toto* the format of the new program that appealed to the old sponsor. Captain Sparks was obviously just an imitation Captain Midnight, and now Little Orphan Annie was simply playing the role of a Joyce Ryan, a supporting sidekick who didn't do much more than gasp "Leapin' lizards!" in awe and admiration when Sparks pulled out of a power dive in his mighty airplane.

The imitation, however, couldn't stand the competition from the original. *Captain Midnight* went on until the end of radio serials. Captain Sparks went down in flames, dragging the pale ghost of *Little Orphan Annie* with him.

One of the first adaptations from a comic strip on radio concluded its run, but when *Captain Midnight* replaced *Little Orphan Annie,* radio proved, just as television would in its own time, that broadcasting could create comic-strip-level programming on its own.

VI

THE STRAIGHT SHOOTER

"The Tom Mix Ralston Straight Shooters are on the air!" cried announcer Don Gordon. "And here comes Tom Mix, America's favorite cowboy!"

Tom Mix called, "Up, Tony, come on, boy!" and launched into what had been one of radio's first singing commercials, always much the same, and to the tune of *When It's Round-up Time in Texas*. The mid-forties version went:

> Hot Ralston for your breakfast
> Start the day off shining bright
> Gives you lots of cowboy energy
> With a flavor that's just right.
> It's delicious and nutritious
> Made of golden Western wheat
> So take a tip from Tom
> Go and tell your Mom
> Hot Ralston can't be beat!

It was a painless pitch, and often without a commercial with a more direct approach to selling, the program would plunge right into the story itself.

We were told one afternoon in 1947 how the boss of the TM-Bar swung his eyes around to look at two of his faithful Straight Shooters caught in the same deadly trap as he was. Wash, the Negro cook, and big, burly Sheriff Mike Shaw were each strung up between a pair of trees half a dozen feet apart, their toes just scraping the dirt. Diabolically, they were tied with thongs of wet rawhide that stretched from their wrists to the limbs of trees on either side of them. Already their arms ached from the strain, and it would get worse!

WASH: Mist' Tom . . .
MIX: Wash!
WASH: Mist' Tom, I . . . I . . .
MIKE: Thank God, he's fainted.
MIX: He'll come to again. Heaven help him, he'll come to plenty of times before he cashes in!

The sun beat down on them, burning their raw nerves. It couldn't go on much longer, we were assured. It might last another hour, an hour of agony that would be many lifetimes to them. An hour in which they could only puzzle over the signs along the trail that led them to death. What was the meaning of the strange drum message Chief Gray Eagle had sent in his desperate fear? Was the terrifying figure of Kahwenga, the Flaming Warrior, really alive? Had he fired his signal arrow of death into the steps of the TM-Bar ranch house?

These were terrible questions to ask a youthful audience, and a frightful scene to describe to them. Such a carefully detailed account of Indian torture would unquestionably be tossed out of any adult, nighttime television drama (and any producer who suggested such a scene for a kiddie show nowadays would probably be thrown out too). Yet because such Indian torture had been a part of reality in the Old West, it was used by *Tom Mix* on radio. The program, inspired by a real hero, always aimed toward a compelling sense of reality, sometimes grim, sometimes rather homey. There were moments of fast-shooting, hard-riding, baffling mystery, broad humor, as well as pathos and pain. The intent was to convince you, the kid listening in, and as I well remember, your mother and father too, that every shot, every squeak of pulling rawhide, every groan, every chuckle was real. The kids were supposed to believe that it was happening; the adults that it could happen.

Just think of it: First Wash, then Sheriff Mike, heroes of one of our programs, had passed out under torture—Mike because he was old and fat, and because he was really human. This concept of humanity belongs to an era of belief, when you could listen to the adventures of a man who had made silent movies forty years earlier, and who now sang a jingle for a breakfast cereal, a man who had friends who could get sick, just like your friends, with their parade of sore throats and colds. Now this concept has seemingly disappeared from popular entertainment. Producers have given up trying to convince the jaded audiences to suspend their disbelief, and more and more everything is turning into either a gentle spoof or a broad spoof of the real thing, the real adventure, the genuine feeling.

Even in the era of radio, not everything was supposed to be taken seriously. *Sam Spade* and the blood-splattered creatures of *Inner Sanctum* would be at home among today's grinning grim reapers of violence. Many of the other detective heroes of radio went through their paces with such predictable routine that they could hardly be consumed without a shakerful of salt. In our hour after school, *Jack Armstrong* and *Captain Midnight* were handled in a nonrealistic manner. Jack Armstrong's Uncle Jim Fairfield must have been about the same age as Sheriff Mike, but no weariness, no human failing touched him. On these shows almost no one got scared, no matter how murderous the peril, because the sponsor didn't want to "upset" the kids, or, more probably, their parents. By comparison to these shows, *Superman* was almost realistic. In spite of the fantastic powers of its hero, the program kept some touch with reality by giving its other characters such human emotions as fear, anger, and pride.

Tom Mix, however, was the master of conviction. Tom Mix and his Straight Shooter pals even knew they were on the radio—many episodes detailed how they studied their scripts and re-created their adventures on the air. One particular *Tom Mix* broadcast was interrupted by a gangster from back East, Caesar Ciano, who didn't like the way he was represented on the show. "I a-have a-no got no a-accento! Let 'em have the chopper!" A blast of machine-gun bullets shattered the On the Air sign. "That won't put us off the air," Tom Mix said complacently. Only one thing could put them off the air, and, at gunpoint, the announcer said it. "This-uh-this is the Mutual Broadcasting System!" (Much later, Tom succeeded in reforming Ciano. He stopped being that stereotype of the gangster hated by all Italian Americans. Ciano became a barber. The cause of Italian-American friendship may not have been significantly advanced.)

The sense of realism this program had was heightened, no doubt, for the audience and on the producers, by the fact that its hero was a real man. The facts of his life are in never-ending dispute, but if half of the legends of him are true, this man of Irish, Jewish, Dutch, and Cherokee ancestry lived one of the most fantastic lives of high adventure since Marco Polo's day. It was no daydream of a radio writer or movie press agent that the real Tom Mix had been a United States marshal, a sheriff in Kansas and Oklahoma, and a secret agent for the United States government. (I received verification of all this from his first wife, Olive Stokes Mix, who lives in a modest Hollywood apartment today.) Furthermore, Tom Mix had an active military career. He fought in the Spanish-American War at San Juan Hill as one of Teddy Roosevelt's Rough Riders, was the second occidental wounded in the Boxer Rebellion, fought on both sides in the Boer War after a change of conviction made him support the Boers, and was wounded again in World War I. Mix paused long enough to catch his breath away from the battlefield and outlaw bullets to win the title of World's Champion Cowboy in rodeo competition. This brought him to the attention of Hollywood moviemakers and soon he was a major star (once the highest paid in the world), in such films as *Riders of the Purple Sage*. While he liked to spend his Hollywood salary lavishly on expensive automobiles and other trappings, he was not content living in the movie capital. In the early thirties he left the West Coast to travel the country with his own Wild West Circus. While he was absent from the screen his agents and licensees kept his name before the public through toy and clothing merchandising, *Big Little Books* of his exploits, and offered radio rights for the adventures of Tom Mix.

The *Tom Mix* radio program went on the air in 1933, with the true life of Tom Mix, and to an even greater degree, the life he led on the screen, serving as its basis. Contrary to folk legend, the quality of Mix's voice was not so poor as to ruin him in talking movies or, for that matter, radio. His voice was a deep baritone and he could deliver lines in a believable, professional manner, as he did in a number of sound films such as the first *Destry Rides Again*. Tom Mix was not interested in working for the low rates paid actors on a daily radio program, however, and the show closed with the information that "Tom Mix" was impersonated."[1]

Even after his death in a 1940 auto accident, his fame and the past successes of the radio series carried it on until 1950, just as the series of Buffalo Bill dime novels went on for years following the passing of William F. Cody in 1917.

[1]Those who "impersonated" Tom Mix from 1933 on over the air were Artello Dickson, followed by Jack Holden and Russell Thorson (yes, the same Thorson who was later Jack on *I Love a Mystery*), and finally, and most lastingly, from 1943 to the end of the series, Joe "Curley" Bradley. Bradley, once a member of the real Tom Mix's corps of stuntmen in Hollywood, later a western singer in the Ranch Boys' trio, played the sidekick, Pecos, before taking over the title role. Others in the *Tom Mix* cast will be only names today, but here are a few you may recognize: "Wrangler" was Percy Hemus; Wash was played by Forrest Lewis; Sheriff Mike Shaw was chiefly Leo Curley, but the role had been taken for a long time by Harold Peary (later *The Great Gildersleeve*); Tom's young wards were Jane and Jimmy—Jane was Jane Webb, and Jimmy was played by young George Gobel, who continued to work in broadcasting.

The broadcast series of *Tom Mix* was created for the Ralston company by a St. Louis advertising agency staff headed by Charles Claggett, who was chiefly responsible for the format and early scripts. The air of conviction came into full force in 1943, however, under the authorship of George Lowther, a good enough writer to have had two plays published. (He was later to script a number of dramas for that fine medium now as lost as radio, live television.) Lowther was fortunate to be able to work from the perfect juvenile Western format developed by Claggett. It had the ideal hero, Tom, his wonder horse, Tony, his ranch, the TM-Bar, where his elderly sidekick (originally the Old Wrangler, and later Mike Shaw) and his two young wards, or adopted children, Jane and Jimmy lived. The format was so good— hero,[2] "wonder horse," ranch, senior citizen, boy and girl— that it was cheerfully copied by at least two other radio programs: *Bobby Benson,* which made the young boy its

[2]The one character among the Straight Shooter cast that was not so perfect was the Negro cook, Wash, a typical stereotype. When the *Tom Mix* program began, the *Amos 'n' Andy* show was in its heyday. It influenced many other radio shows with such famous scenes as the 1928 court trial for breach of promise.

ANDY: I met Mrs. Parker oveh at Ruby Taylor's house one night, but I'se sorry I eveh went oveh dere.
ATTORNEY: That's neither here nor there!
ANDY: Yes, 'tis. It's oveh dere—long 'bout three or fo' . . .
ATTORNEY: Just a minute! . . . Brown, did you ever write Mrs. Parker a letter . . . Is this your handwriting?
ANDY: Dat kind-a look famil'ar to me—I don't make no "A" like dat, though. Maybe I did make it, though. Yessah, I guess dat's it . . .

(*footnote continued on next page*)

central character, underplaying the grown-up hero, Tex Mason, a character name once used by Tom Mix in films, and *Sky King*, whose Flying Crown Ranch had exactly the same layout as the TM-Bar. Schyler "Sky" King used his airplane more consistently than Tom Mix did his, although the radio series set in the fantacized "Modern West" did have Tom taking to the air on occasion.

By its second year the *Tom Mix* show had established the characters but not the characterizations or the style. The program began with thundering hoofbeats and the Old Wrangler crying, "Let's-git-a-goin'!" After the pitch for Ralston, the Wrangler would return to tell the story directly to the young audience. "Howdee, Straight Shooters! Howdee! Huntin' down Killer Mike and his Terrible Six gang was one of the most thrillin' adventures we ever had. . . ." With that kind of assurance, the kids just knew they couldn't go wrong by listening.

In the story, Jimmy and Jane were captured by bandits, and, in the rescue, Tom slid down the chimney of the outlaws' cabin, six-guns in hand, to get the drop on the men

(footnote continued)

Freeman Godsen and Charles Correll created *Amos 'n' Andy* in 1928, two Caucasian performers attempting to add color to the monotones of early radio with that stand-by dialect humor. Publicity releases held that Andy was "domineering, a bit lazy, inclined to take the credit for all of Amos' ideas and efforts." Amos himself was "trusting, simple, unsophisticated. High and hesitating in voice. It's 'Ain't dat sumpin' ' when he's happy . . . and 'Awah, a-wah, a-wah' in the frequent moments when he's frightened or embarrassed."

Wash, Tom Mix's cook, was certainly more like Amos than Andy. But radio did grow up a bit. By the forties, even the images of *Amos 'n' Andy* had improved somewhat, and now while Wash remained "easily frightened" it was pointed out he always "fought down his fear manfully."

inside. Standing there in the fireplace, Tom Mix uttered those timeless words: "Reach for the sky! Lawbreakers always lose, Straight Shooters always win! It pays to shoot straight!"

The bandits had few doubts that Tom Mix knew how to "shoot straight" and surrendered. But that wasn't the end of the story. The rescued Jimmy urgently told Tom, "You only got four of 'em here, Tom! Killer Mike's gone!"

"It's a fight to the finish now, Wrangler," Tom Mix said sternly. "We're going after Killer Mike!"

"Whew!" gasped Jane in open-mouthed admiration, "looks like excitement and adventure ahead!"

As the years went on, the figure of radio hero Tom Mix became less cardboard, moving at least from the dimensions of wood-carved to a semblance of life. As the owner of the TM-Bar Ranch, Tom Mix was in trouble around 1939. He had spent so much of his time rescuing others from rustlers and international spies, and neglecting his ranch business duties, that his ranch was facing the familiar prospect of a Depression foreclosure. (You felt like sending Tom all the dimes from your bank. Every time you dropped a coin, Mickey Mouse saluted you. Or did Popeye punch the bag?) At last, the furnishings of the TM-Bar ranch house were sold off one by one. Tom watched the sale, seeing beloved items go one by one. Finally, a cuckoo clock was coming up for sale. "That," said Tom, "is one thing I'll be glad to see go. Never could stand it." Tom walked off to be alone with his thoughts.

Amos Q. Snood, the owner of Dobie Township's Cozy Rest Hotel, arrived on the scene. Snood was mean, petty, bookish, and he had all the money he needed, but not all he wanted. He was, in short, the symbol of the way the adult world looked to you when you were listening to *Tom Mix.* By inspiration, Wrangler told Snood that the cuckoo clock was priceless to Tom, the one thing he hoped to save from this tragedy. Naturally, giggling in glee, Snood bid the clock up for a fabulous sum; for once, price was no object. The cuckoo clock was the only thing Snood or anyone else was able to get, except for one mysterious stranger who bought everything, including the ranch. Who was he? Why, he was the lawyer for Jane, Tom's ward, who had a fortune in her own right from a gold mine, a fortune Tom wouldn't touch. Jane had sent her representative to buy up everything and give it back to Tom, who could repay her later. You didn't worry about the legalities of a minor having control over a fortune back then. It sounded right. In 1939, your parents might very well have been in financial trouble, and if you had owned a gold mine, you would have helped them out, just as Jane did Tom.

Seeing the possibilities in pathos, the producers next saw to it that Tom Mix's Wonder Horse, Tony, broke a leg. There was nothing to be done but the inevitable. Grimly, Tom got his rifle and a silver bullet he had won as a prize at a rodeo. (No doubt Tom's colleague, the Lone Ranger, presented the award at the competition.) Kneeling beside Tony, Tom loaded the rifle with the silver bullet. He talked softly to Tony of all they had gone through together . . . how Tony had carried Tom to safety after Tom had been wounded in a gunfight with rustlers down around the border . . . how Tom's drawling sidekick, Pecos, had ridden Tony through the flames of a forest fire, with an airplane propeller strapped to Tony's side, a propeller to replace the one on the downed plane in which the fire had trapped Tom . . . and, finally, how they had won the silver bullet together at the rodeo. It was all said then. Tom Mix stroked Tony's mane. He lifted the rifle . . .

Meanwhile, back at the ranch, Wrangler and Jane sat in stunned disbelief, not being able to accept the fact that Tom was actually going to have to shoot Tony. A radio was playing in the background, reporting race results. The winner of the last race had, it was reported, been healed of a broken leg by the techniques of a certain eastern doctor. Wrangler and Jane rushed headlong for the TM-Bar stables. Just then, a shot rang out! What happened? Tom missed! For once, tears had clouded the truest eye in the West.

The TM-Bar Ranch was located just outside the town of Dobie, which was surely one of the most harassed communities in all of fiction. It not only had to deal with the usual assortment of rustlers and gunslingers, but with the fantastic inventions of master criminals of the modern West.

One of the menaces Tom Mix ran into most regularly was an "invisible man." The invisibility itself was fantastic, but the explanations were generally extremely mundane. Several times, the "invisibility" was merely the false testimony of lying witnesses. Once, it was a hidden loudspeaker. Perhaps a bit more originally, the illusion of an "invisible rider" was created by a hat and riding gloves suspended by wires above a saddle, the saddlebags of which contained a walkie-talkie that not only gave the "invisible rider" his voice, but supplied traveling instructions to the specially trained horse, who must have been almost as smart as Tom's Tony.

There were other implications of invisibility in "The Man Who Wasn't There," a story about a man who could escape from watched and guarded rooms that were later thoroughly searched for secret panels. The mystery created so much excitement among the Straight Shooter set that Tom called kids on the telephone to ask for their solutions. Nobody got it. Like many of Holmes' deductions that when explained seemed obvious to Watson, it was fairly ingenious. There were no secret panels in the walls, but one whole wall in each of these specially constructed rooms slid back on a solid track. Tom had figured the wall was too solid. After all, any honest wall would shake a bit when tapped for sliding doors.

"The Man Who Could Work Miracles" presented a character who had the power to invisibly strike people dead on the streets of Dobie. His science fictional secret, a death-ray machine, we would call a laser beam today.

Some of the other tricky and kicky inventions Tom ran into came from his movie career. (Radio's Tom Mix also knew that he had made Western movies, as well as currently being on the air.) A giant wind machine was used to erase the tracks of a stolen herd of cattle in one serial, and in another, a spider-web-making device was used to falsely age a house to divert suspicion from it.

The nice thing about some of the fantastic inventions on the *Tom Mix* program was that Ralston would send you some of them for a box top. Perhaps not death rays or spider-web machines, but you were offered other fascinating devices. Of course, the rings, the badges, the premiums, were always carefully worked into the story, first as a build-up to the offer, and then as an adjunct to it.

In 1940, there was a great to-do about assembling a TM-Bar scrapbook as a surprise for Tom's birthday. With the instinctive sixth sense you developed, you knew this was going to be a premium offer. The page of Western history that Wrangler devised, the magic tricks offered by Wash, were less than exciting. Then—*then*—Pecos came to Jane, who was assembling the scrapbook, and bashfully offered some "chicken tracks" he had drawn—*comic strips!*

Tom Mix *Comics* were offered free for a box top by Ralston. There were twelve issues offering much the same kind of story the radio program delivered. In Book 1, Tom Mix made a classic entrance as a comic-book hero. Two riders pulled up at the TM-Bar corral, ranting about a haunted pass through Ghost Canyon. "No one's ever come back from thar!" opines one rider. "I have!" says Tom Mix, striding forward. What more needs to be said? Tom Mix can go anywhere and do anything. Naturally, he took care of the little matter of the rustlers who were hiding out in Ghost Canyon, using a movie machine to project "ghostly" Indian warriors on the canyon wall.

In the first nine issues of *Tom Mix Comics*, the chief Straight Shooter took care of more rustlers, a few spies, and at least one genuine sea serpent. In the last three numbers, the publication became *Tom Mix Commando Comics*, with Tom, Wrangler, Wash, and Pecos in the U. S. Army fighting such menaces as an army of invisible invaders and a squadron of real flying dragons from Japan.

The radio program was off the air on vacation during this period, and never got so far out, but no matter how fantastic the creatures and devices got on the radio series, the people in the stories always remained recognizably human. Tom Mix on radio was less a symbol of "virtue" than the Lone Ranger or Jack Armstrong. Like the movies made by the real Tom Mix, the radio series was not intended to preach any sermon of morality. It was intended to be fun and to sell the sponsor's product. The way Ralston was sold was fun, of course, and they even managed to incorporate the product's name into the title of the show. The program became a choice blending of credibility, commerciality, and what is now known as "camp." It made us believe and want to find out what happened to our "believable" friends. For instance, how did Tom, Mike, and Wash escape from being strung up on those trees?

They had only an hour left to live, but we were now informed that every second seemed like an hour in itself. Tom Mix, Sheriff Mike, and Wash were baked in the relentless sun. The rawhide dried and stretched tighter. Even as the rawhide stretched, so did their flesh and bones stretch. The pain crawled down their arms into their chests, along their bodies, down their legs. They tried to find some relief by lifting themselves on their toes, to ease the pain in their arms. But solid footing was tantalizingly out of reach. The sun beat down, the rawhide stretched ever more taut.

> WASH: You figure we got a chance, Mist' Tom?
> MIX: I don't know, pardner. I figure death's got a running iron on us at last.
> MIKE: Brandin' us for the Eternal Range.

You bought dialogue like that. How else did cowboys talk? You bought the pain, the agony, the whole bag. Then came information that was hard to believe. Our friend, the announcer, told us straight out that the pain was so great that Tom Mix *groaned.* Imagine—just imagine—the pain that could make Tom Mix cry out!

The frightful pain at this point was caused by the sudden release of his weight jerking against the one wrist that was still tied. Yes, the bounds on the other wrist had been released. What had happened? Had the rawhide somehow broken? No! As Tony lay on the cool grass of the forest floor, he looked up and through the filtered light shining through the tree leaves he saw a flash of color. He saw a feathered arrow sticking in the tree trunk. That was the arrow fired by a mysterious bowman, the arrow that had cut the bonds of Tom Mix, freeing him from the Indian torture trap. (It was convenient to have friends like that, but what decent citizen wouldn't help Tom Mix out of a trap?)

After freeing Mike and Wash, the three of them set off on foot for a friendly Indian village (this is taking place in 1947, remember). Near the camp, Tom spotted one of the renegades that had attacked them and strung them up to die. Tom took out after him.

With the speed of a deer, Tom ran, ignoring leaves and branches lashing at his face, the stubborn forest growth that tried to trip him. The distance narrowed between him and the Indian, just as so many times he had cut down distance between himself and a mounted outlaw as he rode the Wonder Horse of the World, Tony. But even on foot, Tom Mix could overtake any evildoer.

Abruptly, even the renegade Indian realized that it was as hopeless to run from Tom Mix as from Justice itself. The warrior halted and turned to meet Tom, his blade in his strong red hand. When only a dozen feet or so remained between them, Tom came to a halt. He had no weapon, and he knew that there were no greater masters of the knife in the West than the Sioux. But did that stop Tom Mix? Not on your tintype!

Tom had only stopped to gain his breath, to prepare himself to fight. He smiled his familiar, tight smile, and showed his raw, reddened wrists to the Indian who had bound him to the Tree of Death.

> TOM: The last time we met, you spat in my face. I aim to put my brand on you now, *hombre*.

The Indian struck first, but Tom Mix had expected him to do that. Even as the knife flashed through the air, Tom's agile body had flashed aside. Now the knife hand was in the grip of the greatest Straight Shooter of them all. The warrior was huge and heavily muscled, and he fought like a maddened bear, clawing, gouging, trying to bring his knee smashing up. The foul blow never landed. Just like his friends Jack Dempsey and Joe Louis, all Tom Mix had to do was send his fist traveling six inches to a man's jaw, and that man was *out*.

> MIKE: (COMING ON) Bow my legs and call me bandy, ain't thet the critter thet ordered us strung up, the one thet spit in your face, Tom?

MIX: Yes . . . (WALKS TO THE FALLEN INDIAN) Now
hear me! Your treachery, whatever the reason for
it, will bring about your own downfall, Bear Claw!
You seek to lead Gray Eagle's clan into war, when
you know there can only be one result, death or
imprisonment for them all! And like the jackal, you
will stand aside, waiting for the kill, that you may
feed! Be warned. Even the wind changes its course.
Change yours before it is too late!

Those were true and ringing words of a brave and wise
man, as anybody—any Straight Shooter—would know. Only
a fool or a foredoomed lawbreaker would not believe Tom
Mix. I believed Tom Mix, and I believed in him. And now
as I write this, how can I help but have faith in those lines
that closed another adventure three years later that was the
final radio broadcast of *Tom Mix?*

As Tom and Tony rode off into the Valhalla of an echo
chamber, the announcer intoned, "In the heart and the
imagination of the world, Tom Mix rides on, and lives on,
forever."

VII

"FOR JUST A BOX TOP"

Winters in the Midwest are dull gray, washed white from
time to time with snow, cheered by a blue sky every other
Sunday. Last fall is a forest of warpaint a hundred movie
serial afternoons behind you; next summer a green place a
million arithmetic lessons away. Yet sometime during those
school months you could find a flash of color: new gold, or

scarlet, insignia, or the eerie glow of a phantom green eye in the shadows clustered around your dresser in the night. If you were a kid in the thirties or the forties, you knew the breathless ecstasy of waiting, waiting, waiting while Jack Armstrong or Little Orphan Annie or another of the unseen, ever-present champions of Radioland sent you their latest life-saving, miraculous treasure trove that was yours for only one box top, and perhaps the thinnest of dimes.

One day your letter to Battle Creek, Michigan, or Chicago 77, Illinois, or St. Louis, Missouri, would be answered, and there waiting for you on the end table when you got home from school would be a small, husky brown envelope, thick and fat with its prize. You would unclasp it, slide out the protective cardboard, and into your hand would fall something small and glittering, handsome and well-made, something already familiar to you from a dozen adventures. Now, the agony of hearing this miracle (on which life itself often depended) described daily, and of not having it at the ready, was over. And if you were like me, you were not disappointed.

Radio premiums cost nothing but a box top, or maybe a dime, or, at the very most, perhaps twenty cents, and they were worth every penny and pouring-spout flap of it. Sent out by cereal companies to encourage kids to use their products and to listen to their commercial programs on the radio, they were made of good, bright, strong, gold-looking metal, which still looks good after twenty-five years in my trunk. The things did what they said they would do. They whistled, glowed in the dark, imprinted secret emblems, flashed messages, looked around corners, magnified, and "smallified." Each device did one or more or nearly all of these things. They did all this not once or twice or sometimes, or if you spent a few weeks learning just how to make them work, but they did these things the first time, the second time, all the time. And the ones that weren't destroyed by conscientious effort with a sledge hammer, or tossed out in a now regretted moment of cocky adolescence, still work, still faithful servants of the child you once were.

How did it all start? Even before radio, boxers and actresses gave away their photos, sometimes with soap or cigarettes. There were Davy Crockett premiums in his time, and there were those using the names and likenesses of Buffalo Bill Cody and Charles A. Lindbergh. In 1921, when Vincent Lopez was broadcasting his orchestra music over WJZ Newark (by wire from the Pennsylvania Grill in New York), he offered an autographed photograph of himself to everybody who wrote in and requested it. WJZ had to hire a staff just to answer the requests, and the pull of the radio premium was established.

The appeal of the "free offer," something for nothing, was especially strong in the Depression era, and then it really was for nothing. A box top might be requested, or a "reasonable facsimile thereof"—a tracing or drawing—or maybe just the name of the store where you bought the product.

There was one person in 1930 who seemed not to believe in something for nothing—Little Orphan Annie. As the spirit of free enterprise (or at least the spirit of her creator, Harold Gray), she emphasized rugged individualism, and in the comic strips radiating from the Chicago *Tribune* of Colonel Robert R. McCormack, the valiant waif told a starving world that in the face of the greatest worldwide catastrophe since the World War of 1918, all the individual had to do was show a little bit of spunk and he could, presumably, elbow his way to the head of the bread line. Certainly Annie would never have taken anything she hadn't put in good, hard, honest, nine-year-old labor for. Yet, in her radio incarnation (no longer directly connected to cartoonist Gray and his philosophy), even Little Orphan Annie gave away something. That something was perhaps the greatest radio offer of them all, the *compleat* premium. It was the Little Orphan

Annie Ovaltine Shake-Up Mug. What could be better? For just the inner seal from a jar of Ovaltine food-drink, you got a good-looking gadget with a picture of Annie right on it in full color. And when you got it, what did you use it for? Why, for mixing up more Ovaltine! Cereal companies didn't make a big thing of offering spoons just like the one Jack Armstrong used to eat his Wheaties, and you never got a special spreader for your Peter Pan peanut butter, but with Annie kids were begging for Ovaltine seals to get something in which to mix up more Ovaltine! I sincerely hope that the Machiavellian talent who so gladdened the hearts of a generation of children has received the reward he deserves.

By 1936, the Shake-Up Mug cost a dime as well as a seal (things were looking up throughout the country), and Annie was saying: "Leapin' Lizards! For a real treat yuh can't beat a cold Ovaltine shake-up! It's good-tastin' an' good for yuh, too!" ("Arf! Arf!" says Sandy.) "It's Little Orphan Annie's very own shake-up mug," the announcer assured us. "With a beautiful, new and different picture of Annie and Sandy right on it. . . . You put the special orange shake top on when you shake up your ice-cold Ovaltine, then lift the top off, and presto! You have a special Little Orphan Annie mug to drink right out of. You'll be keen about this brand-new two-in-one Orphan Annie Shaker and Mug the minute you lay eyes on it . . . and here's the way you get it. . . . Take out all of the thin aluminum seal you find under the lip of a can of Ovaltine and mail it, together with ten cents (to cover the cost of mailing and handling), to the Wander Company, 180 North Michigan Avenue, Chicago, Illinois. Then in a few days the postman will bring you this brand-new Little Orphan Annie Shake-Up Mug to have and keep for your very own. . . ."

Only the voice of the late Pierre André, ringing with conviction, dripping with enthusiasm, could do that copy justice!

In 1940, the makers of "The Drink of Swiss Mountain Climbers" felt they needed a more rugged image than that of a red-headed little girl, and Captain Midnight was asked to fly for the Wander Company. In his cockpit he carried an Ovaltine shaker. Twenty-five years later, with a still more rugged image, Ovaltine offered a shake-up mug in connection with the 1964 Olympic Games, but it wasn't the same, in size, shape, or special content.

Premiums were probably the most totally sold items on radio. Not only were the regular commercial announcements devoted to the current box top offer, but frequently the entire body of the program was built around the premium. Radio's biggest build-up was not for a star; it was for Captain Midnight's new annual Code-o-graph.

The Code-o-graph was a device with numbered and lettered dials for encoding and decoding secret messages. ("Stand by for another Secret Squadron code session!"). But every year the Code-o-graph was something different, too. The 1946 device was only a gold shield badge with a code dial sporting a glittering mirror suitable for flashing messages and studiously examining loose front teeth. In 1947, Captain Midnight gave us a police-type whistle with a Code-o-graph dial set rakishly on the side; 1948 was not a vintage year for Code-o-graphs. That year it was a clumsy thing, bigger than a pocket watch, with a "secret compartment" big enough to hide the floor plan of the battleship *Maine,* and with a mirror several inches wide on the back. It looked more like a girl's compact than a piece of fighting equipment, and many must have been buried deep in the corners of drawers only to be taken out to decipher the radioed code messages by Tom Moore.

As if to make up for 1948's disaster, the Key-o-matic Code-o-graph was introduced in 1949. It was a winner. The idea of a key to unlock the secret code somehow fit. Once again, the new Captain Midnight Code-o-graph became the central theme of the radio series. If you were hip to the inner workings of the show by this time, you sent in your Ovaltine seal even before the offer was formally made. The Key-o-matic Code-o-graph didn't require a separate commercial; the whole show was one solid pitch for the new premium.

When Captain Midnight and his Secret Squadron crew were shipwrecked by archvillain Ivan Shark, SS-1 told his young aide, Chuck Ramsey, to unlimber his Code-o-graph and contact Washington on his "pocket locator" (a miniature two-way radio they were never able to figure out how to manufacture cheaply enough to offer for a dime and an Ovaltine seal).

CHUCK: Shall I use the new Code-o-graph or the old one, sir?

MIDNIGHT: The *new* Key-o-matic, Chuck.

CHUCK: I'm anxious to use it . . . it's so simple to work, yet so sort of . . . mysterious . . .

MIDNIGHT: Ask Major Steel to send an amphibian down right away.

CHUCK: Captain, my pocket locator is flashing on, and how!

MIDNIGHT: Take down the message as Chuck gets it, Joyce. Ikky, you decode it.

JOYCE: Right away, sir . . . hey, what can I write it down on?

MIDNIGHT: On the back of your hand . . . wait a minute . . . here's an indelible pencil.

JOYCE: Gosh, this mermaid life is sure hard on paper . . . just look at my notebook . . . Okay, Chuck, read it out.

CHUCK: Code F-seven . . . ten . . . twenty-two . . . fifteen .

ANNOUNCER: And a short time later, Ikky decodes . . .

IKKY: Message arrived . . . old Code-o-graph made
ob-so-lete . . . new Key-o-matic being sent to all
members. . . . Anything else I can do? Signed,
Steel.

CHUCK: There certainly is, isn't there, sir?

MIDNIGHT: Yes, there is, Chuck. Ask Major Steel to
have an amphibian flown down right away.

IKKY: Oh boy, will I be glad to see that arrive.

MIDNIGHT: Help Chuck code the message, Joyce.
Use Code B-eight . . .

JOYCE: Just a minute while I fix this Code-o-graph,
Chuck . . . gemini, is this key a slick idea! Okay,
Chuck . . . two . . . nine . . . eight . . . seven . . .

All the advertising agencies seemed to think it was a slick
idea to have something the kids could use right along with
the hero of the show. You could get a Green Hornet ring
that imprinted the seal of the Hornet just like Brit Reid
did on every program. If Jack Armstrong had a pedometer
to tell how far he had hiked to get to the Elephant's Graveyard you could also get one for a Wheaties box top to
tell the dismal distance to that cemetery of summer and
Christmas vacations—school. Some premiums rather stretched
things in their attempt at practical value. One such was a
ring offered by Buck Rogers in the mid-forties. After being
charged with sunlight, it would glow eerily in the palm of
an Earthman when taken into the shadows. It would *not*
glow, however, if held by a Venusian. I never ran into a
Venusian all the time I had it.

Things that glowed in the dark were very big in Radioland. So much so that the feature was thrown in as an
"extra" on a lot of premiums. The Green Hornet's seal ring
also had a band of glowing plastic. Sky King had glowing
plastic on the ring that had a picture of himself that changed
by polarized magic to Sky King in disguise. The ring also

imprinted Sky's brand, the Flying Crown. The versatile Sky King Signascope had its glow-in-the-dark band for night signaling, a mirror for sun-flashing, a secret code on its side, and a combination magnifying glass-signal whistle that slid into the secret compartment.

The biggest of the firefly premiums was the Lone Ranger's. He let you hold up your pants with a whole belt that glowed in the dark. One of the least original was a ring offered by The Shadow that only glowed in the shadows, not even ascertaining the planet of your origin. Of course, The Shadow ring did sport for a setting a miniature of his sponsor's product, Blue Coal.

When Ovaltine and Daddy Warbucks were replaced with new guardians for Little Orphan Annie (Quaker Puffed Wheat Sparkies and Airman Captain Sparks), the aviation theme begat aviation premiums, including pilot's wings glowing with their own pilot light, and a Little Orphan Annie Cockpit, complete with joystick.

From Tom Mix, the uncrowned champion in the field, came premiums of every kind, as fast as if they were fired from the clicking cylinders of his Straight-Shootin' six-shooter. In fact, his six-shooter itself was a premium in a wooden model. (A reasonable facsimile of a gun for a reasonable facsimile of a box top—fair exchange.)

Ralston's favorite cowboy also offered his share of the "glow" premiums, enough to make a camp site of Straight Shooters look like a pack of green-eyed creatures in the dark. Tom's cornucopia fired again and again. BANG! A glowing arrowhead with a compass and a magnifying glass. BAM! A pair of spurs with light-charged star spinners. KA-CHOW! Something really special: a Magic Cat's Eye Ring that apparently used a different kind of luminosity. The fire was *within* a glass tiger's eye, a wild thing captured and flaring out at you. This was undoubtedly the classiest of all the treasures of Radioland that burned with a mysterious power of its own in the dark. The Cat's Eye wasn't the only ring offered by Tom Mix. He must have worn one on every finger. No doubt about it, he had a positive thing about them. More than once, when Tom was in a tight spot, he told the others that he knew his ring could get them through it.

One of Tom's earliest rings was a Lucky Horseshoe Nail Ring; that is, a nail bent into a finger-size loop. It was a "lucky charm" for Tom and had helped him through any number of gunfights with hardened killers, sandstorms in the desert, and even an encounter in which he was bitten by a rattlesnake. But then, if Tom Mix looked on his premium ring as a totem, so did we. We hoped a bit of the fantastic luck of our heroes would be carried to us in the things they sent us. Why shouldn't we believe it? Apparently even the heroes did. For free, we not only got the ring, but part of the magic of Tom Mix's "charmed life." What *wouldn't* Ralson have sent for a dime in hard cash?

Later on, when they did charge a dime "for handling and mailing" they sent plenty—plenty more rings from the fingers of the chief Straight Shooter. There was a Magnet Ring, Periscope Ring, Slide Whistle Ring, Tom Mix Signature Ring, Tom Mix Photo Ring, and a Siren Ring. There was, in short, a ring for every occasion. If someone gave you a check signed by Tom Mix, you could verify the signature from your Signature Ring. If accosted by an imposter claiming to be Tom, you could check on him by consulting the portrait in the tiny magnifying lens of your Tom Mix Photo Ring. You could check behind you to see if you were being followed with your Periscope Ring, and if there were some important papers in the hands of a suspected Nazi spy, held together by a paper clip, you could always pick them up on the sly with your Magnet Ring. When on a stakeout, you could while away the time by playing tunes on your Slide Whistle Ring, and then when the case was ready to break, you could imitate a distant police car with your Siren Ring to trick the crooks into foolhardy flight. Tom's nimble fingers never seemed to be stripped clean of rings for his loyal Straight Shooters.

With some reluctance perhaps, Tom also offered other types of radio premiums. There were badges—a gold-colored decoder badge (perhaps a bit similar to that offered by Captain Midnight), a Straight Shooters' sharp-shooter's medal, and a set of badges with photos on them of different members of the cast. Telegraph sets were big around Dobie; Tom offered at least three different models. I remember one kind, a red and white cardboard box the size of a paperbound book, with a metal clicker and penlight batteries. You strung wires between two of them and they worked. There was a slightly larger model in a blue box with white lettering. The main trouble with all the telegraph sets was that you had to make sure one of your friends also got a set so you could use them together. (Having to eat *one* box of Ralston was enough!)

Perhaps the culmination of all Tom Mix premiums was the Signal Arrowhead. This palm-sized gadget contained not only a compass and a magnifying glass, but the siren from the Siren Ring, a set of multinoted pipes on which could be played more intricate musical selections than on the Slide Whistle Ring, and a reduction lens, termed a "smallifying" glass. I never found a practical purpose for this. Surprisingly, the Signal Arrowhead did not glow in the dark.

The main thing glowing in the dark by this time was millions of television screens in shadowy living rooms. Television was becoming the center of interest, even for kids. Still, for the moment, there were more millions of radio listeners. Advertising agencies were still planning premiums for the radio audiences, so they gave the listeners of the *Tom Mix* radio program what they really wanted—a television set! It was a toy television set, a viewer for tiny film reels. It showed you cartoons, pictures of the *Tom Mix* cast, and several Tom Mix stories in comic-strip form. One of these was "The Television Murder." It had this solution: "Photograph of Mintmore (frame three) shows he needed thick glasses. Why didn't he have them on if he was watching television when he was shot?" When a radio show so freely admitted its audience's chief interest was in television, it had to be near the end for dramatic radio, and it was.

Shortly afterward, Ralston replaced *Tom Mix* with a radio version of their television show *Space Patrol*. It, along with other programs with versions on both radio and television (*Tom Corbett, Space Cadet,* and *Sky King*), continued the practice of offering premiums but, because television shows were made to be rerun long after the premium offer had ended, the TV versions could not be so obsessed with the life-depending indispensability of the premium in their story lines.

By the early 1950s, all the juvenile shows were gone from radio. The soap operas lingered on and continued to give out their premiums as they had for years, the Helen Trent Friendship Lockets, the Aunt Jenny Cookbooks, etc. Here again, the sales talk for the premium was within the show itself. Perhaps soap-opera premiums were not presented as being a matter of life-and-death urgency, but they were presented in even more glowing, syrupy tones. One "premium" episode of a daytime serial was especially memorable. A new actress, fresh from the Broadway stage, was added to the cast and she rehearsed a "premium" speech several times before going on the air. "Helen, darling, what a delightful necklace! It looks as if it had tiny real violets entwined in it. It speaks of springtime and the outdoors. It gives you an aura of freshness and youth, hope and beauty."

Then, forgetting this was no longer a rehearsal, the new actress said, "Do I actually have to say this garbage?"

No one would have to say it long. Even the soap operas stopped offering radio premiums as they lost sponsorship of the entire program by one manufacturer. A few advertisers continued to buy the much cheaper individual one-minute spot commercials on soap operas, but they were not concerned with identifying their products with any one series. Even this minimal advertising disappeared and so did the soap opera from radio.

The traditions started by radio premiums linger on in videoland. But Batman appearing at the end of the show to tell you to send in a Gleem box top for a photograph of him isn't the same as if that photograph played a vital part in the story . . . saved the lives of Batman and Robin time after time . . . was a photograph touched with magic and destiny . . . a photograph that no loyal American would be without for a second longer.

That kind of urgent pressure on you to make you desperately *want* and *need* that premium belongs to a different advertising medium (and to the looser advertising regulations of the past). Never again will we know such shrieking and arm-twisting to get us to send in and get something free. Occasionally, we will see or hear something that can make us remember how it was. In 1963, with little shrillness, Golden West Savings of San Francisco joined a long, ghostly line of fondly remembered names . . . Ovaltine . . . Ralston . . . Wheaties . . . when they sponsored the revival of the old transcribed series *The Shadow* and offered the listeners, free, a small button recalling radio's past glories with the single motto "The Shadow Knows."

VIII

FOR ARMCHAIR DETECTIVES ONLY

"This story begins in Baker Street one March morning in the early 1900s. Holmes and I were seated each side of a blazing fire. Holmes was puffing away at his curved pipe, while I browsed through the *Times* . . ."

The voice of Dr. Watson came to me out of a small bedside radio on Sunday evenings in the winter of 1940, when I was supposed to be asleep by nine-thirty because the next day was a school day. But nine-thirty was too important a time for sleep, so I lay in bed with the covers pulled up around my face, getting steamy hot with my breath, and I listened to the voices hovering in the dark like the shadows of cruising bats.

"The New Adventures of Sherlock Holmes, starring Basil Rathbone as Sherlock Holmes, and Nigel Bruce as Dr. Watson . . . brought to you by the makers of Bromo-Quinine Cold Tablets . . ." the announcer said, introducing the program; and then, slipping out of his role of program host, he would step into the scene of the drama. His footsteps echoed off the cobblestones as he made his way through the fog-shrouded streets of nighttime London, while Big Ben chimed the hour.

At last, our guide sounded the brass knocker at the study of Dr. John H. Watson. We were bid to enter by the throaty voice of Watson, his bumbling British accent a pleasant blur. Inside, near the crackling logs of the fireplace, the announcer would ease into the creaking chair opposite the doctor's. "What tale have you for us tonight, Dr. Watson?" our guide would ask. Whereupon Watson would hem and haw a bit, searching his memory and perhaps some notes, and then begin his tale of Sherlock Holmes.

The story that began one March with Watson browsing through the *Times* was "The Disappearance of Lady Frances Carfax." Holmes questioned Watson on his return from outside.

HOLMES: But why a Turkish bath, old chap?

WATSON: Because for the last few days I've been feeling rheumatic and old. A Turkish bath is what we call an alterative in medicine—a fresh starting point—a cleanser of the system.

HOLMES: You say that you have had it because you need a change. Let me suggest that you take one. How would Switzerland do?

WATSON: Switzerland?

HOLMES: Yes, old chap. First-class tickets to Lausanne, and all expenses paid on a princely scale.

WATSON: It sounds wonderful. But why?

HOLMES: I'm afraid that some evil has befallen the Lady Frances Carfax.

Sherlock Holmes rapped out those words in his clipped, intense speech, and so began a half hour of hansom-cab adventure at the full gallop. First, Lady Frances Carfax had her priceless jewels stolen, then she was abducted by the thief, "Holy Peters, one of the most unscrupulous rascals that Australia has ever evolved," then she was sealed up alive with a corpse in a coffin built for two, and, finally, she was saved from being buried alive just before the last shovelful by the timely intervention of Mr. Holmes of Baker Street.

This radio adaptation of the famous Lady Frances Carfax case was written by two very gifted men, Leslie Charteris, creator in his own right of The Saint, writing under the pseudonym of Bruce Taylor, and celebrated actor-author, Denis Green. Along with mystery novelist and critic, Anthony Boucher, they not only adapted famous stories, they also created the excellent *pastiches* of those tales left unwritten by Sir Arthur Conan Doyle and sealed away in Dr. Watson's black dispatch box.

Some of these "new" adventures concerned "the shocking affair of the Dutch steamship *Friesland,* which so nearly cost both our lives," the hideous tale of the red leech, the remarkable account of the man who stepped back into his house to fetch his umbrella and was never more seen in this world, the singular affair of the aluminum crutch, and the curious experience of the Patterson family on the Island of Uffa.

Many of the most exciting stories involved the villany of one of radio's great archfiends, Professor Moriarty, who was nearly the intellectual equal of Sherlock Holmes but, alas, completely dedicated to evil. Of course, a man whose eyes are half-lidded and set in a great domed head that oscillates from side to side is apt to turn out badly.

"He is the Napoleon of crime, Watson. The greatest schemer of all time, the organizer of every deviltry, the controlling brain of the underworld, a brain which might have made or marred the destiny of nations . . . that's the man!"

Unquestionably, Moriarty's most insidious plot in one of the radio originals was the importation of the bubonic-plague-injected "Giant Rat of Sumatra," which was capable of wiping out life in most of London and perhaps the entire

British Isles. At the finish of the adventure, the pair from 221B Baker Street were locked up with the loathsome rodent in the creaking hold of a ship. Only after agonizing minutes of menace and suspense were they able to save themselves and London from the terror, as I recall, by starting a rat-consuming fire with embers from Holmes' ever-present pipe.

Another wonderfully loathsome beast was "The Hound of the Baskervilles," serialized over eight weeks. I will never forget those evenings, listening to the episodes about the cursed Baskerville family and their private demon, The Hound of Hell, slavering phosphorescently in the gloom of the moor, loping silent as shadow, swift as the racing moon—what a dear, dread nightmare! On radio, he was real—more real than the movies were ever able to make him, for who could match the befanged ghastlies blooming in the imagination of a six-year-old boy and nourished by the genius of some of the greatest of all mystery writers, the stylish melodramatics of a Basil Rathbone, and the matchless skill of an anonymous sound effects man in a cramped radio studio.

On radio, Holmes, always a master of disguises, had many voices, too. When the program was first broadcast in the early thirties, he had the manner of sleek, British, Clive Brook. In 1933, he seemed almost American in the guise of Broadway's Richard Gordon. For a one-time performance on *The Lux Radio Theatre* in the mid-thirties he assumed one of his oldest and most revered disguises, the stage's immortal Mr. William Gillette.

But Sherlock Holmes achieved his master incarnation in Basil Rathbone, playing opposite Nigel Bruce as Dr. Watson. Rathbone and Bruce were ideal, their voices as perfect as their appearances. Doyle's description of the way Holmes looked and sounded fit Rathbone exactly, and if Nigel Bruce wasn't a literal embodiment of the Sacred Books' somewhat younger and brighter Watson, he was the image of the good-natured, faithful bungler we remember in contrast to the brilliant detective. These two had me sold completely. Why, I even wished I could get sick so I could use the Bromo-Quinine Cold Tablets that sponsored Sherlock Holmes!

After Rathbone, through the mid- and late forties, Holmes' countenance changed rapidly through Tom Conway, Ben Wright, and John Stanley.

Today there are still *Sherlock Holmes* radio programs on the air, both in the United States and Great Britain. The two different series, each transcribed a few years ago in London, are heard on various American stations (usually FM) and in one Holmes sounds like a young radio actor named Carlton Hobbs, and in the other, Sir John Gielgud. Thus, in this otherwise uncertain age, we are assured that at some time, morning or night, somewhere, whether in America or Doyle's London itself, the cracking voice of the Master Detective, Mr. Sherlock Holmes, is calling out even now his immortal summons to adventure, "Quick, Watson! The game is afoot!"

Perhaps the best disguise Sherlock Holmes ever donned is Ellery Queen. With Ivy League suit, glasses, rare book tucked under one arm, Ellery Queen emerges as "the logical successor to Sherlock Holmes," according to the Holmes radio scripter Anthony Boucher. To others, Queen simply is Sherlock Holmes in modern dress, although not all penetrate the masterful disguise.

Still active in the printed medium, Ellery Queen lives on, just as Sherlock Holmes does in the belief of the devoted. To these faithful, the Master Detective (in either incarnation) is a living man.

The illusion was cultivated both on radio and in the original books by two men named Lee and Dannay, who used Ellery Queen both as a by-line and the name of the hero of the books. Curiously, the novels are not in the first person, although that seems a logical extension of the idea. Of course, Queen is such a mental superman that a first-person account of his exploits would seem immodest indeed.

On the air, an announcement was delivered that "the entire production was under the supervision of Ellery Queen," and the cast credits were given: "The cast featured Sidney Smith, Santos Ortega, Mandell Krammer. . . ." Only by being mentioned first were you to assume Sidney Smith played the role of Detective Queen. He was, incidentally, only one of several who did play Queen over the years, others being Lawrence Dobkin, Howard Culver, and Hugh Marlowe, who also starred in a filmed TV series based on Queen's exploits.

Yet, these credits aside, Ellery Queen seemed to be a real person, one who talked to other real people, the stock "celebrities" of the broadcasting world (Dorothy Kilgallen, John Garfield, et al), challenging them, at the end of the program, as "Armchair Detectives," to solve the mystery. Many of them seemed to have spent most of the broadcast in the bar, and were a bit fuzzy about what murder was coming off. Still, Ellery Queen's show was the detective program that gave you, the listener, a chance to join in on the fun and games. You were given all the clues and you could solve the mystery—if you happened to be a deductive genius on the level of Ellery Queen.

For noncompetitors, the appeal of the show was merely that of a strong hero, his gruff but lovable police inspector father, a comedy-relief cop named Velie, and Ellery's secretary and girl friend, Nikki Porter. But the real fascination of this long-lived series was in his ingenious examples of deduction.

In "The Adventure of the Murdered Ship," Ellery had to solve the wartime problem of how the enemy found out the sailing time of a torpedoed ship from a few bits of loose talk.

OFFICIAL: So you also solved the mystery of that "Ellery Q" on the enemy sub commander's scrap of paper, Mr. Queen?

ELLERY: (LAUGHING) It wasn't my name. It isn't a name at all . . . the appearance of a name was a coincidence. It's a code.

(NIKKI, THE INSPECTOR, VELIE, EXCLAIM IN SURPRISE)

ELLERY: Let's take the "Q" part first. Which letter of the alphabet is "Q"?

VELIE: (MUMBLING RAPIDLY) A, B, C, D, E, F, G, H . . .

NIKKI: The seventeenth letter, Ellery.

ELLERY: Remember that. Now one of our facts was that the ship was torpedoed at five P.M. In one international system of figuring time, A.M. and P.M. are not used, the hours are numbered from one to twenty-four. By this system, the letter "Q" in the code phrase "Ellery Q" would stand for the seventeenth hour. What is the seventeenth hour in terms of A.M. or P.M.?

INSPECTOR: Five P.M.! The time of the torpedoing!

ELLERY: So we know "Q" is the time instruction given to the commander of the enemy submarine.

NIKKI: But what does the "Ellery" stand for?

ELLERY: Obviously, Nikki, for a word which, when grouped with "Q" or "five P.M.," gives a clear message. Think of it as a group of letters—E, L, L, E, R, Y. Now note that the first and fourth letters are the same, and the second and third. Can you think of another word with a similar construction?

VELIE: (QUICKLY) Who me, Maestro?

ELLERY: Well, Sergeant, what happened at five P.M.? There was an attack on the ship. "Attack"—A, T, T, A, C, K!

INSPECTOR: "Ellery"—the code word for "attack"!

ELLERY: Yes, Dad. "Ellery Q" simply meant to the sub commander, "Attack at five P.M.," which, combined with his other information, gave him all he had to know.

Of course, this part of the puzzle is so simple and obvious that the "official" in the story points out that even the FBI figured that part of it out. Then Ellery gets down to work and solves the hard part of the puzzle.

Some years ago, the collaborative author, Ellery Queen, complained bitterly about one of the actors who played Queen making public appearances (for charity) as "Ellery Queen," when he and only he was E.Q. I don't know how the judge solved that puzzle, but if it was left to me and to many others, it was that cultured, resonant voice coming out of the loudspeaker those evenings in the forties that was the world's greatest *living* detective, Ellery Queen.

By the late thirties, the greatest living mystery story writer was Dashiell Hammett. His novels such as *The Maltese Falcon* and *The Glass Key* are more than outstanding detective novels, they are recognized as being significant works in the mainstream of American literature. "The best detective story in the world," Alexander Woollcott said of the first. Among his other distinctions, Hammett was the only author not in radio production himself to lend his creative efforts to three successful mystery programs.

The Thin Man in Hammett's original novel was the nickname of the murder victim, not the nickname of detective Nick Charles. But Hollywood confused the issue with many William Powell-Myrna Loy vehicles all employing "The Thin Man" in the titles. It was, indeed, a situation similar to the confusion caused by the films about Dr. Frankenstein's monster, where the monster instead of the doctor became known as "Frankenstein." But by the time of the radio show, even Hammett accepted the alias.

Nick and Nora Charles were a fun couple who seemed to take little if anything seriously (unlike *my* parents), except perhaps the revealing of the murderer at the end of each story, and their liquor. Nick, in particular, was the connoisseur. "Martinis are only to be mixed to the rhythm of a waltz," he would dutifully remind Nora, who enjoyed the thrill of the murder hunt much more than husband, Nick, who had retired from private-eye life when they married. But Nora always goaded him into taking "just this one last case, Nickee, please?" And off they'd be on another mystery adventure.

On the radio series, the stars were Claudia Morgan, one of the most beautiful (but alas, unseen) actresses in radio, daughter of comedian Frank Morgan, and her leading man, Les Damon, hero of countless radio thrillers, including *The Falcon.* He and Miss Morgan worked together as late as 1960, when they were co-starring in one of the very last soap operas, *Right to Happiness.* During his World War II service, Damon was temporarily replaced by Les Tremayne, but their voices, and even their names, were so similar, that most of the audience never noticed the switch.

Hammett was not a prolific writer, and all of his handful of novels and a few score of short stories are carefully preserved in hardcover editions. Yet there are radio scripts by him that have gone unnoticed. Less than classics, these scripts are nevertheless interesting examples of a style that has been favorably compared to Ernest Hemingway's as an expression of the American language.

Hammett adapted one *Thin Man* script for the picture magazine *Click,* a rival to *Life* and *Look* in 1942. In it, Nick Charles again proved himself always willing to slip away from wife Nora to help a girl in trouble.

Sonia started to talk as soon as she saw we were alone. "First letters, then telephone calls," she said. "They say they kill me."

I handed her a fresh handkerchief. Hers was in shreds. "Maybe it's just your imagination," I said. Sonia went to work on my handkerchief. "Then comes candy to my house," she said. "I give one to Tovarsh, my dog. He die. I have great fear. I . . ."

A barking pistol cut her short. She fell like a plummet at my feet. I was bending over to help her when I saw that we now had company. Brady, Helen Roberts, Al and Nora were leaning over my shoulder. The bullet had missed Sonia. "Get me some brandy," I told Nora. I held Sonia's head on my arm, tried to force the brandy through her lips. It brought her to. Brady said he could look after his own wife. "No . . . no," Sonia sobbed. "I do not want to go home. Do not let them take me."

Brady started to haul her up. "She wasn't hit, was she?" he said.

"You sound disappointed," I said.

Sonia bit her lip. "He is," she cried, "he wants me dead so he can marry Helen."

Eventually, Nick and Nora would wrap the case up and then wrap themselves up in the covers of their very own trundle bed. There, somehow, it seemed more prelude than finish when Nora uttered that one famous closing line, "Good night, Nickeeee . . ."

In large part it was the well-designed and constantly repeated intros and outros that made vintage radio memorable. Few who ever heard it can forget the opening of another show created by Dashiell Hammett.

"He's walking into that drugstore. . . . He's stepping onto the scales. . . . (SNICK! CLICK!) Weight: 237 lbs. . . . Fortune: *Danger!* Whooooo is he??? The . . . Fat Man,"

rumbled the bass voice of J. Scott Smart, who at times tipped the scale thirty-three pounds more than the specified weight of the character he played.

For some reason, I always identified with *The Fat Man.* Maybe this was because I was a fat kid. Unfortunately though, whenever I put a penny in the weight machine (and consequently tipped the scales usually about twenty-five pounds over what I should have) my fortune never read "Danger!" Instead, that little green fortune card always read "You're too fat!" But I did wonder if thin kids identified with *The Thin Man.* If I'd been a thin kid, I'd sure have wanted to identify with the Thin Man. It was a better show.

The Fat Man was the natural running mate of Hammett's earlier success *The Thin Man.* It was the one property the writer was credited with creating specifically for radio. Without doubt, the title *The Fat Man* and the character's real name, Brad Runyon, were new. Still, the Fat Man seems only to be the name finally given to one of Hammett's earlier famous, yet curiously anonymous, characters, an overweight operator for the Continental Detective Agency. In stories written during the thirties for *Black Mask* magazine, Hammett left the character completely nameless, but his editors began nicknaming this detective "the Continental Op." Finally, on radio, this detective, one of the greatest in the literature of crime, emerged with a memorable name and title.

After Hammett's first few scripts, "setting" the series, the program sank into pedestrian mediocrity and only the great booming voice and sly intonations of the man we knew as the Fat Man still bring the series to mind after nearly a score of years.

The Fat Man appealed to listeners of all sizes and shapes, but the appeal was more in the immense man with an immense appetite for life than in the tough-guy scripts written after Hammett left.

> CYNTHIA: My name is Cynthia Prior. . . . I was told that the Fat Man was the best private detective in town . . .
>
> RUNYON: I'll take the bow sitting down.
>
> CYNTHIA: I imagine you're pretty handy with a revolver, but are you . . . tactful?
>
> RUNYON: I don't embarrass my clients, if that's what you mean.
>
> CYNTHIA: I have a case for you, Mr. Runyon . . . a case of blackmail.
>
> RUNYON: Who's being squeezed? And who's doing the squeezing?
>
> CYNTHIA: A man named George Brandon. He's demanding money from me.
>
> RUNYON: Why?
>
> CYNTHIA: We've been friends up to now, but he's threatened to tell my husband that his friendship was more than a passing fancy.
>
> RUNYON: How did you meet up with this guy?
>
> CYNTHIA: It was accidental, in a cocktail lounge. I dropped my purse and he—
>
> RUNYON: Picked you both up.
>
> CYNTHIA: Mr. Runyon!
>
> RUNYON: No offense intended. I just like my stories straight and to the point.
>
> CYNTHIA: At any rate, he's demanding twenty-five thousand dollars . . .
>
> RUNYON: I guess we'll go up and see George.

CYNTHIA: We?

RUNYON: Sure, you're coming along. We'll have to talk him out of it, and I'll need your help . . .

CYNTHIA: I'm ready, Mr. Runyon . . . here's your fee, in advance. . . . What are you doing?

RUNYON: Checking my gun.

CYNTHIA: Will there be . . . trouble?

RUNYON: In a case like this, Mrs. Prior, there usually is . . .

The Fat Man had known better days, and it got worse when the program was adapted into a motion picture of the same title, starring the bulky J. Scott Smart, who was better behind the microphone than in front of the camera. In the movie a lot of tough-guy-isms were added to his dialogue, along with a whole crew of flunkies. This film's sole claim to lasting fame was that it offered the debut of a new young star in a supporting role. TV listings occasionally offer uncomplimentary confusion by cataloguing "Rock Hudson as *The Fat Man*."

Dashiell Hammett had fared better with *The Thin Man* series as a generally reliable *pastiche* of his work, than with *The Fat Man* program, which was a poor imitation.

The third of his creations came to radio neither as good imitation nor a poor one, but as outright satire. *The Adventures of Sam Spade* was produced and directed by William Spier, one of the most distinctive talents in radio production. His helming of the *Suspense* anthology produced some of the most effective drama in radio history, far more successful in achieving its aims than more serious dramatic attempts on other programs such as *The Columbia Workshop*. But with *Sam Spade*, Spier was trying not so much for drama as for comedy. The result was a show that still seems fresh and alive.

Remember those confused conversations so full of verve

between Howard Duff and Lurene Tuttle as Spade and his faithful secretary, Effie?

> EFFIE: Sam Spade Detective Agency.
> SAM: Sam, sweetheart.
> EFFIE: Oh, Sam, how did it go?
> SAM: Well, it wasn't exactly a ten-in-one outfit, more of a mud show, dog and pony type, rag front, you know.
> EFFIE: Sam, what are you talking about? By the way, where were you last night?
> SAM: Missed the last bus in from the Cow Palace, so I had to do a star pitch. Carny talk, Ef.
> EFFIE: If you think I'm going to ask what a star pitch is, you're mistaken. . . . What were you doing at the Cow Palace?
> SAM: Oh, just bulling around.
> EFFIE: Sam? Uh . . . Sam? *Sam?*
> SAM: You ask too many questions. Sweetheart, in the patter of the carny, I'll be down to spiel my pitch . . . pitch my spiel . . . and make with the canvas on . . . "The Bluebeard Caper."

And immediately after this, the announcer billboarded, "Dashiell Hammett, America's leading detective fiction writer and creator of Sam Spade, the hard-boiled private eye, and William Spier, radio's outstanding director of mystery and crime drama, join their talents to make your hair stand on end with *The Adventures of Sam Spade* . . . presented by Wildroot Cream Oil for the hair."

In this story, Sam was called upon to track down an illusive lady named Sylvia. When she disappeared from a locked room in a skyscraper, Sam was given to complain. "Who is Sylvia? What is she?" Later on, he got a clue.

SAM: What I found on the roof did surprise me a bit.
. . . It was a rope and grappling hook, human-fly
type, which fitted in with the circusy aspect the
caper was beginning to take on . . . but I would
never have taken Sylvia for a stunt woman. . . . I
took a few quick knee bends to get in shape for
what lay ahead . . . slid down the banister to the
top floor, somersaulted into the elevator and rode
it down to the lobby, no hands. Pausing only to
acknowledge the applause of the scrubwoman, I
skated on over to the phone . . .

After a few phone calls and a few lumps on his hard-
boiled skull, Sam Spade found out that Sylvia was not one
but three circus daredevils—that is, she was posing as three
different girls—and that she was collecting on her own life
insurance as one by one each of her identities was "killed"
in a spectacular stunt. Her helper, a rascally southern gentleman, tried to kill off Sylvia's final identity and got bitten
by Sylvia's pet cobra for his trouble.

Such scripts as this, written by Bob Tallman and Gil
Doud, were clearly wild parodies of the taut and often grim
Hammett novels of the thirties. Audiences had been asked
to accept all the conventions of the hard-boiled private eye
for quite some time, and to take them deadly seriously. The
takeoffs by the great comedians, notably Fred Allen's oriental
sleuth, One Long Pan, had prepared them for a somewhat
more humorous approach, and in *Sam Spade*, which began
September 29, 1946, they got it. The program lasted until
the McCarthy frenzy when Dashiell Hammett came into
disfavor for refusing to answer some of the prying questions
of the junior senator from Wisconsin. The radio program
was completely alien to him, using only his name and the
name of his character, but in another case of guilt by
association, it went off the air. The series later returned

briefly with another cast and crew, but the spark was gone, and the radio series came to a final curtain.

When Sam Spade exited there were others to take his place. On radio, there was a detective for everybody—tough, suave, elderly, Chinese, feminine, English, even invisible. There could never be too many detectives and, seemingly, there were never enough. In fact, *everybody* was a detective in addition to his regular line. Comedians Jack Benny, Bob Hope, and Eddie Cantor regularly featured mystery sketches. Ma Perkins was a sweet little old lady during the daytime hours, but she nailed more than one murderer. Helen Trent, Just Plain Bill, Young Widder Brown, and Our Gal Sunday's husband, Lord Henry, all had to find the real killers before the evildoers were sent to the chair for a crime. A bit later in the afternoon, Jack Armstrong and Little Orphan Annie often seemed to be fully as much cops as Dick Tracy.

Along with the host of famous fictional detectives from mystery novels that flooded the halls of radio stations with blood, or, at least, bloodcurdling screams, radio created enough of its own investigators for the evening hours: *Crime Doctor, Mr. District Attorney, Martin Kane, Pat Novak for Hire, Dragnet's* Joe Friday.

The oldest of all fiction series detectives (predating even Holmes), Nick Carter, seemed young and active enough on his Mutual series set in modern times. While Philo Vance belonged to the 1920s, his broad "A" and coldly logical deduction took him through many society murders into the 1950s. Mike Hammer's sex and violence seem almost too recent to be a part of Golden Age radio, but he played his part in the last days.

The ethnic range, too, was unlimited. Charlie Chan, the Chinese detective, represented a deviation from the Caucasian (although he was played by Irish Ed Begley). There was a short-lived series about the Japanese Mr. Moto. Bulldog Drummond was as English as Holmes. Hercule Poirot was Belgian, "not zee French" as he always had to say in heatedly denying the source of his accent. Most of the rest of them were American, but of various backgrounds: Greek (Nick "Charles" was short for "something Greek and unpronounceable"); Slavic (Pat Novak); a number of real police detectives named Levy and Greenberg impersonated on *Gangbusters;* and Ed Jacobs, one of Joe Friday's coheroes on *Dragnet.* Sometimes there was even a Negro detective in a stray *Amos 'n' Andy* sketch.

Some radio detectives were old (Mr. Keen, "the kindly old tracer"), some young (Nick Carter's adopted son in his own series, *Chick Carter, Boy Detective*). Most of them were thin, but some were fat (*Nero Wolfe* and *Peter Salem* as well as *The Fat Man*). The airwaves investigators were generally brilliant, but at least one was pretty stupid (*Johnny Fletcher*). But virtually each and every one of these detectives was male. The private and public eyes might have girl Fridays or even wives, but no woman ever made a success of solving crimes all by herself in a regular nighttime mystery series. The one who came closest was the Mrs. of *Mr. and Mrs. North.* This program was superficially similar to *The Thin Man's* marital adventures, but there was a significant difference. Although she did something of a Gracie Allen dumb act, it was really *Pam* North who was the detective, and her husband, Jerry, a book publisher, was the stooge.

The era of radio drama was a time when everybody saw crime—evil—everywhere. Moreover, all these people, housewives, old men, representatives of minorities, foreigners, and a lot of white male Americans, felt qualified to go out and battle the evil they found. If they—if we—were paranoid in spotting devilish schemes, there was at least optimism about overcoming the menacing danger. It seemed as if it would take everybody to defeat the criminals and murderers in the world when you listened to radio mysteries. But then, that was okay. Back then, we were ready and eager to do our part.

IX

GENTLEMEN OF THE PRESS

Newspapermen were supermen on radio. In fact, Superman was a newspaperman—*Daily Planet* reporter Clark Kent, and the Green Hornet, when not equipped with mask and gas gun, was Brit Reid, publisher of the *Daily Sentinel*. Reporters and editors were always so heroic (in stories generally written by ex-newspapermen) that we were sometimes surprised that Editor Steve Wilson or Casey, Crime Photographer were content to walk around in ordinary, unpressed civilian clothes instead of revealing their true identities in dazzling uniforms as "The Electric Editor" and "The Phantom Photographer."

Steve Wilson of the Big Town *Illustrated Press* even had a ringing oath he delivered before each adventure, similar to the ones spoken by various dedicated comic-book heroes: "The freedom of the press is a flaming sword! Use it justly! Hold it high! Guard it well!" Though Wilson was only the editor of Big Town's foremost newspaper, he was far more the first citizen of that city than was the mayor. He called all the shots, as witness this telephone call on one hectic day in 1938.

WILSON: Hello.

PETE: (FILTER, HOLDS THRU SCENE) This is Pete, Boss, we're up at the State Pen now. Everything under control up here. They've got the fire out and the cons locked in their cells.

WILSON: What about the ones who got away, Pete?
Which way were they headed for?

PETE: Out towards Ridgefield—two cars of them . . .

WILSON: How many made the break?

PETE: Eight . . . six of 'em in one car and two in the
other car they commandeered. That's the one the
warden's in. And, Boss, from what I hear, they
are the toughest mugs that ever crashed out of
stir!

Steve Wilson wasn't one to be as impressed with the
toughness of the convicts as his reporter. He was only interested to know if his "boys" were hot on the trail of the
jailbreakers. Pete assured him they were, and further informed the editor that Toby, the photographer, had some
just "wonderful" pictures of the guards being shot down by
the escaping cons, and a real gem, a picture of the warden
himself being strong-armed into the getaway vehicle.

The boss of the *Illustrated Press* was so enthused over
these four-column cuts that he lavishly promised the photographer a bonus big enough to buy him a "nice little car"
—presumably in those days a Crosley, not an MG.

It was a busy day in the city room. No sooner had Wilson
hung up on good old Pete than in breezed the lovely Lorelei
Kilbourne. Wilson generated his own enthusiasm to his star
reporter.

WILSON: While you were out covering luncheons and
odd leaf teas, Goldilocks, the biggest story of the
year has broken and we've scooped the town! . . .
Here, take a look at the extra!

LORELEI: Let me see! "Wholesale Jailbreak! Convicts
Abduct New Warden!" Wow! What a story!

In the good old days, editors and star reporters didn't
have much time to sit around congratulating each other.

Steve Wilson's phone rang. It was a call from District Attorney Miller with his fawning admiration for the *Illustrated Press'* scoop on the prison break.

> WILSON: Of course I have some of my boys out trying to locate those escaped cons, but I thought you might get news from the police before it comes over the regular teletype. Now if you do, will you give me a buzz? I want the *Illustrated Press* to have the first smack on it.
>
> MILLER: Of course, Steve. I'll do what I can.
>
> WILSON: Thank you, Miller. I'll appreciate it a lot!

Given District Attorney Miller's apparent concern with what the *Illustrated Press* could do for him, it is fortunate there was no Ethics in Government Committee active in Big Town to investigate his relationship with Steve Wilson. There was certainly never any question about the ethics of the star who played the part of Steve Wilson when *Big Town* was founded in 1937. Edward G. Robinson, in a change of pace from his movie gangster roles, was a reformed man as the *Illustrated Press* editor. It was not quite enough of a change. According to published interviews, Robinson wanted less violence and hokum on the radio series, more stories with better acting parts for him and his co-star, Claire Trevor. (Later, Ona Munsen replaced Miss Trevor in the role of Lorelei and played it for years.)

One of the stories that offered Robinson a greater range for his talents I remember vividly. Steve Wilson was blinded by racketeers, forced to quit the newspaper, and gave up to despair, winding up on skid row. Then, he heard a call for help from a burning building, and even though blind, he went into the inferno and led a child to safety. His eyes were damaged again in the fire, and a dangerous, thousand-to-one chance operation was performed. The scene where

Wilson's sight, hope, and job were restored offered an acting tour de force, to say the least!

Even more emotional, less violent drama was attempted, and, not surprisingly, the audience switched to other programs to find its prison breaks and murders. The Hollywood series of *Big Town* went off radio in the early forties.

But fighting newspapermen die hard. By 1943, the staff of the *Illustrated Press* was back at work, now in a program originating from New York and written by former newspaperman Jerry McGill, with Steve Wilson and Lorelei now being played by familiar radio performers Edward Pawley and Fran Carlon. Some of the other citizens of Big Town who worked on its leading newspaper were Fletcher, the gruff but lovable city editor; Dusty Miller, a brash but ingratiating photographer; and Harry the Hack, a cab driver whose accent seemed to indicate that Brooklyn was one of the boroughs of Big Town. When not driving Steve Wilson to the scene of a crime, he was on the lookout for trouble himself, armed with a trusty monkey wrench. Harry was never known to have an argument with a paying passenger—or at least never a very lengthy one. Although he was not a dues paying member of the newspaper guild, he found his scoops and took his risks with the best of them.

In one episode, Harry the Hack witnessed an old flower peddler named Violet having a heated conversation with young reckless Johnny Nolan on one of Big Town's gloomier side streets. She was begging him not to join Chick Larson's criminal gang. Rebuffed by Johnny, the old woman went to boss Larson himself, warning him not to involve young Johnny or she would sing out to the *Illustrated Press* on his activities. Larson, in the courtly tradition of gangland, shoved her down a flight of stairs. (*Crash! Thud! Bounce! Bof-bof-boff! Splat!* went a frantic sound effects man, tumbling a sandbag down a flight of toy stairs with expert care.)

Violet reeled into the city room and blurted out her story to Steve Wilson, who took a hand. He visited the mob leader, warned him, kayoed a hood, and followed Larson's girl friend Lola to her apartment. Called in by Steve, Lorelei used the woman's touch to cajole Lola into revealing that she was interested in young Johnny, and afraid of Larson, a killer. Larson burst in and decided to take everybody in sight (and Johnny, who was on his way) for the long ride. Steve had to fight Larson and his gang of killers with only his bare hands, and easily won, with a slight assist from his driver, Harry the Hack, and the cabbie's skull-busting monkey wrench. Then, not only could Lola and Johnny get together, but Steve arranged the reunion of Johnny and loyal old Violet, who was in reality Johnny's mother. And so ended another day in the life of a typical newspaper editor and his hackie.

While the title to the program about Steve Wilson's exploits always remained *Big Town*, and his newspaper was permanently the *Illustrated Press*, that illustrious publication went through many editors before hitting the final. (Ed Pawley, Mgn. Ed.), and then the Late-Night Final (Walter Greaza as Wilson in the last radio run). With that, the presses of radio's *Illustrated Press* closed down.

A new publisher, television, took over and issued a flashy new tabloid under the old title, however. Steve Wilson was demoted from managing editor to a reporter (played by Patrick McVey). Perhaps sulking because of his change in status, Wilson did practically nothing but observe other people's problems, playing no more active part in the stories than host Rod Serling on *Twilight Zone*. Then, even the new TV tabloid was replated and Steve Wilson, played by movie star Mark Stevens, once again was the managing editor. The new format proved serviceable enough to turn out enough editions to be sold for repeat runs.

It was a long row of editions all in all, and filled with

enough extras to drive the pressmen mad. Certainly the men of the city room had to be good and fairly independent. After all, half the time the managing editor was being held prisoner somewhere at gunpoint.

The *Illustrated Press* was a rugged training ground for aspiring newspapermen. I wouldn't be surprised if Brit Reid and even Clark Kent may have taken their early training there, dodging bullets, catching crooks, and writing a feature story on the back of a matchbook while hanging to the rear bumper of a black sedan. Surely, if any newspaperman wanted to learn how to be a superman, he could do far worse than follow the example of Editor Steve Wilson.

THE TWO-HEADED HERO

The only thing tougher and smarter than one newspaperman on radio was two newspapermen, and one man had the distinction of being two of the greatest newspapermen on the airwaves all by himself.

Staats Cotsworth not only played the lead on *Front Page Farrell,* the story of star reporter David Farrell, on the air five afternoons a week, but on one evening per week he moonlighted as *Casey, Crime Photographer*. His voice did seem to fit the popular concept of a newspaperman perfectly—a rich baritone, but touched with a slurred cynicism.

As David Farrell, radio's complete gentleman of the press investigated the troubles of a girl whose romantic problems involved attempts on her life in a 1948 sequence. "Front Page" and his wife, Sally (to whom he was just plain "Front"), visited the apartment of the girl's aunt for information.

The strange old lady's grandniece had nearly been killed in a fire just the day before. The girl had become engaged to wealthy Clifford Putnam, and old Miss Westwood did not like renewed newspaper publicity for the Westwood family in general. Supposedly, the recluse had threatened to cut off the allowance of the girl, and when that failed, she appeared to have taken even more drastic measures. Now even after the girl had almost died, the old woman still refused to cooperate in the investigation when David Farrell and his wife called on her.

FARRELL: We have to find out who is responsible for what almost happened to your niece. If you won't let us in and talk to us, the police will come. You'll have to talk to them.

MISS WESTWOOD: The police! In my apartment! I won't permit it—

FARRELL: I'm afraid you'll have to. So why not talk to us instead? It'll only take a few minutes, and it can't do any harm. Why, we can't even see your face through that veil!

MISS WESTWOOD: Are you sure? Well, come in then . . . but I won't let you stay long. You've ruined my day! My poor, poor, beautiful day . . . ruined! (SHUFFLE OF FOOTSTEPS: DOOR CLOSES) Sit down.

SALLY: My, how neatly you keep your place, Miss Westwood . . . all spick and span.

FARRELL: Now then, did you know, Miss Westwood, that your grandniece was engaged to marry Clifford Putnam? . . .

MISS WESTWOOD: Certainly . . . But what could I do about it?

FARRELL: You might have sent one of your lawyers to warn Aldin that you were cutting off her allowance if she didn't break her engagement . . .

MISS WESTWOOD: But I didn't! I never heard—

FARRELL: You didn't warn Aldin not to speak to me or my wife? You didn't hire men to drive her away and tie her up in an old house?

MISS WESTWOOD: I never in my life heard such nonsense! I don't hire anyone to do anything, except my lawyers! And I'm getting rid of them very soon, too, don't you think I'm not. And now, Mr. Farrow, if you'll take yourself and your wife and your ridiculous conversation—

FARRELL: The name is Farrell. Okay, we'll go. For now . . .

Did you catch the clue about the thick, black veil? Then you won't be surprised to learn Miss Westwood had something to hide. She was, in fact, hiding the fact that she was not the real Miss Westwood but an impostor who was out to take over the Westwood fortune by eliminating its heiress, the niece, just as she had the aunt. So strong was the impostor's determination that she was able to actually deny a direct accusation of the crime in the way that no guilty suspect on *Perry Mason*, in any medium, has ever been able to do.

On the Thursday evening each week when Staats Cotsworth took over the role of that other stalwart member of the press, *Casey, Crime Photographer,* the labors of the working press seemed closer to the reality of cold print. The program was based on a character from a series of mystery novels by George Harmon Coxe and adapted for radio by Alonzo Dean Cole. Cole was another of radio's outstanding writers who had gained fame early in the thirties with *Witch's Tale*, the *Twilight Zone* of the crystal-set age. His *Casey* scripts contained wit and naturalism missing from many radio thrillers.

As for Casey himself, he was a sarcastic operator of a press camera who spent most of his time in a bar, the Blue

Note, talking to his reporter girl friend, Ann Williams, and the bartender, Ethelbert. When not solving murders, he was mostly concerned with negotiating small loans to tide him over to payday and trying to keep his stomach calm with soothing liquids. He was never known to make a direct pass at Ann, but then the listener might conclude that the time for passing was over, and now he was receiving.

Occasionally he did work at being a news photographer, when his editor at the *Morning Express* forced him to leave the neon-lit cafe that was the Blue Note. His job was clearly demonstrated to be news gathering primarily, with the solving of crimes a forced, if inevitable, necessity. Sometimes his motivation for finding a murderer was to help get the story first for his paper, but often he was just out to protect a friend, or, not infrequently, himself.

In a *Crime Photographer* script called "Blackout," Casey comes staggering into the Blue Note at ten in the morning, with a bloodstained handkerchief, a torn press card, and partial amnesia. Immediately his friends, Ann and Ethelbert, suspected something was wrong. The last thing Casey remembered was having a drink with gangster Needles Jones, trying to get a story on the rackets investigation. Ann seemed a bit suspicious of Casey's account of who he was with the night before, and she went with him to Needles' apartment. There they found Needles knifed to death, and a very live Captain Logan of Homicide. Logan had one clue to the murderer—a torn corner of a press card. By this time, Casey's head was killing him.

Ann and Casey went to his apartment, where they found that the hunting knife he had bought for the kid next door as a birthday present was missing. Things were not, Casey concluded, looking too well for him. Agreeing, Ann went into a messy bunch of hysterics that Casey had to slap her out of. Casey ran, and right into the waiting arms of the underworld. They accepted him as one of them, praising him for the neat job he did on Needles, sure he was working some racket of his own. Through these contacts, Casey pried loose a certain telephone number. From a booth, Casey set up a buy for the murder weapon. He would pay $1000 for that hunting knife. But faithful Ann, who had spotted Casey on the street and watched him go into the booth, overheard the phone conversation. She went to Casey's bartender, who knew him better than anybody, and she and Ethelbert trailed Casey to the appointed meeting place for the sale of the knife.

Things looked bleak for Casey when he guiltily bought the murder weapon. Then, as he counted his money, the gangster gloated that *he* killed Needles because "he talked too much," and pinned the rap on Casey who "found out too much." Of course, the confession was overheard by Ann, Ethelbert, and by Homicide's Captain Logan, who stepped out of the shadows, gun in hand.

Later, as the Blue Note piano tinkled in the background, Casey explained how he set the whole thing up with Logan to trap the killer. Naturally, he couldn't take a hysterical woman like Ann into his confidence. Smiling sweetly, Ann repaid the slap Casey gave her earlier, saying, "In case you ever black out again, here's something to wake you up!"

In another episode, the murder of a social butterfly was occupying the attentions of the *Morning Express* staff. As usual, Casey and Ann discussed the case with their favorite bartender in a way that almost anybody might talk over what was going on down at the office.

> CASEY: Logan believes the same as I do, Ethelbert, that one of the people present when Mrs. Forsythe killed that insect, that butterfly, killed her last night.
>
> ETHELBERT: But which one?

CASEY: Right now it looks like her husband did the job.

ETHELBERT: Robert Forsythe, huh?

CASEY: Yeah . . . Logan's been on the wire to Chicago and Forsythe left there by plane early yesterday morning. He had plenty of time to get out to River-hill last night and bump his wife off.

ETHELBERT: But why should he have done it?

CASEY: Ah, I don't know . . . according to the servants the Forsythes haven't been getting along too well lately.

ETHELBERT: I've heard Forsythe's a big, strong guy. He could have pushed that spear clear through his wife and three inches of hard wall.

CASEY: Easy! The butler, Hendricks, is a skinny, puny old codger . . . Helen Frane, the social secretary, is a small woman . . . which practically rules them out. . . . Incidentally, pal, I'm getting thirsty . . . set me up a drink, huh?

ETHELBERT: Oh, sure . . . (POURS DRINK) there you are . . .

CASEY: Kinda tiny, isn't it? Uh, thanks, pal . . .

ETHELBERT: Here comes Miss Williams . . .

CASEY: Oh hello, Annie.

ANN: (COMING ON) Case, Logan's just called from headquarters. The cops have just located Robert Forsythe and he was in Riverhill last night when his wife was murdered!

Of course, it wasn't that simple. Nothing was ever simple for Casey or any of his colleagues in radio's corps of fighting newspapermen. Even the earliest show gave its reporters assignments that were hardly commonplace. In a 1930 episode of *Front Page Headlines* two reporters were sent by the city editor to cover a football game between inmates of a prison and a visiting team. During the game, a prison break was attempted and a riot got under way. Dodging bullets, the reporters phoned in the story, just as the National Guard triumphantly arrived, with the buglers blowing the cavalry charge. Afterward, the city editor remarked that the home team had lost the football game for an infraction of the rules—too many men on the field at one time.

By the 1940s, radio had learned to deal with the gentlemen of the press in a less obviously comic fashion in a program called *The Big Story*, with dramatizations based on fact. A different, real reporter was featured each week, the only continuing character being the narrator, whose booming voice constantly told the reporter exactly what he was doing, as if it were all news to him. It went something like this: "You feel like taking a walk. It's a nice day. You stroll along Michigan Avenue, tipping your hat to the ladies, nodding to the gentlemen. But there is something wrong, something different about today, something that sets it apart from other days. The people stare at you, whisper, turn away. Suddenly, you sense what it is. It's the machine gun you are carrying to the police lab . . . the proof of your . . . *Big Story!*" Some reporters did more than carry a gun to win their $500.00 Pell Mell Award of Merit. One dressed up like a girl to trap a sex maniac. Another arranged for the surrender of Public Enemy No. One to J. Edgar Hoover. This reporter was Walter Winchell.

Hot Copy was a short-lived series about a girl reporter, but, as with female detectives, the audience preferred its heroes male. Most of the newspaper yarns on the air couldn't achieve the level of popularity of *Big Town* and *Casey, Crime Photographer*. Still there is a strong fraternal feeling among members of the press, and somewhere, no doubt, the established newspapermen share a drink with the *Hot Copy* girl and tolerate the *Big Story* narrator telling them, "You are drinking a martini. It is a very dry martini. You like your martinis very dry . . ."

I know where Steve Wilson and Lorelei go after working hours. I know where all of the radio's members of the press wind up. Casey and Ann found it first, but they told everybody else about the place. Ethelbert polishes the bar, while the Blue Note pianist tinkles away at *Star Dust* or *Blue Moon*. Only newspapermen and women come there. It exists only for them to kill time between murders and to wait for their extras to hit the streets. Maybe Brit Reid drops in for an Orange Crush (sponsor loyalty), and, of course, Clark Kent and Lois Lane split a soda. Maybe Casey even meets himself coming and going as Front Page Farrell. I can see all of them sitting around, discussing business—the business of scoop stories, racket crackdowns, crime exposés—the business that was news reporting during the Golden Age of radio.

X

"CAN A WOMAN FIND HAPPINESS?"

JUST PLAIN MILLIONAIRES

ANNOUNCER: We give you now . . . Stella Dallas—
a continuation on the air of the true-to-life story of
mother love and sacrifice . . . in which Stella Dallas saw her own beloved daughter, Laurel, marry
into wealth and society, and, realizing the differ-
ences in their tastes and worlds, went out of Laurel's life. . . .

Stella and her daughter, Laurel, were in New York investi-
gating the theft of a stolen Egyptian mummy. In a stagger-

ingly long synopsis, the announcer informed us that, having been accused of the theft of the mummy herself by Laurel's mother-in-law, Mrs. Grosvenor, Stella sought the help of the man who brought the mummy to America, Sheik Ahmead. She was unaware that the real Sheik Ahmead had been replaced by his twin brother, Rahshed, who planned to seize power in the sheik's homeland. Stella and Laurel were in the room of Stella's old friend, Ed Munn. Stella did not know that Ed had been blackmailed into being the righthand man of the false sheik.

LAUREL: Mummy, I can't believe even Mrs. Grosvenor would be mean enough to send you to jail for stealing that Egyptian mummy.

STELLA: Ah, Lolly baby, she'd do it in a minute. You know how she resents you and her son, Dick, bein' close to me.

LAUREL: Yes, I know.

STELLA: Besides, having that Egyptian mummy at her party was an important thing to Mrs. Grosvenor. It was somethin' to impress all her big society friends. She blames me for making her look bad to all those people.

LAUREL: But Mummy, anybody who knows you knows you could never steal an Egyptian mummy. Why, you'd never steal anything!

STELLA: Lolly baby, you're my own daughter. Naturally you wouldn't think I would steal the Egyptian mummy, but I reckon I'm just going to have to prove my innocence to everybody else.

The success of the daytime serial, the "soap opera," on radio has been attributed to the fact that the programs presented simple, everyday types of problems anybody could identify with and believe in. This theory may be open to question. Being accused of stealing an Egyptian mummy is not the type of problem the average housewife in mid-twentieth-century America faces frequently. Other sporadic difficulties of everyday life are losing your memory, being paralyzed from the waist down, fighting off a half-dozen wealthy suitors, and being tried for murder. Still Ma Perkins' daughter, Fay, managed to have all of these problems simultaneously, and Helen Trent once had most of them.

While soap operas began with simple, close-to-home domestic problems, time wore out the appeal of such basic plot devices as the sex triangle. The wandering husband, the eager secretary, and the wronged wife soon became subplots, secondary to such real and earnest matters of everyday life as finding a murderer, a jewel thief, or an Egyptian mummy.

Stella Dallas not only located that stolen Egyptian mummy, she restored the real Sheik Ahmead to his rightful position, and, with Lolly, accompanied Ahmead back to his sheikdom. There Stella had to survive sandstorms, attacks (non-passionate) of desert nomads, and a curious cruise through the Suez Canal in a submarine. Captain Midnight seldom had a rougher time of it. But Stella (portrayed by Anne Elstner) and Laurel—Lolly—(Vivian Smollen), survived it all. Meanwhile, Lolly's husband, Dick, was valiantly searching for his wife and beloved mother-in-law.

Actually, Dick had more troubles than anybody on the show. He was portrayed at various times by MacDonald Carey, Frank Lovejoy, and Jim Backus. "They fired you to see if you were paying attention," Backus once observed. To cushion the shock of the transition in actors, Dick was given to frequent attacks of tropical fever, in which he could only mumble incoherently, and the inevitable amnesia, in which he wandered off microphone for months. If Stella had really gone "out of Laurel's life," as the introduction erroneously claimed for some twenty years, the poor girl might have starved to death with a husband like Dick. Poor, inept Lolly was probably the most feather-brained woman in soap opera; however, she was never quite as stupid as the men.

At an early age you realized all the men on the "women's stories" were helpless boobs. Yet there was no offense to be taken. This was "ladies' territory," and when you entered it you realized you had to play by their rules. On your programs—*Captain Midnight, Jack Armstrong, Tom Mix*—the kids played a far more dominant role than you realized you played in real life. In soap-opera land the men were de-emphasized. It was merely a matter of home-team rules. No trauma, no neurosis. Mama's boys weren't created by radio listening.

Stella Dallas was allegedly a story of "mother love and sacrifice," but like most of the problems set up by radio's daytime serials, Stella's sacrifice was a strawman. There was no more a question of Stella actually getting out of her daughter's life than there was of the girl from the little mining town in the West, *Our Gal Sunday,* failing to find happiness as the wife of England's richest and most handsome lord, Lord Henry Brinthrope of Black Swan Hall. Perhaps not complete happiness, but there would be no total marital disaster for Sunday, and no final sacrifice for Stella, because that would be the end of the story and everybody would be out of work. Everybody knew that. Everybody but mothers, it seemed.

Both of these programs, as well as most, literally most, of the soap operas in Radioland, were products of the organization headed by Frank and Anne Hummert. Unquestionably, it was with the Hummerts that the soap opera found its purest and most lasting traditions. The soap opera, as well as the juvenile serial and many of the other staples of radio and television broadcasting, began about 1930 in Chicago at the offices of the Blackett-Sample-Hummert advertising agency. The junior partner of the firm was Frank Hummert, who claimed not to be a businessman, only a simple, creative artist. A one-time news reporter, Hummert had made $50,000 a year with the Lord and Thomas Agency before joining Hill Blackett and Glenn Sample. Cloistered in a secluded office, away from the noise and confusion of the business world, Hummert came up with the million-dollar slogan, "The Skin You Love to Touch," one of his first efforts for the soap manufacturers, for whom he would do so much. The office manager (in fact, if not in name) was Mrs. Anne S. Ashenhurst, who claimed to know only "what women wanted." She also knew what she wanted. She married Frank Hummert.

Perhaps the catalyst that helped Frank and Anne become a creative team was a young newspaper reporter named Robert Hardy Andrews. He applied for a job as a writer just when Blackett-Sample-Hummert was seeking an ideal format for women's radio programs for several soap companies and other makers of household products. The small, well-groomed, self-possessed Anne did not exactly put the young newspaperman at his ease, but she gave him sound advice for writing scripts. "The silence throbs . . . the empty hours are endless . . . then a friend in need is brought into the room by the turning of a dial. . . . Misery loves company. . . ." And then she added tellingly, "Worry, for women, is entertainment."

With this excellent credo ringing in his ears, Andrews adapted one of his recent newspaper serials for radio. *The Stolen Husband* concerned a handsome, but not overly bright, young businessman who was anxious to get ahead in the world; his secretary, who was anxious to give him every aid and comfort; and his wife, equally attractive and as dense as her husband, who didn't realize until too late that no man should be allowed to spend too many evenings at the office with his beautiful secretary. At first, Andrews was simply going to read the story on the air, but his voice was too good—deep, resonant, and professional—and it was thought that the audience wouldn't believe that he was the real author, so an announcer impersonated Andrews, and, then a vaudeville performer, a "man of a thousand voices," filled in for him. The strain of changing his voice dozens of times, with thousands of people listening, proved too much for the actor. He collapsed on microphone. The next morning, a full cast was assembled—men, women, announcer— and the first fully dramatized episode of *The Stolen Husband* was presented. It was 1931.[1]

The next venture of the Hummerts came in 1932, when they developed a new program for WMAQ in Chicago. Pressed to come up with an idea for a "homey" series, Andrews recalled a friendly, if nosy, barber he had known as a boy. He suggested a serial about a barber who lived in a small town called . . . called . . . Hartville! Yes, and he had a daughter named Nancy. Nancy in turn had a suitor named . . . Kerry Donovon. They would call the show "Bill the Barber." "*Just Plain Bill*," corrected the Mrs. Hummert-to-be, who knew what women wanted.

It might not seem that women would be that interested in hearing the exploits of an elderly barber, but *Just Plain Bill* became the first daytime serial with lasting power. It stayed around for over twenty years, surviving almost as

[1]Among the members of that first cast were Jim and Marion Jordan, later to become *Fibber McGee and Molly*. Years before, in the mid-1920s, they had done a program on WENR called *The Smith Family*, a show combining humor with more serious human-interest-type situations. At that time there were other obscure productions of a similar format on other stations scattered across the country. In these, and even in *Amos 'n' Andy*, and its earlier incarnation, *Sam 'n' Henry*, the sources of the soap opera can be found.

long as any radio drama. The first successful soap opera, it was sponsored by Dr. Lyons' Tooth Powder and other products, never a soap.

In the course of time, Bill's daughter, Nancy, married Kerry Donovon. (Bill and Nancy were played right along over the decades by Arthur Hughes, a fine actor who worked hard on his lines and gave depth and meaning to his material, and Ruth Russell. The longest running Kerry was James Meighan.) After the birth of Nancy and Kerry's son, Wiki, Bill found himself spending more time with his old friend, Elmer Eeps, proprietor of the general store. But Bill wasn't just seeking company—there were so many people in Hartville who needed his help in running their lives.

Sometimes Bill had to face far more dangerous situations than the usual domestic ones on which he thrived. In one story he strongly disapproved of the actions of a proprietor of rest homes for the aged who was finishing off his clients for their insurance. Bill's own life was threatened, but his philosophy saw him through.

"You have to stand up to evil and fight it," Bill observed. "You have to be ready for it when it strikes, and never give in to it. If you do them things, son, you can never be whipped by evil men."

The dialogue from one program was indistinguishable from that of another. The only way to make one soap opera protagonist recognizably different from another was through the use of *schtick*—a specialty. It was the same formula comic books would use a decade later. The Hummerts offered suffering in the form of a young widow with two children, *Young Widder Brown.* Then there were the problems of the "older woman" (and a career girl to boot) in *The Romance of Helen Trent,* the story that asked the question, "Can a woman over thirty-five find romance?" Hollywood dress designer Helen found romance past thirty-five for twenty-seven years. For ladies who longed for the glamor of Broadway and Hollywood there was *Mary Noble, Backstage Wife,* "married to matinée idol Larry Noble, dream sweetheart of a million other women." *Our Gal Sunday* appealed to dreams of sudden wealth and social position. *Stella Dallas* was designed originally for those who loved to feel miserable over the ingratitude of their children. To complete their product line, the Hummerts had thirty-six different titles on the air *at once.*

The Hummerts also created certain programs that were not exactly soap opera, but shows that combined soap opera with other attractive elements. *Lorenzo Jones,* a comedy soap, was the story of a crackpot inventor, "a character to the town, but not to his wife, Belle, who loved him." Its contrived comedy was machine-made farce that attempted to appeal to the audience for serials that offered genuine and unique American humor, *Easy Aces* and *Vic and Sade.* In later years, when the number of soap operas on the air decreased, there was no room for such a specialized series as a comedy soap, so Lorenzo developed amnesia and a complete change of character—a serious young scientist with plenty of romantic problems. Fortunately, Lorenzo was Karl Swenson, one of the best as well as busiest actors in radio—Lord Henry on *Our Gal Sunday, Mr. Chameleon,* etc.—and he could almost make the switch come off.

By the forties, many soap operas were dealing in crime and murder, and the Hummerts had developed two that crossed over into the mystery audience in appeal: *Front Page Farrell,* who found mystery and romance every afternoon for years, and *Mr. Keen, Tracer of Lost Persons,* which was originally a late afternoon daytime serial, but eventually became a nighttime half-hour story once a week. The time change did not require changing the story line. The kindly old investigator still mined his bottomless files "of his celebrated missing persons cases" each broadcast. Keen was not really a "tracer," just a detective, and his missing persons almost always turned out to be murdered persons, but with the help of his "partner," Mike Clancy, Mr. Keen lived up to his name. The contrast between the partners, as between Holmes and Watson, was particularly striking.

> MIKE: Sakes alive, Mr. Keen, it's another dead body. And saints preserve us, Boss, it don't have no head.
> KEEN: Yes, Mike, this dead body has been murdered.
> MIKE: You don't mean it, Mr. Keen!
> KEEN: I'm afraid I do, Mike. This doesn't look at all good for our client, Iris Sloan.
> MIKE: But how could the po-lease think Iris Sloan had anything to do with this murdered body?
> KEEN: That phone call I received, Mike. It was from Inspector Heywood at headquarters. Iris Sloan was released from custody three hours ago.
> MIKE: Saints preserve us, Mr. Keen!

Along with Jones, Farrell, and Keen, the Hummerts made an excursion into producing a soap opera for kids and came up with one of the most successful, *Jack Armstrong*. In spite of these triumphs, the Hummerts staple remained the domestic tragedy, the romantic woman-interest serial, and their most lasting creation, first written by the prolific Robert Hardy Andrews (later, when the Hummerts no longer owned the program, it was written by Oran Tovrov), was among the final seven CBS soap operas to leave radio just after Thanksgiving 1960. The program was frankly conceived to be *Just Plain Bill* in skirts. They called it *Ma Perkins*.

Ma Perkins ran a lumberyard in Rushville Center, instead of a barbershop in Hartville. A widow, she had the help of her son-in-law, Willy Fitz, down at the office, along with old family friend Shuffle Shober. (Shuffle and Elmer Eeps would have been fast friends if one of them had journeyed over from the neighboring town.) Ma had a son, Joseph, and two daughters: Evey, who talked the dialect of the natives, and Fay, who seemed to speak urbanese and to attract far more admirers than Evey. Fay, like many cosmopolitans, went through several husbands. They had a habit of dying tragically.

After the death of husband Paul, Fay began choosing a second husband in the mid-forties. One of her current suitors was wealthy, the other poor. Finally, Fay chose the rich one. Ma was somewhat concerned about this, and talked the matter over with old friend Shuffle.

SHUFFLE: Ma, if Fay was making a sacrifice, for the sake of us folks she figures is old and can't take care of ourselves no more, you and me wouldn't let her do it. We'd beat her over the head and lock her in the cellar. But Fay ain't making a sacrifice, she's catching the brass ring . . . she's reaching out her hands and letting the blessings of life fall into 'em . . .

MA: Shuffle, Shuffle, you're right. Here we sit, and upstairs there's Fay, and the circle comes round again. Losing Paul, but here's baby Paulette. Fay gets married, but we get Carl . . .

SHUFFLE: Be happy, Ma. You and me, we've been on this porch a hundred million times, the lights going off in the houses up and down the street. But what I'm saying—of all the times we've sat here and talked the rest of the town to sleep, maybe tonight is best of all.

MA: Oh, Shuffle. He'll be a wonderful husband for Fay. And I couldn't ask for nothing more than that.

Fay was to have still another husband, however—a writer. Evidently she grew tired of wealth and luxury.

One part of Ma's thoughts on that day was repeated some

fifteen years later on the final broadcast of the program. Once again, Ma's thoughts turned to the great circle of all things, "like the turning of stars in the heavens." Looking about her at her loved ones gathered around a Thanksgiving table, "laden with the fruits of this good green earth," she thought, "Oh, someday Fay will be sitting here where I'm sitting, or Evey or Paulette or Janie or Anushka's child. But I find right and peace in that . . . I give thanks that I have been given this gift of life, this gift of time, to play my little part."

"And so," the announcer added, "after more than seven thousand broadcasts and twenty-seven years, we say good-bye to Ma Perkins."

Ma Perkins was always played by Virginia Payne, who is still active in the affairs of the American Federation of Radio and Television Artists. Murray Forbes was Willy, and the original players for Shuffle, Evey, and Fay were Charles Egelston, Bernardine Flynn, and Rita Ascott.

MISERY MILL

There were hundreds of other soap operas *not* created by the Hummerts, but compared to the prodigious output of that couple the rest seem only a footnote.

One of the best was one that depicted people very much like Ma Perkins and her friends as they really might be. Writer Paul Reimers accurately reflected the speech patterns of Middle Western Americans and much of what such people thought and felt. Some called this show a soap opera, some a comedy. Like many of the great programs of radio, it did not fit into any narrow category. The program was called *Vic and Sade*.

Art Van Harvey and Bernadine Flynn played Vic Gook and his wife, Sade (rhymes with "aid"). With their son,

Rush (Billy Idelson), and Uncle Fletcher (Clarence Hart-zell), they drew a picture of the sometimes boring, some-times comforting routine of everyday life.

> FLETCHER: A four-foot length of railroad track makes a fine doorstop . . . a four-hundred an' forty-pound doorstop would hold a door *open* or hold a door *shut*.
>
> SADE: (GIGGLES) I'll say it would.
>
> FLETCHER: Think Mis' Keller *like* a doorstop for her birthday.
>
> SADE: I . . . don't think she could *handle* all that weight.
>
> FLETCHER: Husky *woman*, Mis' Keller. Tips the scales at a hundred an' sixty-six. All beef . . .
>
> SADE: One of my boys must of got home. Heard the kitchen door open.
>
> FLETCHER: Fine.
>
> SADE: (CALLS) You, Willie?
>
> RUSH: (OFF) Both of us.
>
> SADE: Well . . . everybody puts in an appearance simultaneous.
>
> FLETCHER: Fine.
>
> SADE: (CALLS) We got lovely *company*.
>
> VIC: Not Addison Sweeney, the noted high diver?

. Most of the other non-Hummert soap operas followed the lead of the pioneering couple and dealt with people who were unusual, not as "ordinary" as Vic and Sade, certainly.

Joyce Jordan—Girl Interne was typical of the many women and men in medicine on daytime radio. There was also a woman lawyer, Portia Manning, on *Portia Faces Life;* an orphanage manager running *Hilltop House;* and a lady newscaster (who delivered a capsule of *genuine* news on each broadcast) in *Wendy Warren and the News.*

Being a bookstore clerk may sound a rather humdrum profession, but it was held by the heroine of the soap opera whose title became a generic term for all soap opera—*Life Can Be Beautiful.* It was "drawn from life by Carl Bixby and Don Becker." It told the story of Chichi Conrad, who was adopted by kindly old Papa David Solomon, who ran the Slightly Read Book Shop. Papa David was a ridiculously stereotyped Jew (but a *good* Jew) who handed out much the same advice as *Just Plain Bill* or *Ma Perkins* might hand out, but delivered it with a Yiddish accent. Chichi, like most soap-opera heroines, ignored good advice and married a man named Stephen, a cripple in a wheelchair who, perhaps understandably, turned out to have a thoroughly nasty disposition and died a violent death, leaving Chichi a widow with new problems. (Chichi was Alice Reinheart and beneath the *yarmulka* Papa David was Ralph Locke.)

Perhaps the most singular soap-opera heroine of them all was Mary Marlin, a lady senator, busy in Washington with many important affairs, including one with the President of the United States, the fictional Rufus King. Mary had a husband, Joe Marlin, but he was thought to be dead, killed in a plane crash somewhere in remote Siberia. Mary had been appointed to fill Joe's Senate seat by the governor of Iowa, who also seemed to have an eye for her. Casting considerable doubt on the legality of Mary's Senate votes, however, was the fact that husband Joe was still alive. He had hit his head in that plane crash and, it should come as no surprise, was suffering from amnesia. Known only as "Mister X," Joe wandered through Asia having wilder adventures with Chinese bandits than *Terry and the Pirates.*

Written by Jane Crusinberry, certainly the most consistently imaginative daytime serial writer, *Mary Marlin's* "Claire de Lune" theme first tinkled gently on January 1, 1935. In the early years, the cast included one-time silent-movie idol Francis X. Bushman. Later, Joe Marlin was played by Robert Griffith. Anne Seymour, a lady of great talent and dignity (in film and television as well as radio), portrayed Mary for most of the years. On September 11, 1944, Mary found that Joe was still alive. Years of separation and suspense were over, and so was the listener's interest. The show faltered on for a time, but its basic, classic situation was gone. While it lasted, *Mary Marlin* was a great hit with women who secretly wished their husbands would get lost so that they could take over, and with small boys who thought it would be a grand adventure to be fighting bandits in Siberia and known only as the mysterious "Mister X."

It was the search for the lost identity, the missing clue, or the unknown murderer that interested me as a boy, trapped inside on a winter's day with a sore throat and the radio. I had to lie there in numbed misery, too sick to work a jigsaw puzzle or to read a book, or even to look at a comic. The radio was all that kept me from going *mad* with boredom. During the day all I could stand were the soap operas, and some I even got to like. Perhaps too well. If the story lines on a couple of shows got particularly exciting, I would play sick a couple more days to hear the outcome of Lord Henry being accused of murder, just like Sam Spade, and Helen Trent going through the same troubles as Jack Armstrong—being menaced by crooks, shot at, forced down in a crippled airplane on a remote mountain. Only somehow I never did find out how it all ended. Six weeks might pass before I got the sniffles again, or Easter vacation would come up, and when I heard one of the shows again it would seem like I hadn't missed a single day. Absolutely nothing new had happened. "Mister X" was still as lost.

Other programs filled the place left by *Mary Marlin*,

scripted by writers of varying talents. In much of radio, and especially the daytime serials, the writer was the star and often the only person to get name credit. Yet, of all the hundreds of writers in competition to the behemoth organization of Frank and Anne Hummert, only two, Elaine Carrington and Sandra Michael, found great and lasting success.

Elaine Carrington wrote a number of serials at various times and produced at least one major nighttime program, *The Elaine Carrington Playhouse.* Her most successful daytime program was *When a Girl Marries,* "the story of Joan and Harry Davis, and of every girl who has ever been in love." (Soap-opera writers had no bias against using character names that were the same as those of famous people, whether it was a heroine named "Joan Davis," as here, or a hero named "John Wayne," on *Big Sister.*) The Hummerts assigned their plot lines only to lesser-known scripters to turn into finished products; Elaine Carrington talked for eight hours a day, five and six days a week, writing fifteen or more individual scripts per week. Miss Carrington's method of work was to talk the scripts out into a recording machine. "I pour myself into it," she observed. "I give everything. I change voices. I laugh. I cry." She made a million dollars a year. And she worked for it. Miss Carrington's finished products had many of the characteristics that are recalled as being the worst elements of the soap opera. They were sloppily sentimental, totally feminine (without the saving grace of masculine resolve that characterizes most modern women), and would be considered by the average person who habitually reads books of any sort to be totally banal. Yet, Miss Carrington was an intelligent craftsman and she was giving her audience what it wanted and deserved.

In one *When a Girl Marries* script, Joan and Harry are driving down a busy highway, discussing what all married couples discuss at such a time—how much they love each other.

JOAN: I'm just married to a guy I love . . . a man
who hasn't a grain of sense so far as the laughing
of life is concerned. And . . . oh, I guess what I'm
trying to say is that because I love you so much,
it's easy to love and understand anyone who is
the slightest bit like you . . . someone like Steve.
To understand why he loves Betty so much . . .
Harry, look out for that car!

HARRY: Sorry, darling. But I shouldn't even try to
drive when you're sitting that close beside me saying things that make me feel I'm everything in the
world to you, that our love explains everything to
you . . .

JOAN: Nothing matters really, but that we love each
other. Not being separated. Not even death. It's—
why, Harry, it's knowing a kind of immortality . . .
and don't you dare laugh at me!

Miss Carrington needn't have been afraid that Harry, or
her listeners, would laugh at her. Hers was a revered, harm-
less, and no doubt beneficial pornography—the make-believe
fantasy of women about how marriage and sex might be
and perhaps should be, but seldom is after many years.

Sandra Michael was a writer who dealt in matters of
stronger import, perhaps the only matters of any genuine
import ever in a daytime soap opera. Her writings were
often gentle and poetic and struck a note of realism and
truth missing from the work of the financially more successful Elaine Carrington and Frank and Anne Hummert.
Just as Louis Armstrong might do, she took a simple, trite
melody and for a fleeting note blew a note too clean and
sweet to last. It faded before the simple, traditional folk
theme of the radio soap opera itself vanished. With faulty
memory, we sometimes confuse the master player such as
Sandra Michael (or Robert Hardy Andrews at his best)

with the folk theme tinkled and tortured by a thousand other far less capable hands. She still had the sentimentality, folksiness, and simple construction demanded by the format, but she transcended the limitations of the medium in a program called *Against the Storm*. Originally, in the first series, from 1939 to 1942, the program dealt with a subject limited in scope and appeal to the traditional radio-serial audience—the occupation of Denmark by Nazi Germany. After the end of the war, the program was revived with a far more general scope and became, briefly, a novel written for radio revolving around a character from the first series who lived in America, Professor Allen of Hawthorne University. But let's remember what "good listening" the soap opera could be, but so seldom was.

In a dream, Danish refugee Kathy Reimer walked along a street in the town of Hawthorne on Christmas Day in the war year of 1942. Suddenly, the gray and grimy figure of a German soldier appeared before her and greeted her. Beside the soldier stood her old friend, David. But David was a Jew and had died in a concentration camp. Through the mists of the dream, Kathy asked David how he could be walking along, side by side, with this Nazi.

David smiled and shrugged. Dead men were no longer enemies. The soldier had died on the Russian front, even as he, David, had died behind Hitler's barbed wire. Yet they were both victims of the same Nazi poison. Nazism had destroyed David's body, but it had burned away the soldier's power of reason.

The soldier confirmed it all. But death had freed him from the madness of a nation that had become a machine of hate. The insane fantasy was over, ended with his earthly life, and now the soldier could see that he and David were much alike.

As the two figures departed, the form of another friend, Phil, appeared before Kathy and confirmed what she knew.

PHIL: This is a dream, Kathy. You are dreaming.

KATHY: Yes, I know . . . but will they be welcome? Those soldiers are muddy and covered with blood . . . American . . . Russian . . . German . . .

PHIL: Look. You see, Kathy?

KATHY: They have come to the houses!

PHIL: You see? The first one knocked . . .

KATHY: And the door was opened! They are welcome!

PHIL: And don't think they're somber guests on Christmas morning, Kathy. No one should be afraid to think of them today . . . not because we can forget that they died for us, but we can also remember that they lived, and even those who were brutalized and poisoned by Nazism once could have had it in them, like the other, like our own beloved dead to love life and their fellow men. . . . They could have laughed and sung with the others . . . and as the others want all the world to sing and laugh in the future.

KATHY: Listen, Philip . . . is it the soldiers laughing?

PHIL: I think it is. Let's remember them that way—the soldiers, the men and women and children who with their own lives have brought song and laughter for us and for the new world to come. Remember, and welcome them to our hearts today and forever!

BEWILDERING OFFSPRING

"One Man's Family . . . a Carlton E. Morse creation . . . dedicated to the younger generation and their bewildering offspring. . . . Today, Chapter Eleven, Book One Hundred and Nine . . ."

These were the words of announcer Frank Barton in

opening one of the longest running serials of domestic life on radio, and winner by far of the most distinguished awards for such a program. Carlton Morse shared with Sandra Michael the honor of being one of the two authors of the only two serials with continuing characters to win radio's highest honor, the Peabody Award.

In the series, Morse revealed the side of his nature that loved family and tradition, just as his spirit of adventure and rebel-like individuality was displayed in his other famous creation, *I Love a Mystery. One Man's Family* was exactly that, a "family" program, not a soap opera, even though listeners tended to think of it as the king of all those soapy queens. Actually, the writing and production values were as far beyond the daily fifteen-minute soap opera as was the *Family's* "prime-time" slot, one half hour each week, early Sunday evening, during most of the first eighteen years.[2]

In the beginning, Henry Wilson Barbour married Fanny Martin. The year was 1896, and Henry was a clerk in a San Francisco brokerage house. Over the years he rose to become a partner in that establishment and, during that time sired five children: Paul in 1897, Hazel in 1900, Clifford

---

[2] The first of those broadcasts came in 1932 from San Francisco where Morse had assembled a cast comprised largely of players who had been active in the drama club at the University of California and who had appeared in Morse's previous mystery and adventure programs. The actors who were to play the important parts in the saga of the Barbour family were husky-voiced, law graduate Michael Raffetto, who played the eldest son, Paul Barbour; Barton Yarborough, who had a Texas accent that went away when he played Clifford Barbour; serious Bernice Berwin, who played daughter Hazel; laughing Kathleen Wilson, who took the part of Claudia (Clifford's twin); and Page Gilman, who was the youngest son, Jack. For the parents of these Bar-
(*footnote continued on next page*)

and Claudia, the twins, came along in 1912, and finally Jack in 1917.

At about the time Jack was being born, Paul was in France with the Allied Air Service. There, in 1918, he married nurse Elaine Hunter, who died the same year of meningitis. A widower, wounded and embittered, Paul returned to the Barbour family home to begin a long war with his conservative father.

All of these events were brought out in many references to the past when the program picked up the Barbour saga in 1932. In that Depression era, the Barbours offered the consolation to the general audience that even the rich have problems. The Barbours lived in the swank Bay City section known as Seacliff. Henry was a stockbroker, almost as unpopular an occupation in the early thirties as a banker. The children enjoyed all the privileges of wealth and position. None of the Barbours were indolent or arrogant, but they were just as fallible and human as everybody else. One of

(footnote continued)

bour siblings, there had to be imports past student age. Sweet-voiced Minetta Ellen became Mother Fanny Barbour, and one-time candidate for the priesthood, later matinée idol, and always confirmed bachelor J. Anthony Smythe became the head of the clan, Father Henry Barbour. That was the cast in 1932, and twenty-seven years later, J. Anthony Smythe, Bernice Berwin, and Page Gilman were still in their familiar roles. Kathleen Wilson left in the early 1940s and was later replaced by Barbara Fuller as the irrepressible Claudia. In 1955, when his voice became too husky for constant use, Michael Raffetto retired as Paul to be replaced by Russell Thorson, and Minetta Ellen turned the role of Mother Barbour over to Mary Adams. Barton Yarborough died in 1951 and was never replaced as Clifford. In the story, Cliff moved to Scotland and wrote letters home. Of course, after twenty-seven years, there were a lot more Barbours than when it all began.

the earliest problems that plagued the Barbours was girl-crazy Cliff's involvement with a widow, Beth Holly. When it looked as though he was expected to marry the girl, Cliff appealed to his older brother for help. Paul went to see the young woman and something clicked between the suave flier and the widow. They were an item for years, but never married, perhaps maintaining a relationship similar to that between The Shadow and Margo Lane.

Clifford's twin, Claudia, had just as much interest in the opposite sex as her brother. She ran off and married Johnny Roberts, a completely irresponsible young man, interested solely in new kicks. After he found out marriage was not such a kick, Roberts deserted Claudia, went to China to fight a war, and died from a wound. Left with a baby daughter, Joan (born in 1933), Claudia began to take moody walks along the sea wall, staring down at the swirling waters. Father Barbour made bumbling attempts to comfort her, but it was only Paul who had the intelligence and humanity to reach her and pull her out of it. That didn't improve the tension between father and son.

Meanwhile, Hazel, who was the least bit mousy and therefore the favorite of Father Barbour, was dating a fellow named Danny, who, several of the Barbours feared, was as wild as Johnny Roberts. They need not have worried. Hazel was too level-headed. She married William Herbert, a solid citizen and comrade-in-arms of Paul. Hazel and Bill had three children: Henry Barbour "Hank" Herbert and William Martin "Pinky" Herbert, twins, in 1934, and Margaret in 1936, who later (obviously) became Father Barbour's favorite grandchild.

Young Jack, a law student, also married without Father Barbour's blessing (Henry Barbour never seemed to approve of anything or anybody who hadn't been around at least fifty years). Jack and his bride, Betty Carter Barbour, had a few financial problems, the only ones ever heard of in the clan. Even so, they managed to have a flock of children, all girls: Elizabeth Sharon in 1942, Jane in 1943, Mary Lou in 1944, and triplets (multiple births ran in the *Family*), Abigail, Deborah and Constance, in 1949.

Meanwhile, back with the original Barbour twins, Clifford had two disastrous marriages, the first to the fantastically naïve, sex-hating Anne Waite, who died in 1937 while giving him a son, Andrew, alias "Skipper," and then to the more appealing Irene Franklin, who was killed in a 1946 auto crash. Clifford's sister, Claudia, had much better luck in her second marriage, which was to former British Captain Nicholas Lacey.[3] The marriage of Claudia to Nicky Lacey produced two children: Penny in 1938 and Nicky, Jr., some years later. Joan, Claudia's first daughter by the wild Johnny Roberts, was, however, the grandchild of Henry and Fanny Barbour that got most of the story line.

Much of the story of *One Man's Family* was devoted to the problem of incest. It was an adult subject, and the program was for adults. Father Barbour spluttered and muttered about the matter, but no doubt Ma Perkins would have fallen stone dead if the problem had come up in Rushville Center. Joan Roberts Lacey fell in love with her uncle, Paul, when she reached her teens. The matter was complicated by the fact that Paul had adopted a daughter, Teddy, in 1933, and Teddy was also in love with Paul, her foster father.

When her foster father resisted her overtures, Teddy turned to another handsome and distinguished man, Dan Murray, who had asked the now widowed Hazel to marry him and so was about to become Teddy's foster uncle-in-

---

[3] This became the biggest role in the show not taken by one of the original Barbours. "Nicky" was played originally by actor Walter Patterson, and, after Patterson's tragic death, by Tom Collins and Ben Wright.

law! Unlike Paul, Dan seemed to like the attentions of the beautiful teen-ager. She went to Paul for advice.

> PAUL: Teddy, you are old enough to react emotionally to Daniel Murray but not wise enough to see what could happen. When you like a man, you apparently believe in letting him know it and the next man might not be as scrupulous as Daniel Murray . . .
>
> TEDDY: You . . . you don't trust me, Paul?
>
> PAUL: As far as you can trust yourself. How far is that?
>
> TEDDY: As . . . as far as I know . . .
>
> PAUL: Exactly, Teddy, and how far do you know? It's like wading along a familiar shore and then stepping into a deep hole and suddenly finding yourself in over your head. . . . You made a play for Dan Murray. Supposing he had taken you up on it? Supposing he had made a counter proposition, one that you hadn't wanted or expected? Would you have had the courage to back down, to say no, especially after you'd started it? You don't have to answer. I don't want you to. Keep this in your mind and in the future think things through, not just to the beginning, but to the end. . . .

Teddy finally left the Barbour home to get away from the lure of so many attractive older men. She became an army nurse and had a brief, foredoomed marriage to a service dentist, a fink named Elwood Giddings, who Father Barbour thought was a prince of a fellow.

With Teddy gone, Joan must have thought she had a clear field with Uncle Paul. As he did with so many *Family* members, Paul tried to straighten out her psychiatric problems on his unlicensed couch. Finally, giving up on Paul, Joan married a mixed-up mama's boy named Ross Farnsworth, who was at least good for giving Father and Mother Barbour their first great-grandchild, Johnny. Meanwhile, Paul was trying to straighten out Joan's sister, Penny, about this thing she had about her father, the handsome Nicky.

While Paul seemed to supersede Henry Barbour as the real head of the clan—he was a bit more flexible and understanding—as the years passed, the younger Barbours seemed to realize the old man must have had something on the ball to make a few million dollars and bring all of them through to voting age.

The very essence of *One Man's Family* was summed up by Carlton E. Morse through the words of Father Barbour and his clan in a 1938 conversation in the living room of the family home. Those standards hadn't changed by the last broadcast in 1959.

Mother and Father Barbour sat in the big, comfortable living room with all of their children and their closest son-in-law, Nicky. Outside the dismal rain of the Bay area beat down. Clifford stared into the flames of the fire, a bit troubled as usual. It seemed to him that the rain and the gloom outside represented the state of the world and he said so. Thoughtfully, Nicky confirmed some idea of his own along the same line.

Fanny, Mother Barbour, could see nothing wrong in the comfortable, secure world of the Barbour family. Her daughter, Claudia, was even more positive about it.

"It's a good old world, and I like it," Claudia vowed.

Her husband, Nicky, reminded her that there was trouble in the world—for his own country, England, if he had cared to mention it—and no one could really stand aside or stand alone in the modern world of 1938.

It was Paul, as usual, who crystallized the vague thoughts and feelings of the family. It was a time of world crisis and he felt that the family members gathered there should get their innermost ideas out into the open.

CLAUDIA: Isn't that getting in over our heads, Paul?

PAUL: Not when you consider that every world problem has its beginning and its solution in the hearts of men . . . not in some vague, complicated system of which the ordinary person has no knowledge. . . . What's in your heart and what's in my heart is going to have a lot to do with what happens. . . . Dad . . . what one thing is foremost in your thoughts?

HENRY: Why, Paul, I think "family." . . . It's my opinion that the family is the source from whence comes the moral strength of a nation. And disintegration of any nation begins with the disintegration of the family. The family is the smallest unit in society. Millions and millions of these little units make a nation. And the standards of living set up by these family units indicate the high or low standards of a nation. . . . A well-disciplined, morally upright family is bound to turn out good citizens! Good citizens make a good nation.

PAUL: No doubt about that! There's a rising tide of sentiment growing throughout the world, fostered by people who are sick over the way things are going. . . . Perhaps it's the answer we've all been looking for . . . an answer in the hearts of men.

One Man's Family was a maverick in the middle of soap-opera country. It celebrated life and sex and the value and worthiness of the family. Where others preached agony, the *Family* series avowed happiness. The problems were there to be taken into human hands and solved; the sorrows were there to be taken and passed on. The message was that human society was a good thing and the duty of all human beings to make it better. But its business was not really messages; its business was the living of life.

An exception to the typical soap-opera archetype, *One Man's Family* still shared some aspects of the sudsy format, particularly when it became a daily quarter-hour serial from 1950 to 1959 keeping company with *Ma Perkins, Just Plain Bill* and the others.

In writing of such programs as *Just Plain Bill*, James Thurber once stated: "A soap opera is a kind of sandwich. Between thick slices of advertising, spread twelve minutes of dialogue, add predicament, villainy, and female suffering in equal measure, throw in a dash of nobility, sprinkle with tears, season with organ music, cover with a rich announcer sauce and serve five times a week." Within that general outline, a lot of territory could be covered, all the way from *Stella Dallas* to *One Man's Family. Just Plain Bill* sired an infinite number of bewildering offspring: doctors, lawyers, lumberyard operators, stockbrokers. Without their sometimes appalling examples, our lives might have had far different chapters. We might never have known that "Life Can Be Beautiful" if we hadn't known how ghastly it could be for the poor devils in Soapland.

XI

FROM THE STUDIOS OF WXYZ—I

THE MASKED RIDER OF THE PLAINS

LONE RANGER: Padre, you have heard of the many recent attacks on wagon trains, railroads, steamships—

PADRE: Great tragedies!

LONE RANGER: Ace Perigon is behind them . . . he has a powerful organization, Padre. He and the men with him are fighting "Change." They are opposed to progress.

PADRE: But why, amigo?

LONE RANGER: Their own greedy, selfish interests are best served if the West remains unchanged. They know if this country develops and becomes more civilized, there will be more law and order. . . . They want things to remain just as they are—with small communities isolated and easy prey for outlaw armies. . . . That's why they are destroying everything that might develop this country.

PADRE: My son, you may be right. I think you are. What can be done?

LONE RANGER: I'm going to join Ace Perigon's gang and try to work against him from the inside. . . . This mission may be my last. If I am unmasked and my body is found . . .

PADRE: Your grave shall be alongside that of your brother and the brave Texas Rangers who died with him.

LONE RANGER: Easy, steady there, big fellow . . . *hasta la vista*, Padre! Come on, Silver!

Many years before the Masked Rider of the Plains set out to bring to justice the outlaw army of Ace Perigon, six Texas Rangers had ridden out to round up the Hole-in-the-Wall gang of another notorious outlaw (the worst in the West!), Butch Cavendish, and had ridden into a ravine with high walls on each side, a place called Bryant's Gap.

Suddenly, men behind boulders along the rim of Bryant's Gap began firing down at the Rangers. Some men fell immediately, but others continued to fight against hopeless odds. Two of the Rangers firing back at their ambushers were Captain Daniel Reid and his younger brother. Finally, the captain fell with several wounds, which proved mortal. His brother fought on, firing again and again, until, with a final cry, he slumped to the ground. . . . The killers rode off.

Much later, Reid, the young Texas Ranger, regained consciousness, surprised to find himself alive. He was in a cave, and he was not alone. There was a shadowy form in the mouth of the cave, a form that drew nearer. Reid made out that it was an Indian.

The tall red man explained that he had found the fallen Ranger, brought him there, tended to his wounds. That had been days ago. Finally, the Indian identified himself.

TONTO: Me . . . Tonto . . .

REID: What of the other Rangers? They were all my friends. One was my brother.

TONTO: Other Texas Rangers all dead. You only Ranger left. *You lone Ranger now.*

Reid listened to Tonto tell of how he buried five men but had made six graves to fool the Cavendish gang if they returned. As the Indian spoke, the young man remembered meeting him years ago when they were both boys. At that time, the Indian boy had called him "Kemo Sabay," which could be variously translated from Tonto's unique dialect as "Trusty Scout" or "Faithful Friend."

The Ranger needed a friend now, because he knew he could never rest while the killers of his brother and his friends were free to rain death and destruction on the countryside. Marked for death by a huge outlaw organization, he decided to disguise himself with a mask, a mask made from the black cloth of a vest in his brother's saddlebags—cloth that had borne the silver star of justice.

Ranger Reid's youthful face took on the grim lines of determination, of dedication.

REID: From now on, Tonto, my identity shall be forever buried with those brave Texas Rangers who died at my side. I'll *be* the Lone Ranger.

In the young man's gaze blazed a light that through the ages has shone in the eyes of knights and heroes, strong men determined on the right, who fought for honor, for country, for God.

Together, the Masked Man and his faithful Indian companion rode the plains, tracking down first one, then another of the Cavendish gang, to turn them over to be tried by law for their crimes.

They stopped only occasionally for rest, to replenish supplies, and, most importantly, to visit the secret silver mine owned by the Reid brothers and now worked by a retired Ranger named Jim. The old man took only what silver he required for his own needs, as did the Lone Ranger. In addition, the Masked Man fashioned *silver bullets,* bullets that would leave a trail to terrify and panic outlaws, and which, because of their precious metal, would be a constant reminder to the Lone Ranger to shoot sparingly and always to remember the high cost of human life.

At last a clue came as to the whereabouts of the outlaw leader, Cavendish. The Lone Ranger and Tonto closed in on him near a settlement. Seeing him in the distance, they rode hard. Then a bullet cut down the Lone Ranger's horse. The fine animal was dead.

The Lone Ranger knew he would need a new horse. He had heard legends of a great white stallion, the king of the Wild Horse Valley.

The two men went to Wild Horse Valley, where they spotted the big white horse, but he eluded them. Finally, they saw him in a terrific fight with a huge buffalo. Flashing hooves took their toll, but finally the shaggy head of the giant bison was ramming the flashing coat of the horse, turning it crimson with blood. Then silver bullets struck home and the buffalo staggered and fell dead.

The Lone Ranger cared for the wounded horse, even as Tonto had cared for him. After many days, the horse was on his feet. He started to turn back into Wild Horse Valley and freedom. Then . . . he stopped.

> LONE RANGER: Tonto, I'm going to try a saddle on him.
> TONTO: Uhh, no horse like that take saddle.
> LONE RANGER: There never was a horse like that! Just look at him!
> TONTO: Him shine in the sun . . . like silver.
> LONE RANGER: Silver. That would be a name for him. *Here, Silver!*

The Lone Ranger saddled the horse and rode him. He was right. There never had been a horse like this. No hooves had ever beat the plains like these thundering hooves of the great white stallion who seemed to have the speed of light itself!

Wind cutting his cheeks beneath the mask, riding what seemed a silver streak of light, the Lone Ranger lifted his booming voice in a cry of satisfaction and exuberance, a cry that would ring across the years in sagas of adventure and chivalry—"Hi-Yo, Silver, Awa-a-ay!"

Astride the great white horse, Silver, with Tonto at his side on his own fine paint horse, Scout,[1] the Masked Rider

---

[1]Tonto had two earlier horses, first White Feller, then Paint, but in flashing back to the early days of the Lone Ranger's career, the script writer often conveniently forgot (for the sake of simplicity) that the Indian's horse had not always been Scout.

of the Plains cut a trail across seven states, forcing the powers of darkness into the blinding light of justice.

Butch Cavendish was captured and imprisoned. But there were many other criminals on the loose, and the Lone Ranger had learned his own powers, his effectiveness, his life's work.

Years later, he found the son of his dead brother, also thought to be dead. After a wagon-train massacre, the boy had been found and raised by an old woman, Grandma Frisbe. When Mrs. Frisbe died, leaving young Dan Reid alone, the Lone Ranger assumed the care of his nephew. The boy would go to school in the East part of the year. The rest of the time he would travel with the Lone Ranger, to learn the ways of the West and the great heritage left him.

> LONE RANGER: Yes, Dan . . . you have a *great* heritage. You live in a land of equal rights for all . . . governed by laws that are best for the greatest number . . . to strengthen and preserve that heritage is the duty and privilege of *every* American.

The noble Ranger knew all about great traditions and was, in fact, the product of the most durable of all American traditions—the search for success.

The Detroit radio station WXYZ had been bought in 1929 by George W. Trendle and John H. King. King had built the second motion picture theater in the United States in 1905. By 1929, he had twenty theaters and a partner, Trendle, who had risen from King's legal staff. They sold the theaters for $6 million and went into broadcasting, with Trendle taking active control of the company.

In 1932, down to his last million, Trendle took a mighty gamble and dropped WXYZ's affiliation with the Columbia

Broadcasting System to create his own local programming. With his proven business sense (as he explained in a 1939 *Saturday Evening Post* article), Trendle worked out a plan for a program to create a profitable new image for the station.

The program had to be a drama. In these days, before the playing of phonograph records on the air became an acceptable part of radio programming, drama was the cheapest available format. It required no big name comedians, singers, or orchestra leaders. Furthermore, Trendle decided the show would be done for children, not adults. Children were less critical, he reasoned, and were more responsive to the sponsor's messages. WXYZ would have a kid show then—either a detective or a western hero. Finally he decided on a western. Yes, definitely a western.

Time and distance made crime and violence more acceptable to parents and pressure groups, even giving a "wholesome" air of the American spirit forging the West. And cowboy heroes were more exploitable for "merchandising"—premiums, clothes, toys with the hero's brand on them.

Trendle's western hero would be a grown man because the station owner felt kids would prefer to believe they could be a hero when they, too, were grown than to realize that they were far different from a hero their own age. This mature cowboy would adventure in the Old West instead of contemporary rangeland (as *Tom Mix* did) because the contemporary western was growing ever more improbable.

But what would make WXYZ's western hero different, distinctive, successful? The staff of WXYZ discussed the matter around Christmas of 1932. Trendle told them he pictured the hero as being dashing and heroic, like Douglas Fairbanks in *The Mark of Zorro*. His reference to the masked avenger of old California, created by Johnston McCulley before World War I in a series of novels, struck a responsive chord. Someone suggested the hero be given a mask, to be a romantic figure of mystery, a Robin Hood of the Old West.

Trendle nodded. "I see him as a sort of a lone operator," he said. "He could even be a former Texas Ranger . . ."

Someone cried out in inspiration. "The Lone Ranger!"

They went on to decide that the Lone Ranger should have a very distinctive horse, one that would stand out by day or night, and in the listener's imagination—a white horse.

One of the WXYZ staff making suggestions on the creation of the Lone Ranger was studio manager Brace Beemer, the man who would *be* the masked man. One Beemer suggestion: silver shoes for the white horse.

With these and a few other details, Trendle thought it was time to call in a writer. His station had already carried a short-lived western series called *Warner Lester, Manhunter*, written by a young man in Buffalo, New York. Trendle had liked the program. He decided to call in Fran Striker.

Striker's only personal connection with the Old West came from listening to the stories of a great-uncle who had served drinks to Mark Twain and Bret Harte in a Washoe County, Nevada, bar. But he had a good imagination. Given the basic ingredients, Striker pictured the Lone Ranger as being a shade over six feet in height and just under 190 pounds in weight. Striker remembered another radio series he had written about the original Robin Hood. The writer had given him silver-tipped arrows by which all the countryside knew him. "*Silver bullets*" Striker typed out. Silver bullets, silver horseshoes, silver horse. Horse: "*Silver.*"

Striker's first script had the Lone Ranger a laughing swashbuckler, no doubt fulfilling the original inspiration of Fairbanks' Zorro. He was already established as a masked manhunter (the story of Bryant's Gap would be flashed back to in a few weeks). After a fast battle, he trussed the crooks up and rode off chuckling over their chagrin at their forthcoming hanging. The final signature for that original script had the Masked Man calling to his great white stallion. "Come on, Silver! That's the boy! *Hi-yi—ha-ha-ha ha-ha!* Now cut loose, and away!"

Even after fifteen revisions everybody thought it needed work. But they went on the air with the script on an experimental basis.

The pilot broadcast met with mixed reactions from the WXYZ staff. Trendle didn't like the Ranger's high spirits and good humor, and the rest of the staff didn't like the Masked Man's formal, eastern way of speaking. So they compromised. The Lone Ranger lost his sense of humor and kept his formal speech.

Trendle saw him as a "guardian angel," a man who was the "embodiment of granted prayer." The Lone Ranger never smiled again. He certainly wouldn't laugh as he rode away. Striker worked on that. No doubt corrupting the English cry to horse, "Heigh-ho," he came up with a new cry for the Lone Ranger: *"Hi-Yo, Silver, Awa-a-ay!"*

From the first, the stirring "William Tell Overture" was the theme. "The Light Cavalry Overture" was considered, but no more than that. All of the show's music was from the classics—beautiful public domain, royalty-free stuff. Though chosen for economy, the classic themes gave the show a heroic stature hard to beat. (A Los Angeles radio station recently gave a "pop art" concert featuring not only the "Lone Ranger Overture" by Rossini, but "Preludes to a Silver Bullet" by Liszt and "Rustler's Cave Overture" by Mendelssohn.)

The foremost opening to the show was always a string of gunshots and the Masked Man crying "Hi-Yo Silver!" This was followed by the announcer: "A cloud of dust, a galloping horse with the speed of light, a hearty Hi-Yo Silver!—

The Lone Ranger!" It was the secondary opening that evolved over the years. In the mid-thirties this was reworded slightly for each episode on the theory that the audience would tire of the same opening. One of these introductions went:

Gun law ruled in the early West, but here and there, determined men rose up against the gunslingers and outlaws. Foremost among these was the masked champion of justice whose name has come down to us in legend. Across seven states, the fame of the Lone Ranger and his Indian friend, Tonto, was spread. Back to those days when the West was young. Hear the galloping hooves of the great white stallion, Silver! The Lone Ranger rides again!

Finally, by the early forties, this was polished into a bit of prose poetry, unforgettable when delivered by the greatest of all radio announcer-narrators, Fred Foy:

With his faithful Indian companion, Tonto, the daring and resourceful Masked Rider of the Plains led the fight for law and order in the early western United States. Nowhere in the pages of history can one find a greater champion of justice! Return with us now to those thrilling days of yesteryear! From out of the past, come the thundering hoofbeats of the great horse, *Silvair!* The Lone Ranger rides again![2]

[2]And "thundering hoofbeats" you heard. Jim Jewell, the first director of the program, was a perfectionist on sound effects and WXYZ had the best sound men in the business. They made everything seem as if it were actually happening. At first, gunshots were made by striking a cardboard box with a slat. Then, after experimentation, hitting a leather cushion. Finally, by a rat trap striking an empty metal drum. When a horse galloped on *The Lone Ranger* you not only

(*footnote continued on next page*)

The initial three-station hook-up (WXYZ, WGN, Chicago, and WOR, Newark, New Jersey, the basis of the Mutual network) was the result of early sponsorship by Silvercup Bread in those cities. The similarity between the name of the bread and the Lone Ranger's horse was a coincidence. In later years, Gingham Bread wanted to sponsor the show but they wanted Silver to have his name changed to Gingham. Trendle hotly refused. The image of the silver-coated stallion was too deeply ingrained ever to be replaced. *The Lone Ranger* was broadcast every Monday, Wednesday, and Friday evening at 7:30 P.M. Eastern Standard Time, every program a complete story in half an hour.[3]

(footnote continued)

heard its hoofbeats (changing as it crossed different terrain, the sink plungers hitting different soil samples in the "gravel box") but you heard the jangle of its harness, the creak of the saddle, and the breathing of man and animal, the brush of the air, the rustle of the leaf, the rippling water, the cry of the bird. It seemed you could even hear the sun going down, and once an actor blundered and said, "Listen, I hear a white horse coming."

[3]Only two other western programs had any lasting success in copying the format of *The Lone Ranger*. One was *Red Ryder*, the drawling cowboy from the comic strips who had an Indian boy sidekick, Little Beaver, and an aunt, the Duchess, and who called to his horse, "Roll, Thunder, roll!" The other was "O. Henry's famous Robin Hood of the old Southwest, *The Cisco Kid*," which began with pounding hooves and fat, dumb Pancho calling, "Cisco, the sheriff he is getting closer!" and with Cisco answering, "This way, Pancho, follow!" It had a unique ending for a juvenile show; a romantic one. "Ohhh, Ciscooooo . . ." gasped the freshly kissed belle of the town Cisco was passing through. "Ahhhhh, Senoreeeeta!" said Cisco gallantly. Both of these programs were syndicated transcription series, leaving the national networks solely to *The Lone Ranger*.

The first regularly scheduled broadcast of *The Lone Ranger* came on January 30, 1933, after six weeks of work. The role of the Lone Ranger was first played by a man named Deeds. (The exact date or Mr. Deeds' first name have not survived the onrush of history, but one would not be surprised to find out that his first name was Good.)

After six performances, Mr. Deeds was replaced by George Stenius, now known as George Seaton, currently a major motion picture producer (*The Bridges of Toki-Ri, The Counterfeit Traitor*). Seaton was followed after three months by Brace Beemer, who in turn quit after a few months to open his own advertising agency. The role was assumed by Earle W. Graser ("Grah-zer"), the first Ranger to have lasting power, the permanent Lone Ranger until fate decreed otherwise.

The basic requirement of radio was that *everybody* have somebody to talk to. In more adult programs, the hero might talk directly to the audience in a kind of stream of consciousness narration, but stories for children never had a first-person hero—for one thing, he would sound too immodest recounting his daring deeds. A sidekick was an absolute necessity to the Lone Ranger.

Even so, like all radio heroes, the Lone Ranger did quite a bit of talking to himself ("Another down! Took my bullet in his shoulder. I *must* hold the Cheyennes out of this pass —hundreds of settlers counting on me!") or to his horse ("Come on, Silver! We're needed at the Tomahawk Ranch! This is the showdown!") The device of the cowboy talking to his horse had been pioneered in early talking pictures and was adopted by the Lone Ranger in the first few broadcasts. The speech pattern ultimately proved unsatisfactory however. There could be only a monologue, not a conversation. The Masked Man needed a friend, a confidant. Even the monosyllables of Tonto, who entered in the tenth script, were a more positive contribution than an occasional "neigh" from Silver.

The man who spoke the broken English of Tonto, the Lone Ranger's faithful Indian companion, was John Todd, a former Shakespearian actor capable of far more eloquence. He was a thin, gray-haired man who wore stiff collars and string ties. When he began the role, he was in his sixties, and he was past eighty when he acted in the last live *Lone Ranger* broadcast. Todd, it might be noted, was old enough to have actually *been* Tonto in the days of the Old West (if he had only been an Indian). Even so, he had traveled through the still untamed West with a road show of *Hamlet* and had met the real Buffalo Bill.

Since Tonto was actually a part with a minimum of lines, Todd often "doubled" in other parts. Sometimes this provided unexpected dialogue. One of Todd's favorite alternate voices was that of an affected Englishman. During one story, Todd, as an Englishman, was hunting buffalo out West. He was to say, "I think I shall chance a shot." Then he was to wait for the director to throw him a cue that the gunshot had been fired in the separate studio for the sound men, and say, "Ah, a *hit!*" What came out was, "I think I shall chance a shot. Ah, a *cue!*"

In another story, the Lone Ranger and Tonto were searching the upstairs hotel room of a suspected crook. The Masked Man said, "There's nothing in the closet, or in any of these drawers, Tonto. Let's go." Todd responded automatically, "Ugh! Gettum up, Scout!"

Although the star of the show seldom "doubled" another part, in his role of the Lone Ranger he often disguised himself to be what he wasn't, also disguising his voice, of course. The Ranger often donned the sombrero and accent of a Mexican national. At other times he would be a drawling cowpoke or a bearded prospector. Since the Lone Ranger, even transformed, never told a direct *lie*, his disguises depended on misdirection rather than deception. "Yah might call me Dixie if yah was a mind to," he would say. Swinging aboard a train in overalls and trainsman's goggles, the Lone Ranger would begin issuing orders about repelling an outlaw raid. "Say, you must be a railroad detective!" guessed the conductor. "That seems to be a logical conclusion under the circumstances," the Lone Ranger craftily replied. The line was fine, but the Lone Ranger never crossed it.

Other roles in the Lone Ranger were played by a skilled and hard-working WXYZ repertory group. And work hard they did, since, before the use of transcriptions were permitted, the show had to be done *live* three times each episode—once for the East, once for the Central, and once for the combined regions of the Mountain and Pacific Time zones.

The names of the players changed in the stories. The young rancher might be Hank Yandell, or Bart Allenby, or Steve Goodman, but the voice remained the same. Once in a while, you were fooled and the young and handsome voice turned out to belong to a confidence man, a crook. But, in general, a good voice meant a good man.

Back in the thirties the young rancher was often played by John Hodiak. The nasty, black-hearted villain? He was Danny Thomas, the old man, the rancher with the young daughter, the old fellow who always said, "Say, who was that Masked Man anyway?"—that senior citizen was named Frank Russell. Aside from that line, which he said so often, he is also known for a line he said only once, according to a broadcast interview. Playing the part of an elderly sheriff, he had led his posse to the outlaw encampment and it was time to close in. He was supposed to order his men to draw their six-shooters by saying, "All right, gents, get your guns up!" On the third repeat broadcast, Russell was given the cue and out came, "All right, junk, get your jeans up! Err, *all right, jean, get your junt up!* Aww, shoot 'em!"

The man with the deep, deep voice, even more rumbling than the Lone Ranger's, the outlaw mastermind who growled slyly, "Now, here's my plan . . ." his name is Paul Hughes. He played an in-again, out-again character, gruff Thunder Martin, who sounded a lot like Wallace Beery. Thunder Martin's "Marie Dressler," Clarabelle Hornblower, was really the much younger Elaine Alpert, who played just about every other woman or girl on the show as well.

The Masked Man's nemesis, Butch Cavendish, often escaped jail to plague him again. He was really Jay Michael. Once per show, Michael generally said, "All right, boys, you know what to do." And they did.

Two of the henchmen were Roland Parker, the youngest of the renegades, and Ernie Wynn Stanley. Back in 1934, before his voice changed, Stanley had been on the side of the law as young Dan Reid.

There were many other voices on the program—some of them doubled by those just named. It was a common occurrence for Roland Parker as the town sheriff to capture himself as an untamed Indian.

Unquestionably, these actors must have been in it for the money. In the early days, actors everywhere in radio were making something like $12.50 a week, although by 1939 the Lone Ranger himself was pulling down a full $150 each and every week. George W. Trendle later was able to more amply reward those who helped him pioneer WXYZ. Fran Striker, the senior writer on a staff of scripters including Felix Holt, Tom Dougall, Mickey Merrill, and Dan Beattie, contributed at least one of the three Lone Ranger scripts each week, starting out at $10,000 a year, later several times that, though perhaps not as much as $50,000 a year credited him by some sources. All the scripts from the staff were creatively edited in handwriting by Trendle.

The WXYZ dramas produced by George W. Trendle made nearly a million dollars that same year. Only a few years later, prices were better for everybody, thanks to work by the American Federation of Radio Actors, the Writer's Guild, and other unions. But economy was still the watchword at WXYZ. By this time, Fran Striker was making $50,000 a year, but he was still required to type his own scripts. Not only that, he had to make six to eight carbon copies. (Somebody in production felt that mimeographing scripts was an unnecessary expense.) Whoever got the eighth carbon had to be very familiar with the workings of the show so that he could virtually ad-lib his part.

The Lone Ranger rode on and on. His very earliest adventures in 1933 had him saving some drivers on the Chisholm Trail from rampaging flood waters, trapping a crooked Pony Express rider, and recovering the stolen map to a lost mine. As time went on, he met famous historical figures of the Old West—General Custer, President Grant, Wild Bill Hickok, Billy the Kid. His greatest single task may have been a year-long battle against various members of a secret outlaw organization known as the Black Arrow. The members of the Black Arrow were not only thieves and bandits, they sought to seize control of the entire nation. One by one, the Lone Ranger captured the lesser members of the group, finally working his way to the top and to the leader, acting governor of one of the western states.

In 1941, when Earle W. Graser died in an auto accident, a nation mourned briefly and 10,000 people attended his funeral. He stopped drawing his $150.00 a week. You may not remember when Earle Graser died, but if you are over twenty-five years old, you probably remember when the Lone Ranger's voice changed.

In the story, the Masked Man was critically wounded and lay unconscious for days while Tonto carried on without him. As author-critic Charles Beaumont has observed in *Playboy* magazine, you always knew Tonto could do it all alone if he had to, even if he didn't have a mask and guns with silver bullets. You sometimes had the impression that Tonto was the real brains of the outfit. After all, he gave the Lone Ranger his distinctive name, indirectly named the horse Silver, and it was always Tonto who picked up the trail of the rustlers and told the Lone Ranger which way to ride. Tonto was certainly no "Uncle Tom" as a representative of a minority race. Even his language was excused when years later the Masked Man pointed out that Tonto spoke many languages—several Indian dialects and Spanish among them—but somehow he just happened to have difficulty with proper pronouns in English.

Finally, Tonto was relieved of some of his responsibilities as the Lone Ranger grew stronger, being able to speak a few words here and there. The new voice was very similar to the one you had been hearing, but when at last it raised to full power you realized it was deeper, richer, sterner. A lighter, more easy-going naturalness was gone. Like a god, the Lone Ranger arose from death with his purpose intensified, a grimmer angel of vengeance.

The man behind the voice of the Lone Ranger was once again Brace Beemer, who, unlike Graser, was no stranger to horses and guns and feats of heroism in real life. Beemer served in World War I with the Rainbow Division in France. He was a big fellow, six feet two and over two hundred pounds. He had become a sergeant and led men into battle. Wounded in action, he received several decorations—Beemer at this time was only fourteen years old. ("The Lone Ranger" had told a lie—about his age.)

After the war, Beemer became an actor with the Jesse Bornstell Players, a touring theatrical group. In 1922, he went into radio in Indianapolis, and in 1932 he joined WXYZ as station manager and chief announcer. With some time off for other business interests, he was with the station off and on thereafter. After resuming the role of the Lone Ranger in 1941, he played it until the last live broadcast, the 2956th episode, on September 3, 1954. Transcribed programs were rerun for some years on the networks and returned on some thirty independent radio stations in 1966.

When I was a boy in Mount Carmel, Illinois, there was an explorer named Mr. Hall, who wore a pith helmet and had a parrot who cursed. Mr. Hall lived in an otherwise abandoned barn behind our house, well within the city limits. Please understand that Mr. Hall was no figment of my imagination—he was very real and I don't think my mother approved of him. But my father let him set up his cot in the barn and make his illegal wine. I used to like to listen to his stories of eating monkey meat in Borneo almost (but not quite) as well as I liked listening to *The Lone Ranger*.

My father, who was nearing seventy when I was born, knew some stories about the Old West that he told me himself. Although he had a hard, angular face that looked remarkably like Hugh O'Brian's does now, his hair and moustache were white. He had lived through the days of the frontier and he still affected a flat black Stetson and he still carried a Colt six-shooter under his coat. He had occasion to use the gun several times within my lifetime against men who were after the payroll he carried for the men in his construction company.

One of the people who came around from time to time was a family friend I had heard called Marcus. He was as much a friend of my mother's (who had gone to school with him) as my father's. I remember being rather impressed with Marcus—somehow I always thought he was a doctor. He looked very clean, very distinguished. I remember one time he was rather embarrassed after going hunting with my father and failing to bag a single duck.

Once while Marcus was visiting in our parlor (not the living room, please) the subject of *The Lone Ranger* came up. I still remember the joke my mother pulled on me. "Why, Jimmie, you know Marcus *is* the Lone Ranger." I looked at him. No, not hardly, I thought. Marcus had reddish hair, receding a bit. And he was certainly too heavy. I knew the Lone Ranger had black, wavy hair and was as slim as Roy Rogers. Marcus changed the subject. "What do you want to be when you grow up, Jimmie?" he asked. "A map-maker," I said, envisioning traveling to uncharted jungles. "That's good," he said. "People will always need maps."

Years later, something began to dawn on me as slowly and surely as the news about Santa Claus. From things people said around my home town, a strange, inverted disillusionment broke over me.

Marcus was Marcus "Brace" Beemer, who had been born in Mount Carmel and who occasionally returned there. *That man really was the Lone Ranger!*

My experience may be unique. I wonder. Perhaps you went to school with Jack Armstrong and didn't recognize him. Maybe you passed The Shadow and didn't even see him.

Brace Beemer died March 1, 1965. George W. Trendle alone owned the official "Hi-Yo, Silver," but at least Beemer had a white horse. (Not only in the WXYZ sound department, Silver did live, trained and ridden by Beemer in countless parades and rodeos.) Silver, now old and cranky at twenty-seven, seemed in danger of being disposed of for a time, but Mrs. Leta Beemer (the good woman the Lone Ranger did marry at last) has vowed to keep him "forever." The great white stallion with the thundering hooves and the speed of light lives on.

The Lone Ranger and Silver, with Tonto and Scout, live on *together*. They have gone beyond fiction, beyond nostalgia. They have become as much a part of the American legend as Daniel Boone, Paul Bunyon, John Henry, or Charles Lindbergh.

When, sometime back, the Lone Ranger set out on what might well prove to be his last mission, to work against the outlaw army of Ace Perigon from within, he was riding into the second half of the twentieth century. This program was broadcast January 2, 1950. Far from being his last mission, the Masked Man's avowed task of bringing justice to the West was renewed.

Also working inside the Perigon gang was a government agent, a man named Martin, who had been a former Texas Ranger. Despite the Lone Ranger's disguise, Martin recognized his old comrade in arms, the man thought dead. At the cost of his own life, Martin arranged for the Lone Ranger to escape and bring men to crush Ace Perigon's gang. The Masked Man rushed to the side of the fatally wounded government man.

MARTIN: No—no use. I'm going—my job was done when I . . . I . . . passed the word of the attack to you . . . and . . . and let you get away . . .

LONE RANGER: I owe my life to you, Martin . . . but that doesn't count . . . the nation owes you very much . . .

MARTIN: Listen to me—carry on. And train someone to carry on in the twentieth century when—when you join your Ranger pals—and me . . .

LONE RANGER: Dan Reid is going to meet the twentieth century as a man.

MARTIN: Great things lie ahead for this nation—and great tests of strength and courage . . .

LONE RANGER: America will meet those tests as long
as there are men like you, Martin.

MARTIN: Guess I—I'm the only one who knew your
name, eh, Reid? Now I'm going . . .

LONE RANGER: Steady, Martin . . .

MARTIN: You'll just be—unknown—just . . . the Lone
Ranger . . .

XII

FROM THE STUDIOS OF WXYZ—II

THE GREATEST DOG IN THE YUKON

SPIKE: Don't hit me again! I've had enough!

PRESTON: On your feet, Spike Wilson. I'm taking you
to Mounted Police Headquarters. You're going to
pay for the murder of my father, and for your
other crimes.

SPIKE: Beaten! Me=the toughest outlaw in the Yukon
beaten by one kid constable!

PRESTON: I was told to expect my promotion for
bringing you in, Wilson. Before you hang, you'll
call me *"Sergeant* Preston."

In the thirties, George W. Trendle and his *Lone Ranger*
production crew introduced a program called *Challenge of
the Yukon*. ". . . *Gold!* Gold discovered in the Yukon—a
wild race for riches. Back to the days of the Gold Rush with
Sergeant Preston of the Northwest Mounted Police, and his
wonder dog, Yukon King, as they meet . . . *The Challenge
of the Yukon*." The "Donna Diana Overture" that followed
was less impressive and memorable than the Lone Ranger's

"William Tell Overture," but then, so was the program itself. The cast, as well as producer, director, and writer, was the same as on *The Lone Ranger*. Paul Sutton often a Mexican villain or a drawling cowpoke with the Masked Man, became the voice of law and order north of the border, Sergeant William Preston. Even the scripts were frequently only slightly refurbished and, as a boy, I could spot old *Lone Ranger* stories showing up on these episodes of springtime in the Yukon.

The real star of the show, of course, was not Sergeant Preston, but Yukon King (played by the WXYZ sound department). King (as he was called for short, affectionately) was an Alaskan Husky who ran "free lead" with Preston's dog team, darting in and out of the line, nipping at the other dogs, keeping them on the job. He was also very good at nipping and nabbing outlaws. In fact, his instinct for bad men was much better than the Sergeant's. When he growled at a newcomer, Preston would often chain King to the sled to quiet the new man's fears, only to have the crook bash Preston over the head. Let it never be said, however, that Sergeant Preston was incapable of learning from experience. The following is a completely authentic conversation between beast and master (two points for correctly identifying which is which):

> PRESTON: I'm going to have to ride to the Fort for help . . .
> YUKON KING: Grrrrr-bow-wow-wow! Rruff!
> PRESTON: Yes, King—what is it, boy?
> YUKON KING: Bow-wow-wow!
> PRESTON: He's trying to tell me something. . . . Yes, King?
> YUKON KING: Rrruff! Bow-wow! Rrruff!
> PRESTON: He's saying . . . he should go in my place. I should stay here. You're right, King!

In the 1950s, after *The Lone Ranger* went into reruns on the radio and Brace Beemer had no new *Ranger* programs to do, he was moved over as the senior star of the company to do the last live season of the program that had become known by the title we always called it anyway: *Sergeant Preston of the Yukon.* For some reason it was felt appropriate to recap the origin of Preston since he had developed a new, though familiar, voice.

With the narration of Fred Foy (who moved over from *The Lone Ranger* as well, switching allegiance from Cheerios to Quaker Puffed Wheat), you heard how Preston had first joined the Mounties to capture his father's killer and had earned the rank of Sergeant. A later broadcast told you how young Sergeant Preston had found a Husky puppy that had been "kidnapped" and raised by a female wolf, Three Toes. Preston arrived to witness a lynx attacking both the wolf and her adopted cub. The Mountie fired in time to save the young cub, but not the old wolf. (Brace Beemer must have had a curious sensation he had lived all this before, or something very like it, with a giant buffalo and a great white stallion.) Sergeant Preston gathered up the young dog, and then he expressed his world view to the tiny animal. His were good, solid, *Canadian* views, somewhere between British and American. "I'm going to call you Yukon King," Sergeant Preston said to the puppy. "I'll teach you self-control, and how to best use your great strength. Youngster, we're going to be partners. And when you're grown, you are going to be the greatest dog in all the Yukon!"

With Yukon King as his partner, Sergeant Preston led the fight for law and order during the wild days of the Gold Rush. Together, they rescued countless old prospectors from bandits. They saved the furs of trappers and peaceful Indians from thieves. By dog sled, the Mountie rushed through life-saving serum in several epidemics. Preston ventured as far as the Eskimo lands of the Far North to bring the Queen's justice to these innocent folk, and save them from "civilized" invaders. An even more perilous mission took him to the dangerous territory known as San Francisco, where in 1899 he rode in a new-fangled automobile with members of the San Francisco police force in order to catch smugglers sought by all the policemen, mounted and motorized.

No matter what his adventure, Preston had the habit of ending each one with the solemn announcement: "This case is closed." If that clerklike pronouncement lacks the color and thrills of "Hi-Yo, Silver, Aw-a-ay!" then so did the good Sergeant lack the glory and excitement of *The Lone Ranger*.

There was no riding a great white steed with the speed of light into the fading sunset for Sergeant Preston, not even a brisk trot astride Blackie (who Preston later rechristened Rex in, perhaps, a longing for grandeur) or a hearty "mush" with Yukon King leading the dog team across the sparkling Yukon snows. There was only the standing stiffly at attention, and intoning, "This case is closed!"

But once, just once, near the end, but still with Paul Sutton as the Mountie, Sergeant Preston was allowed a stirring climax. It was for a condensed adventure offered on a phonograph record as a premium from the Quaker Puffed Wheat people. The Lone Ranger's live show had been axed —the writing was on the wall, near the door. This was to be a last hurrah and everybody knew it. King had carried through another of his innumerable messages for help. Sergeant Preston was trapped at a trading post under attack by Indians. As soon as King arrived at Northwest Mounted Police Headquarters with the message, Preston's superior, the Inspector (John Todd again!) dispatched a troop of Mounties and men of the Canadian Field Force—regular Canadian soldiers—to the site of the uprising. The Inspector kept the dog with him and awaited word of what the troops might find at the siege. Then, as day was failing, the old Inspector and the dog heard the sound of men singing—singing Canada's national song—"The Maple Leaf Forever," and moving out through the trees, riding four abreast, the Mounties came, scarlet tunics ablaze in the setting sun. Even the horses held their heads high, sharing in the glory of victory. And in the lead, astride his horse, Blackie, rode Sergeant Preston.

Yukon King and the Inspector rushed to meet Preston as he dismounted. "Mission accomplished, sir!" Preston reported. "The Yukon still belongs to the Crown!"

"Well done, Sergeant Preston," the Inspector said, and for once took over the chore of Preston's official duties. "This case is closed!" he said.

XIII

FROM THE STUDIOS OF WXYZ—III

THE GREEN HAR-NUT

"Dad," Brit Reid said to his father, Dan, "I know personally that the Green Hornet is no criminal. In his own way, he fights for law and order. Can you believe that?"

Old Dan Reid nodded his gray head slowly. "I think I can believe a lot more than that. I think I know what you are trying to tell me."

The young publisher met the eyes of the man who had built the *Daily Sentinel* into one of America's greatest newspapers. "Dad, I am the Green Hornet."

"I suspected as much," the elder Reid said.

"How could you? The world thinks I am nothing but an idle playboy, dabbling in the newspaper business."

"Son, you've seen the painting on this wall many times. I gave it to you years ago."

"Why yes, Dad—the picture of the Masked Man on the great white horse."

"Everyone knows who he was—he is a part of American history. But the world does not know that the Masked Man is your ancestor, Brit—my uncle, your great-uncle."

"Then I'm—I'm carrying on in his tradition, bringing to justice those he would fight if he were here today."

"Yes, Brit. He would be as proud of you as I am."

Faintly, the "William Tell Overture" played through this scene on *The Green Hornet*. At the time, this struck me as having tremendous significance, a sense of purpose and continuation, world without end.

The Green Hornet certainly was a descendant of *The Lone Ranger*. George W. Trendle's intention of developing *The Green Hornet* in the mid-thirties was to put the Masked Rider of the Plains in modern dress, and he patterned other aspects of the new program after his established success.

Like the Ranger, the Hornet wore a mask and hid his identity behind a colorful assumed name. (The Green Hornet called himself that because hornets that are green are the angriest and are the most liable to sting.) Again, like the Lone Ranger, who had his great white horse, the Green Hornet had distinctive transportation, his super-powered car, the Black Beauty (complete with a buzzing Hornet horn).

Unusual hand weapons were also the marks of both men. Instead of the Ranger's six-guns loaded with silver bullets, the Green Hornet had a gas pistol loaded with puffs of instant sleep, an even more humane weapon than silver slugs never aimed to kill. Where the Green Hornet departed somewhat from the Lone Ranger mold was that he had a much, much more extensive private life. The Masked Rider of the Plains was a foot-loose orphan, with only Tonto at his side and an occasional visit from his nephew, Dan Reid. The Hornet, Dan Reid's grown son, some thirty-five years later in an only too realistic modern setting, had to cope with a whole "family" of friends, relatives, and employees.

First there was old Dan Reid himself (played by John Todd), who was generally offstage disapproving of his son's playboy life and who had turned over the management of the newspaper to his son to make a man of him.

Then there was Michael Axford, an ex-policeman hired by old Dan Reid to keep an eye on his son and by inference to drag him out of drunken orgies before the cops arrived. Michael was another dumb Irishman, who eventually got a job on the *Daily Sentinel* as a crime reporter even though his apparent intelligence suggested a lack of ability to read, much less write. As an ex-cop, the Irishman hated the Green Hornet, who he considered to be an outlaw, and his one ambition in life was to "nab the Har-nut." He was frequently given to saying to his employer, "Reid, if I were as close to that no good spaul-deen, the Har-nut, as I am to you, why sufferin' snakes, I'd . . ." Gil Shea took the role.

Then there was Miss Lenore Case (Lee Allman), Brit Reid's girl Friday down at the office. She had some romantic interest in the handsome young heir to the Reid family fortune and was no fool in a lot of other ways. Miss Case was the only one of Reid's friends ever to suspect him of being the Green Hornet. Slowly, she seemed to become absolutely convinced of it, although she knew discretion. She would say to Brit Reid, "Mr. Reid, you know, if I were the Green Hornet, I would go to the warehouse and go in by the third rear exit (which I know is unlocked from a girl I know who works there), and then I would go to the fourth floor . . ." In later years, rather anticlimactically, Reid took her into his confidence and gave away his "secret."

Another regular was Ed Lowery (Jack Petruzzi), the star reporter for the *Daily Sentinel*. Like all reporters, he never pressed his suit and had a special contempt for politicians who he invariably referred to as "crooks." He had more than a grudging admiration for the Green Hornet, who, though he might be a crook, at least was a crook with style.

Finally, there was Kato, the oriental houseboy who went along on Reid's missions, driving the Black Beauty. It's a good story that Kato became Filipino the day after Pearl Harbor. Even some of the people on the show tell it. It isn't true, however. Kato was described as being a Filipino of Japanese ancestry as far back as 1940. Once again, the sidekick had much of the brains in the outfit. It was he who developed the Hornet's gas gun with its sleeping potions, and he who had souped up the Black Beauty. It was never revealed why such a chemical and mechanical genius chose to work as a valet. Of course, the pay may have been much better than it appeared on the surface, and the work was interesting. (Roland Parker is the man who played Kato.)

The most familiar voice of the Green Hornet belongs to Al Hodge. Hodge not only sounded but looked the part of a hero. He played Captain Video on television, and continues to play featured parts on the home and theater screens. Bob Hall, then only seventeen, played Brit Reid beginning in the war years when most leading men of draft age were in the Army. Hall is now a New York disc jockey. Jack McCarthy followed him.

When the program first went on the air, it began with the announcer saying, "The Green Hornet. . . . He hunts the biggest of all game—public enemies even the G-Men can't catch!" (Naturally, J. Edgar Hoover objected to this slur and the line became, "Public enemies who would destroy our America!") "With his faithful Japanese valet, Brit Reid, daring young publisher, risks his life that criminals and racketeers within the law may feel its weight by the sting of the Green Hornet!"

After the standard opening, augmented by "The Flight of the Bumblebee," came an almost equally standard story. Through his connection with the *Daily Sentinel* Reid would learn of a racket that the law seemed unable to touch. With Kato, he would step through a secret panel in the rear of his clothes closet and go down a narrow passage built within the walls of the apartment house and enter a "supposedly abandoned warehouse" (in the very earliest shows, a "supposedly abandoned livery stable!" It is interesting to speculate on the neighborhood in which Brit Reid lived, where a luxurious apartment building was back-to-back with a supposedly abandoned warehouse). They would enter the "sleek, super-powered car of the Green Hornet," the Black Beauty. Reid would press a button and a section of the wall would rise automatically. Then the car would swing out onto a "deserted side street" where there was never anyone to see the section of wall closing automatically behind the Black Beauty. The Green Hornet was off on another mission!

On one occasion, having learned of a crime in the making, Reid drove to the home of a suspected crook named Tolliver.

> TOLLIVER: You're masked! What do you want?
> HORNET: *You*, Tolliver!
> TOLLIVER: Y-you are the Green Hornet!
> (TELEPHONE RINGS)
> HORNET: Don't touch that phone. You are coming with me.
> TOLLIVER: I won't leave this room. How did you get in here?
> HORNET: The door, of course. I have keys that fit most doors. We can't waste time. Shall we go with you walking, or shall I carry you?

TOLLIVER: Neither one. I'll be . . . (COUGHS) that gun. Gas in that gun. Knocking me out . . . (COUGHS) Hornet, you devil . . . (BODY SLUMPS TO FLOOR)

Later, Tolliver regained consciousness in a secret hiding place of the Green Hornet's. As he lay bound, Tolliver heard the masked man tell him he knew all about Tolliver's sweet little insurance-collection racket. Tolliver advertised for men who were willing to work outside the United States and who were anxious to learn a new trade. The men who answered were put through a few weeks of training that enabled Tolliver to claim these new men were valuable to his company. He then had a reasonable excuse to take out on them insurance policies up to half a million dollars each, which he would collect when the employee had an unfortunate accident. It was a good racket, all right, and the Green Hornet wanted in on it.

Tolliver's protestations that there was no racket meant nothing to the owner of the Black Beauty. Nothing Tolliver had to say, not even Tolliver himself, meant anything to the Green Hornet. The Hornet didn't deal with small fry, with figureheads. He wanted the name of the man behind Tolliver, the silent partner in the racket. The Green Hornet demanded to be told the name of the boss of the outfit known as Foreign Industries. Still, Tolliver kept his silence.

Cheerfully, the Hornet pointed out the goggle-masked Kato in the corner. He was an Oriental and knew all sorts of interesting things to do with a knife. The masked man retired, apparently to let the crook think over all he had heard of the tortures of the mysterious East.

Let us recall fondly that the Green Hornet *really* wouldn't have sliced Tolliver apart inch by inch. He was not as pragmatic as modern antiheroes in such matters. While not a stickler for the law, and not above a little good-natured boyish blackmail or burglary, Brit Reid stopped short of either messy or neat homicides. He managed to get by on a certain craftiness.

Actually the Green Hornet only wanted to let Tolliver escape and take him to his leader. Tolliver unwittingly complied. Then the Hornet forced the boss, Hendricks, into writing some incriminating notes by a complex maneuver (*The Green Hornet* plots by Fran Striker were more sophisticated than those of supposedly adult radio thrillers). The Hornet also got Hendricks to turn over a good deal of money to him (to be used for good works later).

> HORNET: Listen to me, Hendricks, I've said you should be made to pay in full for what you've done. You *will* be made to pay in full, but I promised you that I would leave here if you signed those notes. Well, I'll keep my word. The *police* will take care of you.
> HENDRICKS: (COUGHS) Gas! Gas . . . I can't . . .
> (BODY HITS THE FLOOR)

Then the Green Hornet dashes off in the buzzing Black Beauty, Kato at the wheel, one step ahead of Mike Axford and the police. Lowery has a great story for the *Daily Sentinel.*

> "Ex-treeee—Ex-treeee! Insurance Racket Smashed!
> *Daily Sentinel* Ex-treeee! Green Hornet Still at Large!"

Time, if not the cops, finally caught up with the Green Hornet. He went off the air in 1952.

The Green Hornet tried to bring the ideals of his archetype, the Lone Ranger, into modern times, and became a hunted criminal. Sergeant Preston brought the ideals of the

Masked Man into a framework of officialdom and became rather a cut-and-dried policeman.

Only the Lone Ranger was able to be his own man in his own time successfully—the perfect man in the perfect show. Of all the great characters created by radio, only the Lone Ranger retains the most consistent popularity in the world of the 1960s—through reruns of the filmed TV series, new animated cartoons, transcriptions of the radio program still playing on some stations, phonograph records, comics and premiums.

Although there may someday be a really dreadful version of him in some medium, the real Lone Ranger is safe in the past of radio where his Silver can never be tarnished. Who was that Masked Man anyway? He was our ideals and our dreams and we have never been content to put him away forever. We cannot forget who he was and who we were then, when we heard that immortal cry: *"Hi-Yo, Silver, Aw-a-ay!"*

XIV

ACES OF THE AIRWAVES

"You three are in my power," the sinister, grinning Oriental known as the Barracuda said to young Joyce Ryan, Chuck Ramsey, and Major Steel, the senior officer of the Secret Squadron. "I also have Captain Midnight and his mechanic, Ichabod Mudd. None of you shall ever return to your home."

"You can't frighten us!" Chuck said to the Flying Fiend of Nippon. "We're not afraid to die for our country!"

"Perhaps not, Chuck Ramsey," replied the Barracuda. "But I can promise you that before Colonel Goto and his men are finished with you, death will seem the desired-for thing on earth!" The Devil Prince of the Rising Sun turned to the older man in the cell. "Major Steel, I'll give you time to reconsider. It is now noon. I'll give you twelve hours to give me the master plans to America's defense. Until . . . midnight!"

The hours passed swiftly for the courageous Americans in the prison. All too swiftly. "The time is almost up," Major Steel said, staring through the bars at the starry sky. He turned to the two brave young people. "I've been thinking of a night a long time ago during the First World War. It was a night when the allied armies faced a desperate situation; a night when a certain young captain . . . flew across the enemy lines taking a thousand-to-one chance that he wouldn't return. But he did return at midnight and he earned the title by which all men who love freedom and justice know him so well—Captain Midnight!"

Captain Midnight's old commanding officer turned back to the window with a sigh. "Tonight, instead of being at the controls of an airplane bringing back information that will crush the forces of terror and oppression, perhaps that captain is in prison as we are. Or he may be . . . well, we can be sure that Captain Midnight would never reveal information that would imperil America, not as long as he lived!"

"Loopin' loops, Major, listen!" cried Joyce.

Footsteps from outside. The heavy tread of the troops of Imperial Japan. "This is it!" Chuck observed. Elsewhere, a steeple clock began to strike the hour—the hour of midnight.

Bong . . . bong . . . bong . . .
Tramp! Tramp! Tramp!
Bong . . . bong . . .
Tramp! Tramp! Tramp!
Bong . . .

221

Rrrrrrrrrrooowwwwww. . . .

"Captain Midnight!" the three members of the Secret Squadron yelled out together.

Yes, high above in the black sky, it was the *Sky King*, the plane of Captain Midnight. He soon effected a rescue of the Secret Squadron agents and the much-deserved destruction of the Barracuda in a *Big Little Book* adaptation of one of the very first Captain Midnight radio scripts.

The fictional birth of *Captain Midnight* was in World War I, but he came into existence on radio in 1940, when for the first time we heard an airplane roaring in over the bonging of a steeple clock and the announcer droning, "Ca-a-ap-tain Mid-d-n-ni-ght!"

The first episode was aired on September 30, 1940, and flashed us back to that incident during World War I that Major Steel recalled in the Japanese cell. It took place in war-torn France. In a darkened room at Air Corps Headquarters, Steel gave valiant young Captain Albright the most important secret mission of the Great War. Not only did Albright have to capture the most despicable villain in—or rather outside of—Christendom, Ivan Shark, but he had to do it within a few hours, before midnight, or the Allies faced defeat. With the total lack of all caution so characteristic of all heroes during their generally brief careers, Albright accepted the commission.

Steel sat alone in the darkness with his commanding general, weighing thoughts of victory, of defeat, of retirement pay.

> GENERAL: Fifteen seconds before twelve . . . looks
> like we're sunk . . . too much to ask of one man . . .
> MAJOR: Listen! Do you hear it?
> GENERAL: Yes, it's a plane! He's done it . . . we're
> saved!
> MAJOR: And it's just twelve o'clock!

GENERAL: Yes! And to me, he will always be—*Captain Midnight!*

We crossed more than twenty years for the next scenes of that initial episode. After having proven himself in countless adventures, the man now known as Captain Midnight has been appointed by the government as a special agent to head the new undercover organization known as the Secret Squadron. His first mission? To once again capture unredeemed Ivan Shark, who has escaped prison after these many years. Elsewhere, Shark plotted with his chief lieutenant, the chap cheerfully known as Fang. The words spoken by Shark that day would prove fateful to Midnight and his Secret Squadron for years to come. "Any organization designed to fight us must be destroyed!" said Shark to the enthusiastically nodding Fang.

Midnight himself was the number one man in the Secret Squadron, SS-1, and a strikingly dressed hero in a black uinform with a winged clock insignia, wearing helmet and goggles. His two chief assistants, oddly enough mere children, were Chuck, SS-2, and Joyce, SS-3. SS-4 was Ikky, the mechanic. The captain's previous commanding officer, Major Steel, of the Army Air Corps was his direct superior in Washington, liaison man to the detached service group headed by the captain.

With the coming of World War II, "SS" men were in questionable taste in America. Although the radio show never changed the designation, when the program spawned a bastard son on television the numbers of the Secret Squadron received new serial numbers as SQ-1, SQ-2, SQ-3, etc.[1]

[1]Not only the code letters were changed. After the first run, sponsored by Ovaltine, the television series became *Jet Jackson*. Every time a character said Captain Midnight, the new name, Jet Jackson, was dubbed in very loudly, very

(*footnote continued on next page*)

The organization headed by Midnight's archenemy had no fancy serial numbers or splendid uniforms. In fact, it had no true name. The pre-SPECTRE and THRUSH organization was merely Ivan Shark's gang, never something like SHARK—Shark's Henchmen, Assassins, Robbers, and Killers. Of course, Shark was such a criminal mastermind, he needed no fancy abbreviations. (It may be noted that Captain Midnight and his fellow heroes are never described as honest masterminds.) Goateed, heavily accented, Ivan Shark was cut from the same bolt of black crepe as Fu Manchu. The resemblance grew with time. At first, obviously Russian—a Red!—Ivan Shark definitely seemed to become oriental during the middle 1940s. True, relatively few "Japs" are named Ivan, but there was a hint that Shark was Eurasian! A half-breed!

Ivan Shark was always up to something. And always it was something evil. Like the time during World War II when he successfully absconded with a U.S. government employee who was working on some terribly Top Secret plans for a new type of aircraft. Shark hid the doped-up government worker in his underground headquarters. There he revived the man only to subject him to the buzzing, zipping, and zapping horrors of a unique machine of Shark's own design. The device hypnotized the unfortunate employee and gave Shark complete control over his free will. Two hours later, the government man was back at his post and stealing the terribly Top Secret airplane plans Shark was going to sell to the Nipponese.

(footnote continued)
poorly, and very obviously. But then this series was a lot more Jet Jackson than Captain Midnight. The reason for all this? Ovaltine wanted to reserve the name Captain Midnight as its exclusive province, some possible future use in mind.

But in the end, Captain Midnight and the Secret Squadron discovered what Shark was up to, de-hypnotized the government man, and saved the day, as well as those terribly Top Secret plans, thus forcing Shark to beat a hasty retreat back to his underground lair.

There was also the time when Shark lured Midnight, Chuck, Joyce and Ikky to a remote island that was like something straight out of an Arthur Conan Doyle novel. Somehow Shark had discovered this lost tropical "paradise" inhabited by dinosaurs and other prehistoric beasts and decided it was a great place to get rid of Midnight and company. All he had to do was get them there. The dinosaurs would do the rest.

Ivan Shark got them there all right, but while the dinosaurs did their best, it just wasn't good enough to get rid of Captain Midnight and his pals in the Secret Squadron, who found good use for the grenades and a couple of flame-throwers they always carried in their airplane.

To add to his list of despicable crimes, Shark was one of the few heroes or villains on radio who had sunk so low as not to be celibate. He actually had cheek enough to have had a daughter.

Fury Shark did not fit the classic role of the beautiful but evil villainess such as the Dragon Lady on *Terry and the Pirates*. Fury was evil but ugly. When she was pictured in advertising, she was a witch with green skin. In your imagination, she was much worse.

Shark's daughter enjoyed demonstrating that the female is deadlier than the male. If Captain Midnight had been captured (which happened a bit too often for an infallible hero), Fury was sure to hiss, "Let's cut his heart out!" Her kindly father would have to restrain her with, "Not now, my dear. After he has served his purpose we will feed him to the crocodiles!"

225

One thing that could be said for Fury, she was man enough for any trouble. She never complained or whimpered or tried to cop out. If Captain Midnight sent the plane in which she and her father were flying spinning down in flames, or if they were lost in the Arctic, or if it looked as if the entire Shark family were headed straight for the electric chair, Fury always had a cheerful snarl, a hideous laugh, an endearing quality of persistence and belief that someday she and Daddy would get to cut out the hearts of Captain Midnight and the brats that tagged along with him.

The Secret Squadron fought others besides Ivan Shark, but the stories that ran on for six months were chiefly devoted to Ivan and Fury and their plots to seize the Secret Squadron's Code-o-graph, a device that decoded and encoded highly classified information. Ivan Shark did everything in the world to get that Code-o-graph. He tried murder, arson, robbery, bribery, in short, he did everything but send in his dime and Ovaltine seal like everybody else.

Those who did send in received their Code-o-graph and Secret Manual fairly promptly. The Code-o-graph was generally, roughly speaking, more or less, a badge. Besides bearing the winged insignia of the Secret Squadron (a clock with hands at midnight), from year to year the Code-o-graph had other distinctive features, one per annum. A magnifying glass, a mirror, a secret compartment that anyone who didn't listen to the radio couldn't find in that curious-looking bulge.

The 1946 Code-o-graph was a gold badge with a winged combination dial. The knob was a mirror suitable for flashing signals. If the circle of code letters was broken into columns with the numbers next to the letters it would look like this:

M	1	E	10	D	19
U	2	P	11	C	20
A	3	Y	12	W	21
G	4	J	13	R	22
H	5	I	14	B	23
T	6	F	15	O	24
V	7	L	16	N	25
Q	8	X	17	Z	26
S	9	K	18		

The code is set for Master Code M-1 now. The M is next to the 1. Master Code U-1 would have U next to 1, and the other numbers going around in circular fashion, M being 26.

At the end of the program, after Captain Midnight had been left up a tree and was being attacked by a dinosaur, Pierre André would say: "And now, another Secret Squadron code session! Set your Code-o-graph for Master Code M-1. . . ." Mr. André would diligently pause for a moment or two while all of us Secret Squadron members frantically searched the drawer for our Code-o-graph. Instinctively, Mr. André knew when we found it and would start reading off the numbers of Master Code M-1 as we dial-turned with sweaty fingers. The message, when copied down, looked like this:

1-14-19-25-14-4-5-6	21-14-25-9	5-10
19-22-14-25-18-9	24-7-3-16-6-14-25-10	

Up until I was nine or ten, I had to prevail upon my mother to write down the code numbers (the announcer went too fast for me). God only knows what would have happened to me if I had been stuck out in the jungle somewhere getting an urgent message from Captain Midnight if I hadn't had my mother around to copy it down for me!

A manual came along with your Code-o-graph and had messages that didn't require deciphering. One was a letter from Captain Midnight. The good captain said:

> I am happy to have you with us as we take off for exciting new missions ahead. . . . You are the keen-eyed fliers of tomorrow, the skippers of giant airliners and atomic-powered ships that will girdle the world. . . . America needs you—healthy, alert, and well trained to guard her future. . . .
>
> *Captain Midnight*

SS-1

Finally, one unforgettable December, Ivan Shark and his devil daughter Fury actually managed to steal a Code-o-graph. With the long-sought-after coding device now in his horrendous hands, Shark's hopes for Midnight's death were villainously high. At last, he and Fury could intercept Midnight's coded messages and plan an attack from which the heroic flying leader could not possibly escape. Unfortunately for Shark, by the time he was ready to put his fiendish plan for Midnight's demise into full operation, December had become January of the New Year and Ovaltine was offering Captain Midnight's *brand-new, completely different* Code-o-graph. Ivan Shark—foiled again!

Shark and Fury were certainly a despicable duo, but, unlike her father, Fury at least had one desirable attribute —her economy. In a number of sequences, the same girl who played Midnight's teen-age companion, Joyce, also played the part of Fury Shark. That actress was originally Marilou Neumayer, who, strangely enough, was a licensed pilot in private life. In later years she was replaced by Beverly Younger.

Chuck Ramsey was in civilian life Jack Bivens. When Jack Bivens was no longer a civilian during World War II, he reportedly was one of the members of the Air Force crew that dropped the atomic bomb on Hiroshima.

I certainly hope that Boris Aplon, who played Ivan Shark, did not pursue similar activities off microphone.

Captain Midnight himself, Ed Prentiss, confined himself pretty much to acting. He and his mechanic, Ikky—really Sherman Marks—are now in television, as an actor and a producer, respectively. Prentiss may be seen on some of the TV reruns of *Dragnet* as a stocky, gray-haired "captain" . . . of the Los Angeles Police Department.

Two men created *Captain Midnight*—Robert M. Burtt and Willfred G. Moore, who together or separately wrote virtually every program on radio having to do with aviation. Besides biographing the leader of the Secret Squadron, Burtt and Moore also wrote *The Air Adventures of Jimmie Allen, Hop Harrigan*, and *Sky King*.

Their first creation was *The Air Adventures of Jimmie Allen*, boy pilot, a popular feature on radio in the early thirties. (The program saw its last original script in 1936, but continued as one of radio's few rerun transcription series into the fifties.) With his companion and idol, veteran pilot and former World War I flying ace Speed Robertson, Jimmie throttled his racing plane, the *Blue Bird Special*, into a whole skyful of adventures involving airmail robberies, kidnappers, spies and saboteurs, even a mad scientist or two. Once he even encountered a flying saucer, not from Mars, as he and Speed shortly discovered, but from Japan. (Perhaps the Japanese had copied a Martian blueprint.)

In the early days of the series, Jimmie was only a pilot trainee at National Airways' Kansas City terminal, but with

Speed's knowledgeable aid and assistance, Jimmie soon became a co-pilot and finally a full-fledged pilot. On the day he officially received his flying wings, Jimmie was also honored at a celebration party tossed by Speed and two of Jimmie's other friends at National Airways, the anecdote-wielding airplane mechanic, Flash, and Jimmie's lithe, raven-haired girl friend, Barbara Croft.

The big excitement during the first year of Jimmie's air adventures was focused on a transcontinental plane race in which, oddly enough, both Jimmie and Speed were entered, pitted against one another. Even more oddly though, since at that time he was still a control-stick fledgling while Speed was a veteran flying ace and certainly the more experienced of the two, Jimmie actually won the air race. But this aerial feat of his hardly put a damper on the strong, hearty friendship that he had built up with Speed.

As the episodes rolled by, afternoon upon afternoon, Jimmie and his pals became involved in more standard radio kid adventures, stories dealing with bandits, swindlers, various enemies of our nation. Late in the series Jimmie saved for the United States a deadly secret invention of a quite mad scientist known as Professor Partenon Proteus, who had developed a unique little pellet that, when dropped from an aircraft, would instantly dissolve and blanket a city with poisonous gas. For many weeks, the boy pilot battled wave after wave of mysterious enemy agents and spies until he finally won out.

But the exploits of the young airline employee and his mentor began to date badly. Jimmie seemed to belong strictly to the Flying Jenny and Spad school. It was hard to picture him piloting a DC-3, much less a jet, and in 1940, Burtt and Moore turned to something that would create a better image and came up with *Captain Midnight*. Still later, they turned to other programs, but the shows proved to be merely dilutions of the perfect formula they had found for aviation on radio.

Unlike both *Captain Midnight* and *Jimmie Allen*, *Hop Harrigan, America's Ace of the Airways* was always a pretty realistic show, with few, if any, mad scientists or fantastic inventions. A World War II member of the U. S. Air Force, Hop's justifiable griping comes to mind, joined in by Tank Tinker, his mechanic and part-time gunner. Just as V-E Day in Europe was dawning, the two of them were transferred to a hotter field of battle, the Pacific. Complaints were understandable.

After the war, unlike many real-life servicemen, Hop adjusted to civilian life admirably and set up a small flying field with a pilot school. Indulging in air races, helping inventors with new types of planes, and, of course, encountering the usual assortment of crooks, spies, and smugglers, Hop and Tank managed to fill an interesting quarter hour, though few episodes were particularly memorable. Indeed, about the most memorable thing from the show was the opening with Hop flying in for a landing, talking to the base radio operator. "CX-4 to control tower, CX-4 to control tower . . . this is Hop Harrigan, coming in!"

When Burtt and Moore got around to creating *Sky King* in the middle forties, they were merely trying to combine the western elements and character prototypes from *Tom Mix* with their proven format of *Captain Midnight*.

Sky King was the tale of a modern-day rancher with a young boy and girl and an old "hand" on his spread. The boy and girl were Sky's niece and nephew, Penny and Clipper, and the old hand was foreman Jim Bell.

In the early radio serials about the Flying Crown Ranch, Schyler King (his name was Sky King, he wasn't a mystery man known as the Sky King) was just out of naval aviation in World War II and he had come back to his ranch only to encounter a fantastic menace with the name of Dr. Shade, who was, not at all surprisingly, at times invisible. Later, in 1950, when all the kid programs began copying *The Lone Ranger's* complete-in-a-half-hour format instead of fifteen-minute serials, *Sky King* became even more fantastic and had the most condensed adventure shows I ever heard. In twenty-five minutes, Sky King packed in as much plot and travel as Captain Midnight used to take a whole year for!

Always starting and concluding with western elements such as cattle stampedes, gunfights, and hard-riding horseback chases, the middle of Sky King's story might concern a flight to Europe to track down a Paris stool pigeon with some information, then a flight across Africa in the prop-driven *Song Bird,* or the jet *Black Arrow,* a crash landing, Sky and Clipper swinging Tarzan-like through the trees, fighting off hostile natives, reaching Algiers to be treated to intrigue there, and, finally, returning to America for a cowboy shoot-out in the streets of Grover, Arizona.

Sky King's headgear must have been a ten-gallon hat, equipped with goggles and possessed of many of the qualities of a pith helmet. Of course, during the air-minded thirties and forties, almost all of radio's heroes carried flying helmets in the pockets of other uniforms. Normally concerned with football padding and safari hats, *Jack Armstrong, the All-American Boy,* put in his flying time in Uncle Jim Fairfield's amphibian, a marvelous type of aircraft that was large enough to include lavish sleeping quarters, a laboratory, a private brig, and a small but representative zoo. The plane was quite good for stunting and dogfighting, though it was ordinarily used as a camping site in the middle of some tropical river from which Jack and all his friends could make scouting forays against the cannibals and to which they would usually return in a hail of poison darts.

Tom Mix was a cowboy, of course, but in the contemporary setting he enjoyed on radio he was also a pilot, and a frequent passenger on other occasions.

Terry Lee and Pat Ryan winged over the Orient on *Terry and the Pirates*. Their comic-strip compatriot, Inspector Dick Tracy, not infrequently took over the stick from Pat Patton (who was "not as good" as Dick). In later years, even *Little Orphan Annie* was co-pilot to aviator Captain Sparks.

Captain Silver, another sub-major class character, carried the *Sky Hound* on the deck of his ship *The Sea Hound*, and another sailor, *Don Winslow of the Navy*, did more flying that sailing during radio's afternoon hours.

Even *I Love a Mystery*'s Jack Packard brought his aircraft down safely near the Temple of Vampires with "as pretty a piece of flying as you could want to see."

All these memorable shows had flying sequences, but there was only a small band of full-time flying heroes on radio: Sky King, Jimmie Allen, Hop Harrigan, and Captain Midnight, who was what Harrigan only claimed to be, "America's Ace of the Airways."

Aviation was part of the American dream for a brighter, cleaner future. Charles A. Lindbergh was the spirit of the dream in the flesh, but as commercialized and stereotyped as he was, Captain Midnight was the culmination, the apex, of thirty years of aviation fiction—a hero heard on the air itself, known to us as SS-1, the champion of all our favorite American ideals—Truth, Justice, and Motherhood—who at the striking of midnight roared into aerial action with his Secret Squadron, defending our United States from those who would conquer it.

In whatever sky you now fly, Captain Midnight, let me wish you, as your announcer wished us at the end of each show, "Happeeeeee land-innnnnnnnnnn-gs!"

XV

THE ALL-AMERICAN BOY

"Say, Billy, we've got to be careful!"

Jack Armstrong's voice is youthful, but already it carries the authority that will mark him as a leader of men.

"Have you thought how terribly important this cruise of ours may be? I mean, if we let that uranium fall into the hands of the wrong kind of people?"

"I know, Jack," says fun-loving Billy Fairfield, trying desperately to be as serious and mature as his best friend. "This isn't just like hunting a chest of gold, or buried pirate's treasure. Maybe with that supply of uranium they could split the atom—and then invent engines that could take airplanes all around the world without stopping."

Jack and Billy are rowing toward Uncle Jim Fairfield's yacht, the *Spindrift*, that rides in the warm waters of the Sulu Sea. The oars creak, the water splashes, a gentle breeze lifts. The eyes of Jack Armstrong see farther and more clearly than those of his young companion. "Billy, when I think of this country of ours, with millions of homes stretching from sea to sea, and with everybody working and pulling together to have a nation where people can be free, and do big, fine things—why it makes me realize what a terribly important job we've got ahead!"

"I'll say!" Billy agrees readily.

"If we can get that uranium for our scientists at Hudson High, and discover where those pitchblende deposits are located, why we'll learn how to use all that energy in the atom. And we'll use it for the good of the whole world!"

Jack Armstrong, the All-American Boy, has not been revised and modernized for a television appearance. These were his exploits and his philosophy back in the 1940s when he was one of the most popular of all radio heroes. In those days, atomic energy was part of a dream of a Utopian future envisioned by many writers, not a nightmare reality for headline composers. Everything seemed better back then—ideals were nobler, friendship truer, courage surer, and certainly those high school science teachers who were going to crack the atom after Jack and Billy's triumphant return with the uranium ore were more proficient than some of today's muddlers. Of course, the teachers at Hudson High had to be really good, if for no other reason than to live up to the fame of the football team captained by Jack Armstrong (when he wasn't off to the South Seas or the African jungles).

It was one of the school's cheerleaders who started off a "steam engine" for the team's captain that gave the show its classic opening.

"Jack Armstrong . . . Jack Armstrong . . . Jack Armstrong . . . JACK ARMSTRONG!" the cheer built. (In the very dawn days, there were "Rah-rah-rahs" among the string of name calls.) Then, of course, came the fight song of Hudson High.

> Wave the flag for Hudson High, boys,
> Show them how we stand!
> Ever shall our team be champions,
> Known throughout the land!

Following these heroic stanzas, announcer Franklin McCormack would launch into a Wheaties commercial. After the Hitlerian war had begun, commercial zeal was combined with an equal helping of patriotic zest.

ANNCR: It's the big question—the question that's troubling boys and girls all over America as our country fights this war . . .

BOY: What can I do? How can I help to win the victory? I'm too young to join the Army or Navy. They won't even take me in the Home Defense Corps. . . . What can I do?

ANNCR: Train to be an American! Follow Jack Armstrong's rules for physical fitness: (1) get plenty of fresh air, sleep, and exercise; (2) use lots of soap and water every day; and (3) eat the kind of breakfast America needs in times like these—milk, fruit, and Wheaties—Breakfast of Champions!

BOY: Okay, Mr. McCormack—you've given us something to do to really help America—and you can bet we'll be ready to do our best . . . when the time comes.

Yes, nothing you could do to help the war effort was more important than eating your Wheaties! The patriotic character of the serial was further reinforced at the closing of the program when the Hudson High fight song urged you:

Won't you try Wheaties?
They're whole wheat with all of the bran.
Won't you buy Wheaties?
For wheat is the best food of man.
They're crispy, they're crunchy,
The whole day through,
Jack Armstrong never tires of them
And neither will you.
Won't you try Wheaties,
The best breakfast food in the land!

The ideals of Jack Armstrong shifted a bit from a concern for the welfare of "the whole world" before World War II to a super-nationalism encouraging the fattening of cannon fodder during the conflict, but at least he always had some kind of ideals or goals destined to help some part of his fellow men. Indeed, Jack Armstrong was the most idealistic, the purest hero of them all. In the words of the creator of the program, Robert Hardy Andrews, "He was a decent fellow, had a sense of responsibility, and didn't preach like Horatio Alger. In short, if you were like him you were a pretty good kid." And, hopefully, you might grow up to be a pretty good man or woman.

Andrews recalled that when Frank Hummert, the radio producer and advertising executive behind the creation of such soap operas as *Just Plain Bill,* gave him the task of creating sort of a "soap opera for kids" to be sponsored by General Mills, he came up with the title by studying the box of Arm & Hammer soda on his sink. "The All-American Boy" needed a strong arm (like the one pictured on the soda box) and presumably plenty of "jack."

After Robert Hardy Andrews left the show to write such books and movies as *If I Had a Million* (later to become the television series *The Millionaire,* another all-American fantasy figure), the far-traveling adventures of Jack Armstrong were mostly done by Colonel Paschal Strong (a real man, even if he sounds more like a character Jack might meet) and by Jim Jewell, also the producer-director, and the first director on *The Lone Ranger* radio series years before.

The year Jack Armstrong began his adventures was 1933, and kids as well as grown-ups needed something in which they could both believe, and which offered escape.[1] The

[1]When the program began in 1933 the earliest actors to play the part of Jack were Jim Ameche, brother of the movieland inventor of the telephone, and St. John Terrell.
(*footnote continued on next page*)

country was in the depths of economic depression, with seemingly hardly anyone working, and many starving. In that era, Jack Armstrong was an unqualified success. The captain of the team, the leader of his class, Jack always went to the top. Later on, he was bound to be president of the local Chamber of Commerce. He could handle anything, even a depression. Of course, he had some help from Uncle Jim Fairfield, who was a captain in Army Intelligence (retired or inactive), the owner of a large aircraft factory and the possessor of a giant airplane, an amphibian, *The Silver Albatross*.

Jim Fairfield was the uncle of Jack's buddy, Billy Fairfield, and of Billy's sister, Betty. The younger Fairfields had the courage of their uncle, but considerably less brains. Jack and Uncle Jim were always having to pull them out of the

(footnote continued)

The role was taken briefly by two other actors, Stanley Harris and Michael Rye. But the man to play the All-American Boy longer than any other was Charles Flynn. In 1939, the seventeen-year-old Flynn took over the part, and he was the last to play it in 1951. (Today he is a Michigan advertising executive. Only Jim Ameche stayed active in radio as a high-salaried disc jockey.)

Betty Fairfield was played first by Shaindel Kalish, later by Sarahjane Wells. Her brother, Billy Fairfield, was John Gannon before he retired from Hudson High on social security to make way for Dick York, the star of TV's *Bewitched*. Uncle Jim Fairfield seems always to have been James Goss. Paul Douglas was the first to announce for the Breakfast of Champions before going on to star in movies, along with Tyrone Power, who did small parts on the show. Douglas was followed by Franklin McCormack, then by Bob McKee, and the last announcer the program had was Ed Prentiss, who, when his own series was getting ready to fold, left the role of Captain Midnight to become the narrator on *Jack Armstrong*. (*Sic transit gloria mundi.*)

238

messes they got themselves into. Dick York, who was one of the actors to play Billy, recalled that as Billy he "always had the answer to the problem first and it was always wrong. I did what Jack said not to do. I usually apologized by saying, 'It's all my fault. I shouldn't have done it.' " Billy wasn't really stupid, but he and Betty—even Uncle Jim!—always suffered in contrast to the infallible Jack, just as the courageous and chivalrous Dr. Watson always seemed a boob in contrast to the great Sherlock Holmes.

In a devastating satire entitled "Jack Strongarm, All-Boy American," the comedy team of Bob and Ray in the 1950s had their own "Uncle Jim" say to their hero, "Jack, I'm a colonel in G-2, owner of one of the world's largest aircraft plants, and at least thirty years your senior, but *you* have all the brains in this outfit—*you* make the decisions!" The line was more *pastiche* than parody. Change it slightly to "I believe you can judge this situation better than I can—I suggest you outline a plan of action," and it would literally fit into a real *Jack Armstrong* script. Uncle Jim showed wisdom in trusting in Jack, because Jack never made a mistake.

Jack was infallible even before Uncle Jim came on the scene. In the early years, Jack went to school at Hudson High in the town of Hudson, U.S.A. His best friends, Billy and Betty Fairfield, were fellow students at Hudson. Their five-day-a-week adventures revolved around the football field and the basketball court. For a short time, there was even a sixth episode on Saturday consisting of nothing but a fictional ball game of some sort. The dialogue went something like: "Hey, Billy, I'm in the clear—throw me the ball!" "Here it is, Jack!" "And here goes . . ." "Hooray! Hooray! Hudson High has won again!" Sensing a limitation in dramatic possibilities, the Saturday games were discontinued.

Inevitably, Jack came in contact with crime and criminals.

He was called upon to find out who stole the big-game box-office receipts, and who burgled the dean's office for the answers to the exams. His greatest trouble in making justice triumph and winning the big game came from Monte Duval, the bully of the school, and his equally villainous sister, Gwendolyn Duval. Monte and Gwendolyn were constantly scheming to make it appear that Jack had broken training so Monte could take over and be the big man on the team. They were not even above keeping a suitcase of money they found in the stands, a suitcase Jack had seen and dutifully reported. But they were always so thoroughly defeated in the end by Jack Armstrong, they became shamefaced dropouts after a year or so.

With the Duvals' departure, Uncle Jim arrived with his amphibian airplane. He invited his nephew and niece, Billy and Betty, and their friend Jack to accompany him on a trip around the world. Who could refuse? After that, Jack never really came back to Hudson High for more than a week or two. Although he was supposed to "keep up his studies," with the help of Uncle Jim, I'm afraid he became as much of a dropout as the black-hearted Duval pair.

The lure of far places was too great even for sober, sincere, reliable Jack. The places were far indeed, out of this world into such "lost worlds" as those created by H. Rider Haggard and Edgar Rice Burroughs. Even in Jack's time, the area on this planet available for "lost worlds" was shrinking. Just as a Hilton Hotel stands on the stump of Tarzan's tree home, and United States radar bases are on sentry at the entrance to the "Hollow World" inside the earth, the site of one of the Jack Armstrong adventures in 1939, the surging, gigantic "Lake of Fire," as awesome a sight as mortal man has seen, has probably been drained dry by the pipes of some Near East oil consortium.

I was intrigued by the method used by Jack and his friends to cross this cauldron of flame. They swung across it on ropes. It now seems remarkable, but hardly unique. Radio's first swinger was *Tarzan of the Apes* in the 1930s, and it seemed to become a union regulation for heroes to be able to swing. The practice of vine-vaulting was observed not only by the Lord of the Jungle and by Jack Armstrong, but also by Jack Packard and the Lone Ranger, Captain Midnight, and Tom Mix, when the occasion demanded. Presumably during summer vacation the loin-clothed Lord Greystoke had instructed all his hero-colleagues in Radioland on the art.

Tarzan of the Apes came to radio just a year or two before Jack Armstrong, it might be noted, scripted by his creator, Edgar Rice Burroughs, in a syndicated, transcribed fifteen-minute serial. Burroughs' daughter, Joan Burroughs, and her husband, one-time movie Ape Man, James Pierce, played Her Jane and Him Tarzan. Pierce had no lines, only grunts, during the first few weeks until Jane taught the ape-raised Tarzan to speak.

During those weeks of grunts, Tarzan managed to polish off the shipload of mutineers who had stranded Jane and her father, Professor Porter, on his jungle isle. He rescued the girl from a few lions and tigers (Burroughs was never scrupulous on his African zoology) and became her captive of love.

Later sequences took Tarzan through other adventures Burroughs had covered in his books, finally to the Lost Caves of Opar where he met the only other woman he ever desired, even temporarily—the Priestess of Opar. However, Tarzan resisted her lure and that of the wealth of the Jewels of Opar and returned to Jane and their tree home, from where he possibly conducted those vine-tingling classes.

Eventually, Jack's adventures swung him not only across the "Lake of Fire" but away from it entirely to another "lost world." This one was "The Elephants' Graveyard."

It was a desirable thing to find "the place elephants go

to die" since that place would be a storehouse of priceless ivory tusks. In this story, Jack, Billy, Betty, and Uncle Jim were being raced to the treasure by the villainous Lopez. All were opposed by the mystical Elephant Man, Boo-loo-la, who devoted his life to protecting the final sanctuary for the greatest of all land beasts. Between Boo-loo-la and Lopez, our side had to cope with an attack by the poison arrows of Pygmies, the fangs of leopards guarding a lost city, and the hairy arms of a tribe of giant gorillas.

At one point, the map that showed the way to the treasure was stolen (but, naturally, Jack had had the foresight to memorize it first), and their plane was forced down in the jungle when the gas tanks of the amphibian had been punctured by Lopez. Jack won a trial-by-combat with a native chief through the employment of "the science of modern wrestling," and, at last, the group reached the legendary Elephants' Graveyard. It was then explained to Boo-loo-la that the ivory would be used to help preserve the living species of the elephant, and everybody but Lopez was happy. Everyone but Lopez and me.

Jack Armstrong had wound up another one, but I personally felt little triumph in identifying with him. Jack was a little too damned infallible for me. I lost grocery lists and couldn't even remember them, much less memorize treasure maps to the Elephants' Graveyard. And I certainly wasn't able to win all my fights with the secrets of "modern wrestling." Other heroes on the air occasionally broke down and became human. On the radio, Tom Mix was such a lousy businessman he was in danger of losing his TM-Bar Ranch. The Lone Ranger occasionally lost his temper. He once delivered a terrific beating to a mangy owlhoot after the bad man discovered the Masked Man in one of his disguises as an old man—a "cover" on which many lives depended on his keeping—and forced him at gunpoint to lick his boots. Even Superman occasionally took on something he couldn't handle, such as the time he came too close to the sun while flying between planets and had to fight what seemed a losing battle against being pulled to a fiery doom by the awesome gravitation.

Of course, Jack Armstrong never had occasion to fly between planets; but I was sure he could do it if the necessity arose, and if caught in the gravitational pull of the sun he would twist free by a scientific wrestling secret. He hadn't gotten around to buying a ranch, but certainly he would never have any business difficulties with it. Somehow, I *knew* he was a whiz at arithmetic in school. As for losing his temper, *nobody* who got plenty of fresh air, sleep, and exercise, used soap and water freely, and who ate Wheaties would do a thing like that.

A fellow who was much more *my* type in the same age group as Jack Armstrong was Henry Aldrich, heir to the dubious fortunes of *The Aldrich Family.* Henry was not really stupid or blundering, just young and inexperienced, in a condition of ignorant bliss from which the process of life would remove him soon enough.

In publicity photographs, Henry Aldrich even looked like me, certainly more than the champ of Hudson High resembled me. The fellow in the photographs was really cheerful but undeniably chubby Ezra Stone. I felt that on top of all his other troubles, "Henry" joined me in the Weight Watchers' League.

The rest of the Aldrich family who helped Ezra Stone eat so well were father Sam, mother Alice, and older sister Mary. All of them were products of the pen of Clifford Goldsmith, a serious playwright of some note. Goldsmith's original intention in the 1930s had been to present the problems of a boy growing up as a bittersweet tragicomedy, but the line proved too fine for subsequent staff writers to meet. The program became outright comedy.

There seemed to be less and less difference between Henry and his best friend, his Watson, his Tonto, although like most sidekicks Homer Brown had originally been intended to make Henry look good by comparison. His voice (the voice of actor Jackie Kelk) did crack worse than Henry's. If we could have seen Homer, I'm sure his case of acne was more developed than Henry's. Yet, as time went on, Henry began to seem no brighter than Homer.

The two boys could no more escape trouble than Henry could escape answering the signature call of *"Henry—Henry Aldrich!"* by having his voice crumple on "Coming, Moth-er!"

When Henry was given the task of delivering a dress form of his mother's, it was inevitable that Homer would suggest they wrap the life-size figure in a blanket so it wouldn't be conspicuous. Then, in the published adaptation, a passerby looked on in growing alarm as the two boys loaded the stiff, life-size form into Homer's car.

HENRY: Gosh, I'm glad you happened along! This really takes a load off my mind! See if you can get it down out of sight, Homer.

HOMER: That's about as far as it will go, Hen—

HENRY: Hey, what's the spade doing here, Homer?

HOMER: Oh that. Gosh, I almost forgot. . . . My mother wants me to get some grass sod to cover that bare spot in our yard . . . she can't grow grass on it since I spilled the punch there last year . . .

HENRY: I remember the punch you made for your party, Homer. . . . If you hadn't insisted on putting vinegar in it . . .

HOMER: I told you before, Henry, that it was cider vinegar and I thought it was different from ordinary vinegar . . .

Naturally, the boys couldn't understand, when they un-loaded the blanket-wrapped dummy to get at the shovel and started spading up the sod, why people fled in panic, or why the police came, or why their fathers had to be called.

I can't imagine Henry Aldrich attending Jack Armstrong's Hudson High, but I can imagine him being sent there to deliver some interschool reports to Jack's principal. The two boys, Henry and Jack, might have met on the campus.

Henry's voice would crack as he asked the worldly, self-assured Jack the way to the principal's office. With kindly condescension, Jack would give Henry detailed but simple instructions on how to reach his destination, instructions that even a retarded Zulu could follow without effort. Then fifteen minutes later, Jack would meet Henry again and have him ask for better directions. And a quarter hour after that—

Finally, Jack would inquire, "Say, you don't have a cousin —or something—named Fairfield, do you?"

Of course maybe Henry would outgrow his inferiority to Jack Armstrong. Maybe even I would outgrow mine.

Ultimately, I decided to give Jack a second chance, which I felt was considerably more than he would give me. (Billy Fairfield's ideas like "Let's rush 'em" always seemed pretty good to me, until Jack patiently demolished them.)

In "The Mystery of the Iron Key," Jack, Billy, Betty, and Uncle Jim Fairfield set off on a new adventure, this time in a giant dirigible, *The Golden Secret*, which Fairfield Aircraft Company had constructed for the Maharajah of Rawal Doon, and which Jim Fairfield himself was going to deliver. En route, the traveling companions were startled by a strange, whining vibration, which they quickly established as coming from the ceremonial iron key given to Jack for finding the location of still another lost treasure in the previous serial story. The key, it developed, had been carved from an iron meteorite with certain mystic powers, including the ability to signal when certain sinister powers were at work. (The sound effects crew developed a special noise for the vibrations of the iron key and used it throughout the serial about occult science of the Far East. Another sound effect developed for this story is the one single effect that has been called to my attention by people recalling the old days of radio more than any other that wasn't a *permanent part* of the program, such as the train "flashing past the long red row of tenement houses" to *Grand Central Station,* or the footsteps of *Bulldog Drummond* coming through the fog-shrouded night. In the serial, Jack was assigned a personal bodyguard by the Maharajah—a bodyguard who followed him around constantly sharpening a saber—*snick-snick-snick* went the whetstone against the razor-sharp blade of the saber . . . *snick-snick-snick!* . . . SNICK-SNICK-SNICK! What, you wondered, what was he finally going to do with that incredibly finely sharpened saber? For this story of India the sound men also came up with thunderbolts, tiger shrieks, the bugling of the charge, and nerve-shattering explosions. *Sound* seemed to dominate the story so much that, when a premium was offered for a Wheaties box top, it turned out to be a Jack Armstrong Sound Effects Kit, with materials and instructions for creating the sound of a fire by crinkling cellophane [red—so it even looked like fire], rolling BB shot around inside a blown-up balloon to imitate the distant roll of thunder, and other goodies.)

They certainly could have used the key in World War II, which proved to be an awkward time for Jack and his friends. True, Jack and the Fairfields had a long-running fight with the master spy Weissoul, who had a thousand faces (thanks to his skill at makeup) and a thousand voices (thanks to actor Herb Butterfield). The All-American Boy did prevent Weissoul and other Axis agents from getting African tribesmen to revolt and destroy Allied nations' air bases on the dark continent, but, really, this never seemed like a job for an All-American Boy. *Hop Harrigan, America's Ace of the Airwaves,* seemed a more fitting choice to handle the matter. Even the *Terry and the Pirates* gang seemed better equipped for trouble like that.

After the war, in the fall of 1946, a drastic change was made in the format of the *Jack Armstrong* program. For thirteen years, the program had been broadcast for fifteen minutes each Monday through Friday afternoon, with the stories running no prescribed length, perhaps running on for months, or half a year. Now it was assumed the young listeners couldn't hold still for a story for more than six weeks. (Later it was cut to three weeks.)

One of the shorter postwar adventures was "The Devil's Castle," a place lined with secret passages, haunted by a mad hermit, and the resting place of a "cosmo-tonic generator" destined to be used to release *"electrical* atomic energy." This last term shows the desperation of radio writers following World War II. Just as Jack Armstrong had sought the secrets of atomic energy in the Sulu Sea of 1940, other heroes had been involved with fictional atomic energy for decades. When true atomic energy came into all too familiar usage, the writers could think of no new scientific miracle, so their heroes could only search for the secrets of *sub-*atomic energy or *electrical* atomic energy, or other such sub-literate nonsense.

Far more disturbing, however, than AC/DC nuclear power in "The Devil's Castle" was the introduction of a new character, Vic Hardy, "a scientific crime investigator." No longer could kids—or at least those who wrote for kids—accept kindly rich uncles who owned amphibian airplanes. The father figure for the postwar generation had to be not so significantly a scientist, but the representative of a governmental police agency.

Vic Hardy turned out to be the director of the Scientific

Bureau of Investigation. The initials of that agency sound more familiar than its full title—SBI. Soon, Jack, Billy, and Betty were employees of the SBI, working for benevolent Vic Hardy. Uncle Jim flew off into the sunset in one of his planes or dirigibles and was heard of no more.

From being a clean-cut American Boy, Jack Armstrong quickly became an efficient agent of this secret police organization. The SBI was so efficient, it was no longer credible for its agents to take six weeks or three weeks or even one-week to wind up a mystery. By 1948, *Jack Armstrong, the All-American Boy*, was broadcast three days a week, each program being a complete story in a half hour's time.

The illusion of reality was gone forever. It was disillusioning to find that the stories about people like Jack Armstrong (and later Captain Midnight, Tom Mix, and all the rest) were just *stories* and could be hacked and crammed into thirty minutes, instead of having to be *lived* day by day.

Strangely enough, I listened to the complete half-hour stories of Jack Armstrong more faithfully than I had the serial in years. Now I knew Jack wasn't real, and he was no longer a threat to me with his smug superiority. I was more comfortable with the phony half-hour Jack Armstrong than I had been with his "real" fifteen-minutes-a-day self.

To delve into the psychic personality of a cardboard hero is a cute trick, a coy bit of fakery, but if Jack Armstrong were a real man, he would have to be among the bitterest living. Anybody who winds up a member of the secret police of any government must be bitter, especially when in his youth he believed in building big, fine dreams for the good of all mankind.

I prefer to remember him that way—a boy who was better than I was or knew I could be—who really *was*, in the words of his creator, "a good kid." I remember the Jack

Armstrong who, on a spring day in 1939, listened to the words of an ancient lama in Tibet.

"Tell the boys and girls of the United States," said the old priest in a thin, fine voice, "this world is theirs, and they may use it as they will. As they are, so shall their world become. If they have hearts of gold, a glorious new golden age awaits us all. If they are brave, they shall find a world of chivalry. If they are honest, all riches shall be theirs. If they are kind to one another, they shall save the whole world from the malice and the meanness and the war that is tearing its heart. Will you take that message to the boys and girls of the United States, Jack Armstrong?"

Jack stood tall and alone in the great throne room of the "wisest man in the world." After only a moment he said, "Yes, sir, I'll be proud to do it. I'm going to spend the rest of my life trying to live that message!"

The dream tarnished over the years. That boy, in the last years he was to know, became a semianonymous creature known only as *Armstrong of the SBI*, helping in the manner of *Les Miserables'* Jauvert to bring the gigantic forces of government down not only on gangsters and killers, but on people guilty of such nefarious crimes as game poaching on federal land and falsifying weather reports! His existence as a half-alive robot ended in 1951, mercifully.

There is a relationship between Jack Armstrong, we who shared his life, and the American Dream. To some extent, all three elements failed the others. The time when all three were new and known to all to be infallible is a time that will always seem a little better than it was. That was the time when *all* of us were going to do "big fine things" for the good of "the whole world"—the time of *Jack Armstrong, the All-American Boy.*

AFTERWORD

CHECK YOUR LOCAL RADIO LOG

The heroes of Radioland offered us a certain variety of standards in which to believe.

Jack Armstrong upheld every law and regulation on the books—except the one that demanded everyone under sixteen attend school regularly. Jack, Doc, and Reggie played by their own rules, and, in so doing, had not the slightest doubt of winning. Sam Spade was a bit dubious of winning, especially if he played by the strict rules of law and order, and Spade's colleague in crime detection, Pat Novak, was resigned to not winning at all, no matter what rules he used —he just knew that as long as you were in the game, you had to keep playing.

After the doubters, came the pretenders: The Shadow, the Green Hornet, the Lone Ranger all pretended to accept all the rules of their society and to uphold them, but in reality they went outside society to defend it. Clearly, however, they were *not* in the same category as Klansmen. While they gave lip service to the most conservative of traditions, they *acted* on the liberal concept that unjust laws may be broken.

Within the territory marked at either end by Jack Armstrong and by the Green Hornet lay the basic philosophy of Radioland. There were some things believed in by all our heroes. Call it "transcendental utopianism" or "super-humanism," radio morality said that it was wrong to kill people, and right to help them.

It was not a complex philosophy, only a standard interpretation of the basic Judeo-Christian ethic. As you grew up, you learned that these standards had to be modified by reality, to be reinterpreted in the light of mature experience, but not completely demolished.

Popular entertainment today has become notably short of even these basic ideals, confused by the complication of a modern adult world into discarding *all* standards of behavior. Today, there are few strong men with high ideals, men who are real heroes. Ian Fleming's spy, James Bond, is the model for the age in books and films. On television, a character inspired by Fleming, *The Man from U.N.C.L.E.* is a spy who owes allegiance to no country, but only to his own organization. U.N.C.L.E. is a gang that fights another gang known as THRUSH. The United Network Command for Law and Enforcement considers the Technological Hierarchy for the Removal of Undesirables and the Subjugation of Humanity to be evil, but no doubt THRUSH thinks the same of U.N.C.L.E. "Good" means "us," and "bad" means "them." The goal is "survival," the prize is "success," and no one on either side thinks or speaks of honor, decency, or justice.

Clearly, television is a different world from that of Golden Age radio. Nostalgia for the past is not the only division between these two worlds. There are some early TV shows as old as some late radio programs, but they are of a clearly different species.

The very stuff of radio was imagination, the very antithesis of television. Radio drama absolutely required imagination and those series that best provided it were rewarded with the greater success. *The Shadow* asked us to see an invisible detective—and gained higher ratings than the mundane private eyes. Jack Benny invited us into his fantastic subterranean bank vault where he kept all his hoarded loot, and came in ahead of the routine situation comedies about dumb fathers.

Radio was at once willing to preserve the best of the past and to constantly experiment for better new shows. The basic prototypical programs lasted nearly the entire history of dramatic radio—*Amos 'n' Andy, The Lone Ranger, Jack Armstrong, The First Nighter.* Yet every week there were dozens of new plays with new characters on the host of dramatic anthologies.

With a lower scale of profits than enjoyed by television, radio cut their profits even finer to serve the minority audience for quality programming. Radio's successor, television, in a frantic scramble, finds no room for Sid Caesar or Jack Benny, *The Defenders* or *Playhouse 90*, managing to discard the best of the old and find the worst of the new.

Goodman Ace, of the *Easy Aces* radio show, and a top television comedy writer, recently observed in the *Saturday Review*, "Thirty-five years ago the Messrs. Paley, Stanton, Sarnoff became the proud proprietors of a class entertainment medium. TV 1966 finds them operating a run-down, second-run movie house open all night and showing B pictures along with quickie, two-reel comedies for which the Phoenicians will have to invent another letter."

Bud Collyer, a successful performer in both mediums, has pointed out that, since radio and television were operated by the same people, it was a conscious decision on the part of the networks to discontinue "big-time" radio programming. There was a selective audience for traditional radio even in the age of television. "Radio gave up too easily," Collyer said.

In Great Britain, where at least one network is operated in the public interest and not for profit, radio drama and comedy still retain an important share of the general audience, some radio shows competing successfully with TV. And no one can argue that any country that can produce both The Beatles and Herman's Hermits is that far ahead of the United States in cultural standards.

Television in America has taken over radio's duties of

providing drama and comedy and has consistently failed to provide entertainment with either the quality of the more serious radio plays or the magic appeal of radio's great thrillers and fun shows. Today's radio happily abdicates providing drama for even a minority audience. Radio proudly proclaims that it is making more money than ever through the playing of phonograph records with up to twenty-five minutes per hour taken up with commercials. This information thrills me as much as if I learned my favorite saloon had increased its profits 50 percent through watering the whiskey twice as much.

Some radio stations experimented briefly with old transcriptions of *The Shadow, The Lone Ranger,* and others. Some of the language and stories had dated. Some had serious technical difficulties, scratches and clicks that obliterated words. They were not a fair test of the basic appeal of radio drama.

A few old radio shows continue with new broadcasts. *Arthur Godfrey Time* and Don McNeil's *Breakfast Club* appear immortal. Producer-host C. P. MacGregor continues nearly forty years of dramatic broadcasts by still transcribing a weekly story based on Salvation Army activities called *Heartbeat Theatre.* The only promising new activity on the radio horizon is the advent of "conversation" radio, which becomes more listenable the more it relies on the in-studio guest on art, politics, or science and less on the telephone calls of a rather loudly uninformed listening audience. Conversation is, however, only debatably an art. The true art of radio was its drama, which has faded back into the darkness whence it came.

Radio today, and its newer broadcasting companion, television, both reflect the same lack of standards of taste and behavior evidenced by the heroes of the contemporary scene. In doing so, our popular culture is only mirroring back our own current attitudes. We could be assured that this would not be happening if Jack Armstrong were alive.

If you have missed any full-length U.N.C.L.E. adventures starring Napoleon Solo and Illya Kuryakin, ask your newsdealer for them, or use order form on this page and the following page:

ACE BOOKS (Dept. MM)
1120 Avenue of the Americas, New York N.Y. 10036

Please rush me:

......copies 51683, **THE MAN FROM U.N.C.L.E.** #8, *The Monster Wheel Affair* by David McDaniel.

......copies 51685, **THE MAN FROM U.N.C.L.E.** #9, *The The Diving Dames Affair* by Peter Leslie.

......copies 51687, **THE MAN FROM U.N.C.L.E.** #10, *The Assassination Affair* by J. Hunter Holly.

......copies 51689, **THE MAN FROM U.N.C.L.E.** #11, *The Invisibility Affair* by Thomas Stratton.

......copies 51691, **THE MAN FROM U.N.C.L.E.** #12, *The Mind Twisters Affair* by Thomas Stratton.

......copies 51693, **THE MAN FROM U.N.C.L.E.** #13, *The Rainbow Affair* by David McDaniel.

......copies 51695, **THE MAN FROM U.N.C.L.E.** #14, *The Cross of Gold Affair* by Fredric Davies.

......copies 51697, **THE MAN FROM U.N.C.L.E.** #15, *The Utopia Affair* by David McDaniel.

......copies 51699, **THE MAN FROM U.N.C.L.E.** #16, *The Splintered Sunglasses Affair* by Peter Leslie.

......copies 51700, **THE MAN FROM U.N.C.L.E.** #17, *The Hollow Crown Affair* by David McDaniel.

......copies 51701, **THE MAN FROM U.N.C.L.E.** #18, *The Unfair Fare Affair* by Peter Leslie.

......copies 51702, **THE MAN FROM U.N.C.L.E.** #19, *The Power Cube Affair* by John T. Phillifent.

I enclose 50¢ per copy, plus 10¢ handling fee for each book.

NAME ....

ADDRESS ....

CITY .... STATE .... ZIP CODE ....

Don't miss these edge-of-the-chair novels of the most talked about TV series in years:

67900 — 60¢

THE PRISONER #1

by Thomas M. Disch

67901 — 60¢

THE PRISONER #2

by David McDaniel

"Number 6" had escaped from The Village.
  (Hadn't he?)

Then why was he imprisoned there again.
  (Or was he?)
